应用型本科通用教材

信息类行业英语阅读教程

胡家英　主编

中国林业出版社
China Forestry Publishing House

内 容 简 介

《信息类行业英语阅读教程》着眼于新时期国家对应用型人才的需求以及信息类人才可持续发展需要。内容上选择了与信息类专业学生发展相关的话题，包括人工智能、数字技术、生态网络、AI 技术，太空科技等，结合了 15 篇相关行业英语应用文实践阅读。旨在把信息类专业课程和英语课程交叉理念落地生根，实现学科交叉融合。提升学生英语应用能力，助力学生成长为引领行业发展和创新的高素质、复合型、应用型人才。增强他们在各自行业领域内的竞争力和素养。本教材语言原真，内容贴近科学技术发展前沿，具有很强的可读性和实用性。

图书在版编目（CIP）数据

信息类行业英语阅读教程/胡家英主编. —北京：中国林业出版社，2024.6
应用型本科通用教材
ISBN 978-7-5219-2715-3

Ⅰ．①信… Ⅱ．①胡… Ⅲ．①信息技术-英语-阅读教学-高等学校-教材　Ⅳ．①G202

中国国家版本馆 CIP 数据核字（2024）第 095848 号

责任编辑：高红岩　王奕丹
责任校对：苏　梅
封面设计：睿思视界视觉设计

出版发行　中国林业出版社
　　　　　（100009，北京市西城区刘海胡同 7 号，电话 83223120）
电子邮箱　cfphzbs@163.com
网　　址　www.cfph.net
印　　刷　北京中科印刷有限公司
版　　次　2024 年 6 月第 1 版
印　　次　2024 年 6 月第 1 次印刷
开　　本　787mm×1092mm　1/16
印　　张　15.5
字　　数　413 千字
定　　价　48.00 元

《信息类行业英语阅读教程》编写人员

主　　编：胡家英

副 主 编：于　丽

编写人员：胡家英（东北农业大学）

　　　　　于　丽（哈尔滨信息工程学院）

　　　　　张佟菲（哈尔滨信息工程学院）

　　　　　王　月（东北农业大学）

前言
Preface

　　《信息类行业英语阅读教程》是应用型本科院校信息类专业学生的英语教材。本教材的设计和编写基于应用型本科院校信息类专业学生的实际英语水平培养人才，旨在提升从事信息类行业人才和信息类专业学生的行业英语能力，力图满足新形势下国家和地区应用型人才培养的需求。

　　本教材兼具新颖性、趣味性和知识性，本教材突出人文和理工特色，融合科技文化知识，内容涉及信息科技在生态、计算机、艺术和新能源等领域的应用。单元内的主题和文章选择均包含时尚科技元素，能够极大吸引学生的注意力，并引发强烈的思考与讨论。本教材全面贯彻 OBE 成果导向的教育理念，以使学生成长为具有信息类行业英语能力的应用型人才为培养目标，教学内容上选择设计与信息类专业相关的主题内容，强调英语和专业知识的融合和应用，把现代信息技术融入语言学习，开展文理交叉，为学生提供综合性的跨学科学习，以实现知识扩展和创新思维，从而为应用型本科院校新工科建设服务。

　　本教材共 15 个单元，每个单元分为 4 个部分：Part A 为信息类文章精读，Part B 为信息类文章泛读，Part C 为信息类产品说明书的阅读与翻译，Part D 为工作坊话题。每单元除单词表外，还列出了相关短语、语言点讲解及课文注释，并配有大量练习。

　　本教材主编胡家英教授负责 1～4 单元的编写，副主编于丽教授负责 5～8 单元的编写，张佟菲老师负责 9～12 单元的编写，王月老师负责 13～15 单元的编写。在教材的使用过程中，我们希望能够得到更多宝贵意见和建议，从而使其不断完善，更好服务于教学工作。

编　者
2023 年 11 月

目 录
Contents

前言 Preface

Unit 1　Web Life Today ··· 1
   Part A　I'm Toast in the Battle Against "Smart" Appliances ················· 1
   Part B　30 Days Without Internet－a Self-Experiment ························· 5
   Part C　Product Manual ··· 10
   Part D　Workshop ·· 14

Unit 2　Arts Technology ·· 15
   Part A　Artifacts Come Alive With Technology ···································· 15
   Part B　Online Exhibitions ·· 19
   Part C　Product Manual ··· 25
   Part D　Workshop ·· 28

Unit 3　E-commerce ··· 30
   Part A　Amazon Gets Physical ··· 30
   Part B　Autonomous deliveries ··· 34
   Part C　Product Manual ··· 39
   Part D　Workshop ·· 42

Unit 4　High-tech ··· 44
   Part A　How Can Big Data Save the World ·· 44
   Part B　High Technology at the Beijing Winter Olympics Venues ········ 49
   Part C　Product Manual ··· 56
   Part D　Workshop ·· 59

Unit 5　Artificial Intelligence ·· 61
   Part A　Technology in Science Fiction ··· 61
   Part B　Robot-proof: Higher Education in the Age of Artificial Intelligence ······ 65
   Part C　Product Manual ··· 70
   Part D　Workshop ·· 74

Unit 6　Energy Technology ··· 75
   Part A　Energy and Public Safety ·· 75
   Part B　Earth Resources Technology Satellites ··································· 79
   Part C　Product Manual ··· 85
   Part D　Workshop ·· 89

Unit 7 Technology and Future — 90
- Part A "Iron Man" Armor Might Actually Come into Our Lives — 90
- Part B Building Better Ultralight Computers — 95
- Part C Product Manual — 101
- Part D Workshop — 104

Unit 8 Technology and Communication — 105
- Part A Facebook Wants to Emulate WeChat. Can it? — 105
- Part B Challenges for a Webbed Society — 110
- Part C Product Manual — 115
- Part D Workshop — 119

Unit 9 Space Technology — 120
- Part A The US Rover Perseverance Has Successfully Landed on Mars — 120
- Part B The Scientific Exploration of Space — 127
- Part C Product Manual — 132
- Part D Workshop — 137

Unit 10 Technology and Brain — 139
- Part A Musk: Technology that Connects the Human Brain to Computers Is Not Far Off — 139
- Part B Is It True that The Human Brain Is Only 10% Developed? — 145
- Part C Product Manual — 151
- Part D Workshop — 155

Unit 11 The World Is Changing Fast — 157
- Part A What Is Digital Economy? — 157
- Part B The Future of Information and Education — 162
- Part C Product Manual — 168
- Part D Workshop — 172

Unit 12 ChatGPT — 173
- Part A ChatGPT Is a Tipping Point for AI — 173
- Part B ChatGPT: Student Builds App to Sniff out AI-written Essays — 178
- Part C Product Manual — 184
- Part D Workshop — 186

Unit 13 Eco-network — 188
- Part A US Launches Eco-network — 188
- Part B Experts Are Warning AI Could Lead to Human Extinction — 193
- Part C Product Manual — 199
- Part D Workshop — 202

Unit 14 Technology and Entertainment — 204
- Part A Why Hollywood Really Fears Generative AI — 204
- Part B Applications of AI in the Media & Entertainment Industry — 211
- Part C Product Manual — 218
- Part D Workshop — 220

Unit 15　Technology and Home Security ·· 222
　　Part A　AI: the Future of Home Security ·· 222
　　Part B　Don't Put Home Security Cameras in These 3 Places ·· 227
　　Part C　Product Manual ·· 233
　　Part D　Workshop ·· 235

Unit 1   Web Life Today

I'm Toast in the Battle Against "Smart" Appliances

Recently, *The Washington Post* printed an article explaining how the appliance manufacturers plan to drive customers up the wall. Of course, they don't SAY that exactly. What they SAY they want to do is to have us live in homes where "all appliances are connected to the Internet, sharing information", and that appliances will be "smarter than most of their owners". For example, you could have a dishwasher that "can be turned on from the office", and a refrigerator that "knows when it's out of milk".

But listen, appliance manufacturers: we don't NEED a dishwasher that we can communicate with from the office. If you want to improve our dishwashers, give us one that senses when people leave dirty dishes on the kitchen table, and shouts, "Put that bowl in the dishwasher right now or I'll get your shoes all wet!" Likewise, we don't need a refrigerator that knows when it's out of milk. We already have an effective system for determining that: we ask our husbands or wives. A real improvement would be a fridge that refuses to let us open its doors when it senses that we are about to eat our fourth piece of pie in two hours.

Here is what really disturbs me about these new "smart" appliances: even if we like the features, we won't be able to use them. We can't use the appliance features we have NOW. I have a feature-packed telephone with 43 buttons, at least 20 of which I am afraid to touch. My phone is probably equipped to communicate with the dead, but I don't know how to operate it, just as I don't know how to operate my television set, which has features requiring TWO remote controls. One control (44 buttons) came with the television; a second (66 buttons) came with the VCR (Video Cassette Recorder).

So, when I want to watch television, I'm faced with a total of 110 buttons, identified by such helpful names as PIP, MTS, DBS and JUMP. Though there are two POWER buttons, there are times — especially if my son and his friends have changed the settings — when I cannot figure out how to turn the television on.

I stand there, holding two remote controls, pressing buttons at random, until eventually I give up and go turn on the dishwasher. It has honestly been years since I have successfully recorded a television program — that is how "smart" my appliances have become.

And now the appliance manufacturers want to give us MORE features. Do you know what this means? It means that some night you'll open your "smart" refrigerator, looking for a beer, and you'll hear a cheerful recorded voice declaring, "Your milk is out of date." You will not know how your refrigerator knows this, and, what's worse, you will not know who else your refrigerator is informing about it.

Yet, to make the refrigerator stop, you'll have to read a whole book written in terms that are beyond comprehension.

Dear customers, is this the kind of future you want? Do you want household appliances that are smarter than you? Of course, you don't!

So, I am urging you to let the appliance industry know that when it comes to "smart" appliances, you say "NO", but you need to act quickly, because as you are reading this, your microwave is saying "YES!"

Words and Expressions

smart/smɑːt/*adj.* 聪明的，明智的；智能的
toast/təʊst/*n.* 烤面包片，吐司；*v.* 祝酒
appliance/əˈplaɪəns/*n.* （尤指家用的）电器用具；设备
manufacturer/ˌmænjuˈfæktʃərə(r)/*n.* 制造商
sense/sens/*n.* （对某物的）感觉；道理，判断力；*v.* 感觉到，觉察到；（机器）检测出
dishwasher/ˈdɪʃwɒʃə(r)/*n.* 洗碗机；洗碗工
refrigerator/rɪˈfrɪdʒəreɪtə(r)/*n.* 电冰箱
effective/ɪˈfektɪv/*adj.* 产生预期结果的，有效的；生效的，起作用的；给人深刻印象的
improvement/ɪmˈpruːvmənt/*n.* 进步；提高；好转；改善的事物，改进，改善
disturb/dɪˈstɜːb/*vt.* 打扰，麻烦，干扰；破坏，搞乱，弄乱；惊动，惊扰，使不安，使心烦意乱
feature/ˈfiːtʃə/*n.* 特征，特色，特点；特殊部件，附加部件；特征（模块）；（报纸等的）专题报道，特稿，特写；专栏文章；（电影）正片，故事片；特别节目；专题节目；（区别性的）特征
pack/pæk/*n.* 包，包裹，背包；大量，大堆；（纸牌的）一副；（尤指捕食性动物的）群，队；一伙，一帮；（尤指）犯罪团伙；全体前锋；（童子军的）一队；包，箱，盒，袋
button/ˈbʌtn/*n.* 纽扣，扣子；按钮，操作按钮
equip/ɪˈkwɪp/*vt.* 配备，装备（必需物资等）；使有能力；使具备知识；使穿戴；打扮
remote/rɪˈməʊt/*adj.* 远的；（距离或空间上）遥远的，偏僻的；边远的；（时间上）久远的；关系远的；无关的；微乎其微的；（机会或可能性）渺茫的；疏远的；孤高的；冷淡的；（计算机）远程的；遥控的
cassette/kəˈset/*n.* 磁带盒；盒式录音带；盒式录像带；胶卷暗盒；底片盒；盒式胶卷
recorder/rɪˈkɔːdə/*n.* 记录人，记录员；记录器，录音机；直笛；竖笛；记录法官（英国皇家刑事法庭的兼职法官）
identify/aɪˈdentɪˌfaɪ/*vt.* 把…等同于；把（自己）与…密切联系；认为（自己）与…有

关联；确定（植物或动物）的类别

press/pres/*vt.* 压榨；挤压；熨平；熨烫；强烈要求；催促；敦促；竭力推行；坚持；推举；用重物压死；重压；强征…入伍；*n.* 新闻从业人员；印刷机；（通常用于名称）出版社；拥挤的人群；推挤；压；按

comprehension/ˌkɒmprɪˈhenʃən/*n.* 理解；理解力；包含；理解力测验；内涵

microwave/ˈmaɪkrəʊˌweɪv/*n.* 微波；*vt.* 用微波炉烹调

Notes

1. *The Washington Post*： 1877 年，斯蒂尔森·哈钦斯创办了《华盛顿邮报》。《华盛顿邮报》是美国华盛顿哥伦比亚特区最大、最老的报纸。《华盛顿邮报》今天属于华盛顿邮报公司。该公司还拥有一些其他媒界或非媒界的企业，包括《新闻周刊》。

2. PIP： picture-in-(a-)picture，画中画，指数码式电视机屏幕的一角能显示第二个画面。

3. MTS： Multichannel Television Sound，双语立体声系统。

4. JUMP： 跳台（电视机遥控器上的功能键按钮）。

Exercises

I. Getting the Message

Read the questions and complete the answers according to the text.

1. What does the author mean by "drive customers up the wall?"

_____

2. What does the author think a good refrigerator should do?

_____

3. What is the greatest problem with the appliances we have now?

_____

4. What is the worst thing about a refrigerator that tells you when the milk is out of date?

_____

5. What does the author try to tell us in writing the text?

_____

II. Languages Focus

A. *Match the following words in left with their explanations in right.*

1. toast   a. a business for printing (and sometimes also for selling) books, magazines etc.

2. appliance   b. an apparatus, instrument or tool for a particular purpose, esp. an electrical machine that is used in the house

3. manufacturer   c. a large box or cupboard in which food and drink can be stored at a low temperature, but without being frozen

4. dishwasher   d. the act of understanding or ability to understand

5. refrigerator   e. recognize as being a particular person or thing; find out exactly what the cause or origin of something is

6. effective   f. (a result of) the act of making better or the state of being better or more acceptable

7. improvement   g. producing the desired result

8. identify   h. a firm that manufactures goods

9. comprehension   i. a machine that washes dishes or a person whose job is to wash dishes in a restaurant

10. press   j. bread made brown by being placed close to heat, usually eaten hot with butter

B. *Fill in the blanks with the words or expressions given below. Change the form where necessary.*

likewise	comprehension	helpful	disturb	effective
probably	urge	manufacture	feature	identify

1. He is a manager in a big company that _____ car parts.

2. I'm sorry to _____ you, but my car has broken down and I am wondering if I could use your phone.

3. The most surprising _____ of the house was a large room as big as a swimming pool.

4. He was too far away to be able to _____ faces.

5. Just water these plants twice a week, and _____ the ones in the bedroom.

6. How she manages to fit so much into a working day is beyond my _____.

7. I'll _____ start off for Hong Kong next week, but I'm not quite sure.

8. Sometimes, e-mail can be the most _____ form of communication, for messages can be exchanged within a very short time.

9. It was such a beautiful place that we had an _____ to stop and enjoy the scenery.

10. It was very _____ of you to do that for me.

Ⅲ. Translation

Translate the following sentences into Chinese.

1. You are toast if you don't take the doctor's advice.

_____

2. The alarm clock is driving me up the wall. It rings whenever it pleases.

_____

3. I don't want your money. Likewise, I won't accept your apology.

4. He hid in the shadows, pressing his back against the wall.

5. I noticed that she was sad and had a sudden urge to tell her the whole truth.

IV. Discussion

Directions: *You must have heard of some so-called "smart" household appliances with many new features, and they are supposed to make our life more comfortable and convenient. Now it is said that in the near future we would live in homes where all appliances are connected to the Internet. Would this be possible? Work in pairs and ask each other the following questions.*

1. In your opinion, what "smart" appliances would be available in the near future?
2. What are the advantages of "smart" appliances?
3. What are the disadvantages of "smart" appliances?

30 Days Without Internet—a Self-Experiment

For many of us who use the Internet to connect with our friends, buy things online and gather important information for our jobs and studies, it might be quite a challenge to live without the Internet just for a week.

That's the reason I hit on the idea to start this self-experiment: to plug off the Internet for one month. I wanted to know how being completely offline would affect my life.

On the morning of the first day, I got up, ate my breakfast, glanced through the headlines of the newspaper and read the sports section. I was disconnected, cut-off and separated. And this wouldn't change for the next 30 days.

Internet withdrawal doesn't feel good; it's uncomfortable and unpleasant. There is this uneasy feeling that you are missing something very important, which is quite a struggle, especially in the first week.

In fact, you are going to miss major news and updates that are interesting to you. I became the last who got to know about current developments in the world; mostly my friends would inform me and anything else could be found in the newspaper the next morning.

From day one I realized that being offline is much better to deal with when you are distracted, especially while being at home. Distracting myself by the use of a TV was not an option for me, as that would be like replacing one vice with another. I did however discover some old, yet amazing, books I read with interest.

Remaining distracted at home can be a challenge at times. I realized that the longer I was away from home, the easier it was to accomplish my challenge of being disconnected for 30 days.

One of my strategies to deal with being offline would be to work longer, step into the library more often or call one of my friends to do something together.

After a while, you get used to the state of being disconnected. Even more so, you fully begin to accept it, as the advantages of being offline present themselves right in front of your eyes. Surely, the need to reconnect will come up every now and then, especially when you urgently need certain information. But the online-activities like checking your e-mails begin to look less and less important to you, once you accepted the fact of not being able to connect to the Internet.

Instead of surfing the Internet for entertainment, I would sit down to meditate. I would open an interesting book or have a good conversation. I would hold my camera, discover new places and take amazing shots of architecture on the streets. I've never had the time to admire. Also, I would just sit around and reflect deeply on my life. I became absorbed in my own thoughts, and not in those of another person.

Living disconnected from the Internet in a society where everyone is online can be a rough ride, but it is possible. Moreover it can be a very valuable experience. You will notice that you spend more time with yourself, instead of thinking about the actions of others.

Being offline gives you the opportunity to get to know yourself much better and to meet friends you haven't seen for a while in real life. And it will help you to be more focused on the important things in life, to be more determined about your real goals and all the projects you have successfully delayed for the last months.

Words and Expressions

experiment/ɪkˈsperɪmənt/ *n.* 实验，试验；尝试，实践；*v.* 进行实验，做试验；试，尝试
plug/plʌɡ/ *n.* （电）插头，（电）插座；*v.* 插入；用插头接通电源；推广，宣传
offline/ˌɒfˈlaɪn/ *adj.* （计算机）未联网的，不在线的；（计算机设备）脱机的，离线的
disconnect/ˌdɪskəˈnekt/ *v.* 切断（机器或设备电力、煤气、水等的供应）；（尤指因未缴费而）停止供应（电、气、水、电话等服务）；使（电话）断线，将（电话）中断；切断（与系统、网络的）联系；*n.* 断开连接；差异，缺乏联系
development/dɪˈveləpmənt/ *n.* 发育，成长，发达；发展，进步；动态，进展；开发
accomplish/əˈkʌmplɪʃ/ *v.* 完成，实现
meditate/ˈmedɪteɪt/ *v.* （宗教中）默想，冥想；思考，沉思（meditate on/upon）；暗自策划，谋划
architecture/ˈɑːkɪtektʃə(r)/ *n.* 建筑设计，建筑风格；建筑学；结构；架构
focus/ˈfəʊkəs/ *n.* 重点，中心点；关注，注意；意图；焦距；*v.* 集中，注；聚焦，调焦
project/ˈprɒdʒekt/ *n.* 项目，计划；研究项目；*v.* 预计，推算；计划，规划；伸出，

突出；投掷，喷射；投射，投影；展现，表现
strategy/'strætədʒi/n.（尤指为获得某物制定长期的）策略，行动计划；战略，战略学
update/ʌp'deɪt/v. 为…增加最新信息，更新；使现代化；向…提供最新信息；n. 最新报道，最新消息；（计算机软件的）更新；新型，新版

 Notes

Meditation：冥想，是瑜伽中最珍贵的一项技法，是实现入定的途径。一切真实的瑜伽冥想术的最终目的都在于把人引导到解脱的境界。一名练习瑜伽者通过瑜伽冥想来制服心灵（心思意念），并超脱物质欲念，感受到和原始动因（the Original Cause，万源之源）直接沟通。瑜伽冥想的真义是把心、意、灵完全专注在原始之中。随着科学的发展，西方对冥想体系进行了进一步的挖掘，使其告别过去晦涩神化的背景，通过简单的练习，即可帮助人们告别负面情绪，重新掌控生活。

 Exercises

I. Comprehension of the Text

Read the text and answer the following questions. Write the answers on the lines.

1. Why did the author do the self-experiment of plugging off the Internet for one month?
_____
2. How did Internet withdrawal make him feel in the first week?
_____
3. How did the author get to know about the current developments in the world?
_____
4. When did the author feel the need to reconnect to the Internet?
_____
5. What will being completely offline help us to do, according to the author?
_____

II. Main Details Comprehension

Directions: *In this section, you are going to read a passage with ten statements attached to it. Each statement contains information given in one of the paragraphs. Identify the paragraph from which the information is derived. You may choose a paragraph more than once. Each paragraph is marked with a letter.*

A South Korean city designed for the future takes on a life of its own

A) Getting around a city is one thing — and then there's the matter of getting from one city to another. One vision of the perfect city of the future: a place that offers easy access to air travel. In 2011, a University of North Carolina business professor named John Kasarda published a book called *Aerotropolis: The Way We'll Live Next*. Kasarda says future cities should be built intentionally around or near airports. The idea, as he has put it, is to offer businesses "rapid, long-distance connectivity on a massive scale".

B) "The 18th century really was a waterborne century, the 19th century a rail century, the 20th century a highway, car, truck century — and the 21st century will increasingly be an aviation century, as the globe becomes increasingly connected by air," Kasarda says. Songdo, a city built from scratch in South Korea, is one of Kasarda's prime examples. It has existed for just a few years. "From the get-go, it was designed on the basis of connectivity and competitiveness," says Kasada. "The government built the bridge directly from the airport to the Songdo International Business District. And the surface infrastructure was built in tandem with the new airport."

C) Songdo is a stone's throw from South Korea's Incheon Airport, its main international hub. But it takes a lot more than a nearby airport to be a city of the future. Just building a place as an "international business district" doesn't mean it will become one. Park Yeon Soo conceived this city of the future back in 1986. He considers Songdo his baby. "I am a visionary," he says. Thirty years after he imagined the city, Park's baby is close to 70 percent built, with 36,000 people living in the business district and 90,000 residents in greater Songdo. It's about an hour outside Seoul, built on reclaimed tidal flats along the Yellow Sea. There's a Coast Guard building and a tall trade tower, as well as a park, golf course and university.

D) Chances are you've actually seen this place. Songdo appears in the most famous music video ever to come out of South Korea. "Gangnam Style" refers to the fashionable Gangnam district in Seoul. But some of the video was filmed in Songdo. "I don't know if you remember, there was a scene in a subway station. That was not Gangnam. That was actually Songdo," says Jung Won Son, a professor of urban development at London's Bartlett School of Planning. "Part of the reason to shoot there is that it's new and nice".

E) The city was supposed to be a hub for global companies, with employees from all over the world. But that's not how it has turned out. Songdo's reputation is as a futuristic ghost town. But the reality is more complicated. A bridge with big, light-blue loops leads into the business district. In the center of the main road, there's a long line of flags of the world. On the corner, there's a Starbucks and a 7-Eleven — all of the international brands that you see all over the world nowadays.

F) The city is not empty. There are mothers pushing strollers, old women with walkers — even in the middle of the day, when it's 90 degrees out. Byun Young-Jin chairs the Songdo real estate association and started selling property here when the first phase of the city opened in 2005. He says demand has boomed in the past couple of years. Most of his clients are Korean. In fact, the developer says, 99 percent of the homes here are sold to Koreans. Young families move here because the schools are great. And that's the problem: Songdo has become a popular Korean city — more popular as a residential area than a business one. It's not yet the futuristic international business hub that planners imagined. "It's a great place to live. And it's becoming a great place to work," says Scott Summers, the vice president of Gale International, the developer of the city. The floor-to-ceiling windows of his company's offices overlook Songdo Central Park, with a canal full of kayaks and paddle boats. Shimmering glass towers line the canal's edge.

G) "What's happened is, because we focused on creating that quality of life first, which enabled the residents to live here, what has probably missed the mark is for companies to locate here," he says. "There needs to be strong economic incentives." The city is still unfinished, and it feels a bit like a theme park. It doesn't feel all that futuristic. There's a high-tech underground trash disposal system. Buildings are environmentally friendly. Everybody's television set is connected to a system that streams personalized language or exercise classes.

H) But *Star Trek* this is not. And to some of the residents, Songdo feels hollow. "I'm, like, in prison for weekdays. That's what we call it in the workplace," says a woman in her 20s. She doesn't want to use her name for fear of being fired from her job. She goes back to Seoul every weekend. "I say I'm prison-breaking on Friday nights." But she has to make the prison break in her own car. There's no high-speed train connecting Songdo to Seoul, just over 20 miles away.

I) The man who first imagined Songdo feels frustrated, too. Park says he built South Korea a luxury vehicle, "like Mercedes or BMW. It's a good car now. But we're waiting for a good driver to accelerate." But there are lots of other good cars out there, too. The world is dotted with futuristic, high-tech cities trying to attract the biggest international companies.

J) Songdo's backers contend that it's still early, and business space is filling up — about 70 percent of finished offices are now occupied. Brent Ryan, who teaches urban design at MIT, says Songdo proves a universal principle. "There have been a lot of utopian cities in history. And the reason we don't know about a lot of them is that a lot of them have vanished entirely." In other words, when it comes to cities — or anything else — it is hard to predict the future.

_____1. Songdo's popularity lies more in its quality of life than its business attraction.

_____2. The man who conceived Songdo feels disappointed because it has fallen short of his expectations.

_____3. A scene in a popular South Korean music video was shot in Songdo.

_____4. Songdo still lacks the financial stimulus for businesses to set up shop there.

_____5. Airplanes will increasingly become the chief means of transportation, according to a professor.

_____6. Songdo has ended up different from the city it was supposed to be.

_____7. Some of the people who work in Songdo complain about boredom in the workplace.

_____8. A business professor says that a future city should have easy access to international transportation.

_____9. According to an urban design professor, it is difficult for city designers to foresee what will happen in the future.

_____10. Park Yeon Soo, who envisioned Songdo, feels a parental connection with the city.

III. Translation

Translate the five following sentences into English, using the words or expressions given in brackets.

1. 当时的局面很艰难，但她顺利地应付过去了。（deal with）
_____
2. 学校和家长不应该只关注考试的结果。（focus on）
_____
3. 我们应该明白，年轻人时不时地犯错是很正常的。（every now and then）
_____
4. 这位母亲从不在孩子们面前说中文，他们因此习惯了听她说英语。（be used to）
_____
5. 当闪光灯闪烁时，你不能插入记忆棒。否则，可能导致系统数据损坏。（plug to）
_____

Product Manual
产品说明书及其文体特点

产品说明书是生产厂家向消费者介绍说明商品性质、性能、结构、用途、规格、使用方法、保养、注意事项、质量保证、销售范围和免责声明等时使用的经济应用文书。产品说明书以文本的形式对某产品进行相对的详细描述，使人们认识、了解某产品，往往和产品附加在一起，是一种说明或宣传资料，属于应用文体中的说明文。产品说明书主要使用文字、数字、图案、符号和标记等表述。产品说明书也称为商品说明书、使用说明书、使用指南或产品使用手册。

一份成功有效的英文产品说明书，可以对产品进行全面详细的介绍，给消费者带来实质性的指导和帮助，还能提升产品的知名度和美誉度，促进产品的海内外销售，对产品能起到良好的宣传和推广作用。

产品说明书的文体有以下4个特点。

（一）客观性（Objective）

产品说明书的客观性是指在描述产品功能、性能和操作方法等方面应该准确、清晰且公正，避免使用主观性较强的词汇和语句。这样可以让用户更好地理解产品，并正确地使用产品。

（1）在描述产品功能时，应使用客观的词汇和语句，如"This product can automatically detect and remove dust from the air", 而不是 "You will feel fresher and healthier with this product"。

（2）在描述产品性能时，应提供具体的数据和指标，如 "This laptop has a processing speed of 2.4 GHz and a 16GB RAM", 而不是 "This laptop is very fast and powerful"。

（3）在描述产品操作方法时，应提供详细的步骤和说明，如 "To turn on the microwave oven, press the 'Power' button and set the time and temperature using the control panel", 而不是 "Just press a few buttons and you're good to go"。

（4）在描述产品的优点和缺点时，应保持客观公正，如 "This product has a long battery life and a high-resolution screen, but it may be slightly heavier than other similar products", 而不是 "This product is the best and nothing else compares"。

（二）专业性（Professional）

产品说明书是一种专业的应用文体，用词专业性是其一大突出特点。这种特殊文体有较固定的结构要素，如名称、型号、功能、特性、用途、注意事项和安装方式等，因此会频繁使用一些固定的名词词组或动词词组。

例如，active stereo loud-speaker（立体声有源音箱），bass reflex system（低音反射系统），class D amplifier（D 类功率放大器），woofer（低音喇叭），dome tweeter（圆顶高音喇叭），frequency range（频率范围），crossover frequency（交叉频率），mains input voltage（电源输入电压）和 max peak power consumption（最大峰值功耗）等。

（三）简明性（Concise）

产品说明书不属于文学性质较强的文体，其目标读者是普通大众，能简洁明了地描述物品并将产品的相关用途等简明说清楚即可。

(1) Temperatures to 65℃.
温度达 65℃。
(2) Usage and dosage：6g，twice a day.
用法用量：6g，每日 2 次。
(3) Power cord must be changed only at the qualified service shop.
需要更换电源线时，须送到专业维修店，不可擅自处理。

（四）呼唤性（Appealing）

产品说明书的呼唤性是指在编写说明书时，要注重语言的亲切、简洁、明了，让用户能够轻松理解并按照指示操作产品。

（1）使用简单明了的词汇和语句。

例如，"Press the 'Power' button to turn on the device", 而不是 "Please activate the equipment by pressing the 'Power' button"。

（2）使用主动语态，让用户感受到指导和帮助。

例如，"Plug in the charger to charge the battery", 而不是 "The battery should be charged by plugging in the charger"。

（3）避免使用过于专业的术语。

例如，"Connect the cable to the port"，而不是"Attach the cable to the interface"。

（4）使用直接、简洁的命令句。

例如，"Open the lid and place the disk inside"，而不是"Please open the cover and insert the disk into the drive"。

（5）在需要解释的地方，使用通俗易懂的语言。

例如，"The indicator light will turn on when the device is connected to the power source"，而不是"The status indicator will illuminate when the appliance is connected to the electrical outlet"。

1. *Read the following paragraphs and then answer the questions.*

Operating Instructions of VR Headset

Headset Control Mode
If the Controller is not connected, you can interact with the home screen by moving your head to direct the crosshairs over your intended selection and clicking the Volume Up/Down button on the VR Headset.

Switch the pointer of the master Controller
In the home screen, short press the Trigger of the corresponding Controller to switch the pointer of the master Controller.

Screen re-centering
Wear the VR Headset and look straight ahead, press and hold the Home button of the Controller or VR Headset (or the Volume Down button of the VR Headset in head control mode) for more than 1 second to re-center the screen.

Disconnect the Controller
Press and hold the Home button until the status indicator turns red and the Controller vibrates.

Controllers will automatically shut down to save power in the following cases:
- When the VR Headset enters deep sleep (a while after the VR Headset is taken off)
- When the Controller is unpaired
- When the VR Headset is powered off

Add a new Controller
If you need to add a new Controller (the VR Headset can only connect one left Controller and one right Controller) or reconnect with an unpaired Controller. Go to "Settings" ▶ "Controller", click on "Pair".
Press and hold the Home button and the Trigger of the Controller at the same time until the red and blue lights of the Controller flashing alternately, and then follow the instructions on the VR Headset screen.

Sleep / Wake up
Option 1 (Proximity Sensor) Take off VR Headset for automatic sleeping: wear the VR Headset for automatic waking up.
Option 2 (POWER Button) Press the Power button of the VR Headset for manual sleeping or waking up.

Hardware reset

VR Headset reset
If the visual in the VR Headset freezes, or the VR Headset does not respond after short press the Power button, you can press the Power button of the VR Headset for more than 10 seconds to reboot the VR Headset.

Controller reset
If the virtual Controller, the Home button or any buttons of the Controller doesn't respond, remove and reinstall the battery case to restart the Controller.

The VR Headset Adjustment
This device has no myopia adjustment function. The VR Headset allows wearing most standard glasses with a frame width of less than 150mm.
to install Glasses Spacer to increase the space. You can install or not according to your situation.

Unit 1　Web Life Today 　　13

(1) Does this device have myopia adjustment function?

_____

(2) What should you do if the controller doesn't respond to pressing the Home button or any button, or if the virtual controller in the helmet doesn't move?

_____

(3) What should you do if the helmet fails to respond to a short press of the helmet power button or the helmet screen gets stuck?

_____

(4) How to disconnect the controller?

_____

(5) How to add a new controller?

_____

2. *Map reading and translation.*

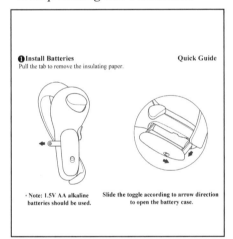

❶_____

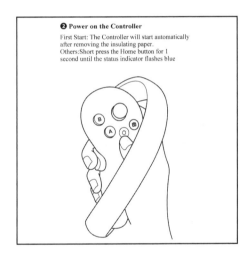

❷_____

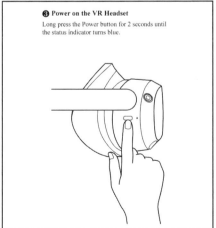

❸_____

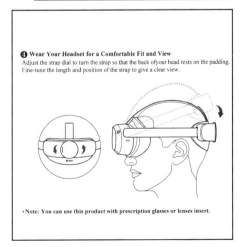

❹_____

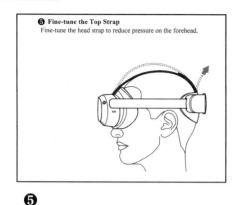

❺ _____

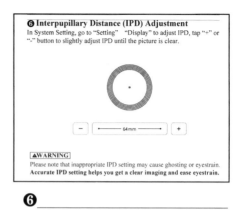

❻ _____

Workshop

Background

With the widespread of Internet, people seem to depend on it greatly. Since we have Internet, our life changes a lot. Each day, we can get information of other countries or places of the updated information. We can share our experiences with others, enjoy a lot of good things and learn much knowledge from Internet.

Firstly, we can obtain knowledge from Internet. There are numerous web sites contains different knowledge relating to skills or theories. If we want to learn certain things, the entire thing we have to do is to click mouse and then we will get the information we want. Besides, lots of people put lots of short video on Internet to teach others.

Secondly, by Internet, we can contact anyone we want. Internet offers us a passage to contact with others by some applications. The only thing we need to do is to download some soft wares and install them so that we can contact with our families or friends. Besides, we can use many free resources by checking the Internet.

Task

How many learning software do you know? What is the function of this software? What software did you use for your recent study and how did it work? Share the software you think is very useful with other groups.

Process

Step 1. The whole class is divided into several groups, each group containing 3－4 students.

Step 2. Each group has a discussion on a new learning software. Each member shares his experiences as well as their thoughts with group members.

Step 3. Group members write a report about how to use this learning software

Step 4. Each group sends a representative to make a report.

Unit 2　Arts Technology

Artifacts Come Alive With Technology

　　Xu Shaoqing stood in front of a large screen as a picture of a golden earring the size of a basketball appeared. "The jewelry dates to the Warring States Period (475－221 BC)," the caption read. Xu took out his phone, scanned a QR code beside the illustration, and a link with information about the earring opened on his phone.

　　The presentation is part of a new experience offered by the latest exhibition at the provincial museum in Fujian province. A 4-by-2-meter high-definition touch screen displays facts about more than 300 artifacts from an exhibition about the Maritime Silk Road. "If visitors miss the real exhibition, they can still enjoy it on the screen," said Gong Zhangnian, deputy director of the museum. "You can even browse the exhibition at home or on your phone." Technology is making its way to more Chinese museums these days.

　　Atmospheric music welcomes visitors to Cave 220－part of the Mogao Grottoes of Dunhuang. Suddenly, the cave becomes very bright, and the beautiful murals painted some 1,400 years ago are fully revealed in impressive color and extraordinary detail. But this is not a real cave－it's a virtual environment created by the ALiVE team. The result is so realistic that it might become the only way to "see" endangered historic sites and monuments in the future.

　　"You wouldn't be able to see any of this in the real cave because light exposure is so damaging," says Jeffrey Shaw, director of the ALiVE team. His team created the virtual cave by mapping the original structure using laser scans and ultra-high resolution photography. Many experts say the result is more visually appealing and accessible than the real thing.

　　The technology enabled the team to augment reality, enhancing color and magnifying detail. They are also experimenting with animation: Dancers spring from the wall and perform movements. Musical instruments are magnified and turn in three-dimensional form while the sound plays from hidden speakers.

　　"This project has been driven by the challenges of preservation and conservation. The caves are an extraordinary heritage site, but they are under enormous environmental threat. There is also increasing stress from the number of tourists who now want to visit. The human traffic can cause great damage to fragile sites, increasing wear and tear through erosion and light exposure," says Mr. Shaw. Mr. Shaw thinks that the best way to preserve the Dunhuang caves is to close them, and that the digital reconstruction will give the viewer an alternative and very strong experience of the caves.

An immersive exhibition at Panlong Tiandi of Shanghai is showcasing Buddhism and pagoda art in ancient China. The exhibition will run till March 2024.

Three digital art pieces created by the Harvard FAS CAMLab team are on show at the Kaimu Theater in Cheng's Ancestral Hall, a historic building in Shanghai's Panlong Tiandi.

The exhibition culminates with the third piece Embodied Architecture, which shows the interior, structure and scriptures found in the Pagoda of Fogong Temple in Yingxian county of Shanxi province, the tallest and oldest surviving pure wood-framed pavilion-style structure dating back to the 10th century.

Using digital technologies such as photogrammetry, digital modeling, and CG animation, the artwork takes viewers on a virtual tour of the pagoda during which they can experience the spiritual journey.

Words and Expressions

caption/ˈkæpʃ(ə)n/*n*. （图片的）说明文字；（电影或电视的）字幕；*v.* 给…加文字说明

QR code 二维码

illustration/ˌɪləˈstreɪʃ(ə)n/*n*. 插图，图解；说明，例释；实例，示例

atmospheric/ˌætməsˈferɪk/*adj*. 有关大气的；有神秘（美）感的，富有情调的

mural/ˈmjʊərəl/*n*. 壁画，*adj*. （似）墙的，与墙有关的；

appealing/əˈpiːlɪŋ/*adj*. 吸引人的，有感染力的；恳求的，可怜的

accessible/əkˈsesəb(ə)l/*adj*. 可到达的，可进入的；易得到的，可使用的；可以理解的，易懂的；平易近人的，随和的；易受影响的

augment/ɔːgˈment/*v*. 增加，增大；加强，补充

heritage/ˈherɪtɪdʒ/*n*. 遗产，传统，世袭财产；植物种类）纯种的，老品种的；特殊（或个人）的所有物，（该有的）一份

reconstruction/ˌriːkənˈstrʌkʃn/*n*. 再建，重建；改造；复兴

alternative/ɔːlˈtɜːnətɪv/*n*. 可供选择的事物，替代物；*adj*. 可替代的，备选的；非传统的

culminates/ˈkʌlmɪneɪt/*v*. （以…）结束，告终；到达顶点，达到高潮

pavilion/pəˈvɪliən/*n*. 运动员席，看台，更衣室；临时建筑；大型文体馆；凉亭，阁

photogrammetry/ˌfəʊtəʊˈɡræmɪtri/*n*. ［测］摄影测量法；摄影制图法

Notes

1. the Mogao Grottoes of Dunhuang： 敦煌莫高窟，俗称千佛洞，坐落在中国河西走廊西端的敦煌。始建于十六国的前秦时期，历经十六国、北朝、隋、唐、五代、西夏和元等历代的兴建，形成世界上现存规模最大、内容最丰富的佛教艺术地。莫高窟地处丝绸之路的一个战略要点。它不仅是东西方贸易的中转站，同时也是宗教、文化和知识

Unit 2 Arts Technology

的交汇处。莫高窟的 492 个小石窟和洞穴庙宇，以其雕像和壁画闻名于世，展示了延续千年的佛教艺术。

2. CAMLab：哈佛大学中国艺术实验室（Chinese Art Media Lab，CAMLab）属于哈佛大学文理学院（Faculty of Arts and Sciences，FAS），由哈佛大学洛克菲勒亚洲艺术史终身教授汪悦进（Eugene Wang）创立。

3. CG：计算机图形学（Computer Graphics，CG），是通过计算机软件所绘制的一切图形的总称。随着以计算机为主要工具进行视觉设计和生产的一系列相关产业的形成，国际上习惯将利用计算机技术进行视觉设计和生产的领域通称为 CG。它既包括技术也包括艺术，几乎囊括了当今计算机时代中所有的视觉艺术创作活动，如平面印刷品的设计、网页设计、三维动画、影视特效、多媒体技术、以计算机辅助设计为主的建筑设计及工业造型设计等。

Exercises

I. Getting the Message

1. What might become the only way to "see" endangered historic sites in the future?

2. What do many experts say about the virtual cave?

3. Please find the description about virtual Cave 220 in the article.

4. What is Embodied Architecture?

5. Please find some information about the influence of technology on art in the article.

II. Languages Focus

A. *Match the following words in left their explanations in right.*

1. accessible   a. relating to or located in the atmosphere
2. mural   b. the process of making maps or scale drawings from photographs, especially aerial photographs
3. caption   c. the activity of constructing something again
4. appealing   d. large and often sumptuous tent
5. alternative   e. any attribute or immaterial possession that is inherited from ancestors
6. heritage   f. serving or used in place of another
7. pavilion   g. able to attract interest or draw favorable attention
8. reconstruction   h. brief description accompanying an illustration

9. photogrammetry   i. a painting that is applied to a wall surface
10. atmospheric   j. capable of being reached

B. *Fill in the blanks with the words or expressions given below. Change the form where necessary.*

| scan | caption | alternative | appealing | culminate |
| heritage | atmospheric | accessible | digital | augment |

1. While searching for a way to _____ the family income, she began making dolls.

2. Their summer tour will _____ at a spectacular concert in London.

3. What is it about Tom Hanks that cinema-goers find so _____?

4. Pictures are scanned into a form of _____ information that computers can recognize.

5. All now buildings must be made _____, and existing facilities must remove barriers if the removal can be accomplished without much difficulty or expense.

6. There are _____ sources of nutrition to animal meat.

7. To serve as responsible stewards of the planet, we must press forward on deeper _____ and oceanic research.

8. The local paper featured me standing on a stepladder with a_____, Wendy climbs the ladder to success.

9. Your bladder needs to be full for the _____.

10. Charmouth _____ Centre is the place to discover more about the natural history of the area.

Ⅲ. Translation

Translate the following sentences into Chinese.

1. "The jewelry dates to the Warring States Period (475－221 BC)," the caption read.

_____

2. A 4-by-2-meter high-definition touch screen displays facts about more than 300 artifacts from an exhibition about the Maritime Silk Road.

_____

3. Suddenly, the cave becomes very bright, and the beautiful murals painted some 1,400 years ago are fully revealed in impressive color and extraordinary detail.

_____

4. His team created the virtual cave by mapping the original structure using laser scans and ultra-high resolution photography. Many experts say the result is more visually appealing and accessible than the real thing.

_____

5. The exhibition culminates with the third piece Embodied Architecture, which shows the interior, structure and scriptures found in the Pagoda of Fogong Temple in Yingxian county of Shanxi province, the tallest and oldest surviving pure wood-framed pavilion-style structure dating back to the 10th century.

IV. Discussion

Modern science and technology provide new material and technical means for art, and promote the emergence of new art types and art forms. modern science and technology have created an unprecedented cultural environment and means of communication for art, providing a broader world for art. It is manifested in the combination and mutual penetration of art and technology, aesthetics and science, which has a profound impact on human life and promotes the development of science, technology and literature and art themselves. Major discoveries in the field of science have had a huge and profound impact on artistic concepts and aesthetic concepts, such as system theory, cybernetics, information theory, fuzzy mathematics and other viewpoints and methods, have been applied to art creation and art research, and become the viewpoints and methods of some art theories and art criticism.

1. Please talk about the penetration and influence of modern science and technology on art.
2. Please give us some examples of the combination of science and art and how it has influenced our lives.

Online Exhibitions

Like all cultural institutions, galleries and art fairs are adapting to a new reality.

Art Basel Hong Kong, Asia's biggest contemporary-art fair, was canceled because of COVID-19, but anyone who had planned to visit last week could enjoy an experimental alternative: the viewing room. At the click of a keyboard, you could enter a panoramic but private visual salon, without having to brave the airless Hong Kong Convention and Exhibition Centre.

Participating galleries were told that, for a quarter of the original fee, they could have a slot in the online fair. Over 90% of the line-up — 231 galleries — gave it a whirl, offering more than 2,000 works worth $270 million in total. The viewing room was a telling indication of how art might be shown (and sold) in the future, in a pandemic-stricken era or if travel is otherwise restricted. It offered encouragement — and some lessons on digital engagement.

There, on one webpage, was Jeff Koons riffing on Botticelli's "Primavera" in a tribute to the history of painting at David Zwirner Gallery. Ota Fine Arts offered one collector the chance to acquire an "infinity room", one of the most instagrammed artworks of recent years — the creation of the psychedelic, nonagenarian Japanese artist, Yayoi Kusama. White Cube presented an array of international works by Andreas Gursky (German), Theaster Gates (American) and Beatriz Milhazes (Brazilian).

But not every artist, gallery and form showed to equal advantage in this alternative fair. Not surprisingly, simple two-dimensional works in bright colors came across best. No sculpture or conceptual art was included. Subtle pieces, such as Lucas Arruda's impressionistic desert-scapes, which seem as much a mood or a state of mind as a physical depiction when you see them in real life, had little impact when viewed remotely.

Besides depth and texture, there are aspects of gallery-hopping that a website is unlikely to replicate. One is serendipity — the sense of wandering between artworks and encountering the unexpected. Another is sociability. Art is a communion between artist and viewer, but galleries and fairs are also places to swap opinions and share enthusiasms.

There are ways to compensate for these inevitable deficiencies. As they shut their physical doors, some of the world's finest galleries and museums are offering whizzy interactive visits, 360-degree videos and walk-around tours of their collections, all without queues and high ticket prices. One of the best is laid on by the Rijksmuseum in Amsterdam; its tour allows visitors to view its Vermeers and Rembrandts, including the magnificent "Night Watch", far more closely than would normally be possible. Another standout offering is from the Museu de Arte de São Paulo, which has an even broader collection. On its virtual platform, its paintings, spanning 700 years, appear to be hanging in an open-plan space, seemingly suspended on glass panels, or "crystal easels" as the museum calls them, ideal for close-up inspection.

But such wizardry may be beyond most galleries and artists. For Art Basel, Tracey Emin, a British artist at White Cube, exhibited a heartfelt demand spelled out in icyblue neon: "Move me". At a distance, that is hard.

Words and Expressions

panoramic/ˌpænəˈræmɪk/*adj.* 全景的
salon/ˈsælɒn/*n.* [法] 沙龙；客厅；营业性的高级服务室
depiction/dɪˈpɪkʃn/*n.* 描述
texture/ˈtekstʃə(r)/*n.* （织物）质地；（材料）构造；结构；肌理
replicate/ˈreplɪkeɪt/*v.* 折叠，复制，模写；*n.* 同样的样品；*adj.* 转折的
sociability/ˌsəʊʃəˈbɪləti/*n.* 好交际，社交性，善于交际
swap/swɒp/*n.* 交换；*vt.* 交换，用…作交易
compensate/ˈkɒmpenseɪt/*vt.* 补偿，赔偿；酬报；*vi.* 弥补，补偿；抵消

inevitable/ɪn'evɪtəb(ə)l/*adj.* 不可避免的，必然发生的
interactive/ɪntər'æktɪv/*adj.* 相互作用的，互相影响的，（计算机）交互的
inspection/ɪn'spekʃ(ə)n/*n.* 检查，审查，检阅
slot/slɒt/*n* 名单，日程安排或者广播节目表中的位置，时间和机会
pandemic/pæn'demɪk/*n.* 流行病，大流行病；*adj.* 普遍的，全世界的

Notes

1. Art Basel：原香港国际艺术展（ART HK）被国际知名的巴塞尔艺术展收购，2013 年正式命名为香港巴塞尔艺术展。巴塞尔艺术展主要展示和销售当代艺术，于 1970 年在瑞士创办，2002 年于美国迈阿密举行首展，2013 年登陆香港，掀开亚洲艺术市场的新一页。该艺术展现在每年于巴塞尔、迈阿密和香港三地举行，被认为是最具代表性的国际艺术博览会。

2. Rijksmuseum：国立博物馆是荷兰最大的博物馆，其丰富的收藏包括伦勃朗名闻遐迩的《夜巡》（*Night Watch*）、维米尔的《倒牛奶的女仆》（*The Milkmaid*）等著名画作。国立博物馆建于 1798 年，于 1800 年正式对公众开放。那时它坐落于荷兰海牙的豪斯登堡，是女王碧雅翠克斯的皇宫，后国立博物馆于 1808 年迁至阿姆斯特丹达姆广场的皇宫，并增添了伦勃朗的著名画作《夜巡》。1885 年，博物馆又迁至现在所在的富有华丽装饰的古老建筑，并成为阿姆斯特丹的一座标志性建筑。在市立近代美术馆（1896 年）、梵高博物馆（1973 年）相继建成后，国立博物馆也成为了博物馆广场的中心。

3. Museu de Arte de São Paulo：葡萄牙语，意为圣保罗艺术博物馆，在当地常简称为 MASP，是巴西最重要的艺术博物馆，设立于 1963 年。主要收藏了大量的画作，但也有收藏第二次世界大战后雕刻家的作品。此博物馆位于巴西圣保罗圣保罗人大道，由 Pietro Maria Bardi 和妻子 Lina Bo Bardi 所成立。经费来自于巴西人民的捐献，其中多数的捐款来自于圣保罗州的人民。

Exercises

I. Comprehension of the Text

Read the text and answer the following questions. Write the answers on the lines.

1. Why has Art Basel Hong Kong, Asia's largest contemporary art fair, been canceled?

2. What are the possible ways in which art could be displayed (and sold) in the future, in an era of viruses, or when travel is restricted?

3. Besides depth and texture, what are some aspects of gallery browsing that websites are unlikely to replicate?

4. Where paintings spanning 700 years seem to hang in an open space, seemingly on glass panels that the museum calls "crystal easels", perfect for close inspection?

_____

5. Are participating galleries expensive? How many works are in the online exhibition?

_____

II. Main Details Comprehension

Directions: *Each of the following statement contains information given in one of the paragraphs. Identify the paragraph from which the information is derived. You may choose a paragraph more than once. Each paragraph is marked with a letter. Answer the questions by marking the corresponding letter in the blanks.*

Is Breakfast Really the Most Important Meal of the Day?

A) Along with old classics like "carrots give you night vision" and "Santa doesn't bring toys to misbehaving children", one of the most well-worn phrases of tired parents everywhere is that breakfast is the most important meal of the day. Many of us grow up believing that skipping breakfast is a serious mistake, even if only two thirds of adults in the UK eat breakfast regularly, according to the British Dietetic Association, and around three-quarters of Americans.

B) "The body uses a lot of energy stores for growth and repair through the night," explains diet specialist Sarah Elder. "Eating a balanced breakfast helps to up our energy, as well as make up for protein and calcium used throughout the night." But there's widespread disagreement over whether breakfast should keep its top spot in the hierarchy (等级) of meals. There have been concerns around the sugar content of cereal and the food industry's involvement in pro-breakfast research — and even one claim from an academic that breakfast is "dangerous".

C) What's the reality? Is breakfast a necessary start to the day or a marketing tactic by cereal companies? The most researched aspect of breakfast (and breakfast-skipping) has been its links to obesity. Scientists have different theories as to why there's a relationship between the two. In one US study that analyzed the health data of 50,000 people over seven years, researchers found that those who made breakfast the largest meal of the day were more likely to have a lower body mass index (BMI) than those who ate a large lunch or dinner. The researchers argued that breakfast helps reduce daily calorie intake and improve the quality of our diet — since breakfast foods are often higher in fiber and nutrients.

D) But as with any study of this kind, it was unclear if that was the cause — or if breakfast-skippers were just more likely to be overweight to begin with. To find out, researchers designed a study in which 52 obese women took part in a 12-week weight loss program. All had the same number of calories over the day, but half had breakfast, while the other half did not. What they found was that it wasn't breakfast itself that caused the participants to lose weight: it was changing their normal routine.

E) If breakfast alone isn't a guarantee of weight loss, why is there a link between obesity and breakfast-skipping? Alexandra Johnstone, professor of appetite research at the University of Aberdeen, argues that it may simply be because breakfast-skippers have been found to be less knowledgeable about nutrition and health. "There are a lot of studies on the relationship between breakfast eating and possible health outcomes, but this may be because those who eat breakfast choose to habitually have health-enhancing behaviors such as regular exercise and not smoking," she says.

F) A 2016 review of 10 studies looking into the relationship between breakfast and weight management concluded there is "limited evidence" supporting or refuting (反驳) the argument that breakfast influences weight or food intake, and more evidence is required before breakfast recommendations can be used to help prevent obesity.

G) Researches from the University of Surrey and University of Aberdeen are halfway through research looking into the mechanisms behind how the time we eat influences body weight. Early findings suggest that a bigger breakfast is beneficial to weight control. Breakfast has been found to affect more than just weight. Skipping breakfast has been associated with a 27% increased risk of heart disease, a 21% higher risk of type 2 diabetes in men, and a 20% higher risk of type 2 diabetes in women. One reason may be breakfast's nutritional value — partly because cereal is fortified (增加营养价值) with vitamins. In one study on the breakfast habits of 1,600 young people in the UK, researchers found that the fiber and micronutrient intake was better in those who had breakfast regularly. There have been similar findings in Australia, Brazil, Canada and the US.

H) Breakfast is also associated with improved brain function, including concentration and language use. A review of 54 studies found that eating breakfast can improve memory, though the effects on other brain functions were inconclusive. However, one of the review's researchers, Mary Beth Spitznagel, says there is "reasonable" evidence breakfast does improve concentration there just needs to be more research. "Looking at studies that tested concentration, the number of studies showing a benefit was exactly the same as the number that found no benefit," she says. "And no studies found that eating breakfast was bad for concentration".

I) What's most important, some argue, is what we eat for breakfast. High-protein breakfasts have been found particularly effective in reducing the longing for food and consumption later in the day, according to research by the Australian Commonwealth Scientific and Industrial Research Organization. While cereal remains a firm favorite among breakfast consumers in the UK and US, a recent investigation into the sugar content of 'adult' breakfast cereals found that some cereals contain more than three-quarters of the recommended daily amount of free sugars in each portion, and sugar was the second or third highest ingredient in cereals.

J) But some research suggests if we're going to eat sugary foods, it's best to do it early. One study recruited 200 obese adults to take part in a 16-week-long diet, where half added dessert to their breakfast, and half didn't. Those who added dessert lost an average of 40 pounds more — however, the study was unable to show the long-term effects. A review of 54 studies found that there is no consensus yet on what type of breakfast is healthier, and concluded that the type of breakfast doesn't matter as much as simply eating something.

K) While there's no conclusive evidence on exactly what we should be eating and when, the consensus is that we should listen to our own bodies and eat when we're hungry. "Breakfast is most important for people who are hungry when they wake up," Johnstone says. "Each body starts the day differently — and those individual differences need to be researched more closely," Spitznagel says. "A balanced breakfast is really helpful, but getting regular meals throughout the day is more important to leave blood sugar stable through the day, which helps control weight and hunger levels," says Elder. "Breakfast isn't the only meal we should be getting right".

_____1. According to one professor, obesity is related to a lack of basic awareness of nutrition and health.

_____2. Some scientists claim that people should consume the right kind of food at breakfast.

_____3. Opinions differ as to whether breakfast is the most important meal of the day.

_____4. It has been found that not eating breakfast is related to the incidence of certain diseases in some countries.

_____5. Researchers found it was a change in eating habits rather than breakfast itself that induced weight loss.

_____6. To keep oneself healthy, eating breakfast is more important than choosing what to eat.

_____7. It is widely considered wrong not to eat breakfast.

_____8. More research is needed to prove that breakfast is related to weight loss or food intake.

_____9. People who prioritize breakfasts tend to have lower calorie but higher nutritional intake.

_____10. Many studies reveal that eating breakfast helps people memorize and concentrate.

Ⅲ. Translation

Translate the five following sentences into English, using the words or expressions given in brackets.

1. 亚洲最大的当代艺术博览会——香港巴塞尔艺术展因COVID-19而被取消，但任何上周计划参观的人都可以享受一个实验性的替代选择：放映室。（cancel）

_____

_____

2. 参与展览的画廊被告知，只需原有费用的四分之一，就可以在网上展览会上占有一席之地。（have a slot）

_____

Unit 2　Arts Technology

3. 观景室生动地表明，在未来，在一个病毒肆虐的时代，或者在旅行受到限制的情况下，艺术品展示（和出售）的可能的方式。（restrict）

_____

4. 一些世界上最好的画廊和博物馆在关闭实体馆的同时，还提供了令人眼花缭乱的互动参观、360 度全景视频和藏品巡展，所有这些都不用排队，也不用支付高昂的门票。（walk-around tour）

_____
_____

5. 在虚拟平台上，跨越 700 年的画作似乎悬挂在一个开放的空间里，似乎悬挂在博物馆称之为"水晶画架"的玻璃板上，非常适合近距离观察。（virtual platform）

_____
_____

 Part C

Product Manual
信息类产品说明书措辞特点

英文产品说明书的特点之一是具有较高的专业性，这主要体现在使用专业性术语、缩略词和复合词来描述产品的功能、性能和操作方法等方面。

（一）专业术语

电子产品说明书是一种相对专业的应用问题，措辞专业性强是其一大突出特点。例如，名称、型号、功能、特征、安装步骤和注意事项等。同时，某一技术领域中特有的"行话"或"俚语"也会使用，而且行业词汇会相对固定。例如，在翻译数码相机说明书时，常常会遇到这样一些术语，film 常指"电影"，此处指"胶卷"；digital zoom 指"数字范围"，此处译为"数码变焦"为宜。

有些词是特定领域内的专业词汇，具有明确的含义。例如：
（1）通信领域的专业词汇
modem（调制解调器）、transceiver（收发器）、antenna（天线）等。
（2）电子设备领域的专业词汇
battery（电池）、charger（充电器）、display（显示器）等。
（3）软件工程领域的专业词汇
algorithm（算法）、encryption（加密）、decryption（解密）等。

（二）缩略词

缩略词是由单词的首字母或前几个字母组成的新词，用于表示某个概念或缩写。缩略词由于书写简单，便于识记，经常出现在科技英语的文本中，尤其在产品说明书中更为常见。说明书的信息须尽可能简明扼要。为了体现其专业性、规范性和简洁性，产品说明书尤其是专业设备的使用说明书，不可避免地会使用一些缩略语。例如，CPU（中央处理器）、GPU（图形处理器）、USB（通用串行总线）、GSM（全球移动通信系统）、Wi-Fi（无线局域网）、蓝牙（Bluetooth）、IP 地址（IP 指互联网协议，Internet Protocol）、CAD（computer aided design）、max（maximum）、temp（temperature）、HMI（human machine interface，人机界面）、BIOS（Basic Input and Output System，基本输入输出系统）、FIFO（First-In，First-Out，先进先出）、VCR（Video Cassette Recorder，录像机）、ERP（Energy Related Products，能源相关产品）和 HF（Hands Free，免提）等，这类词第一次往往以完整形式出现在文本中后，后面将会以其缩略形式出现。

（三）名词复合词

在英文产品说明书中，复合词的使用非常常见。复合词是由两个或更多个词组合而成的新词，通常用来表示一种特定概念或功能。例如，power bank（移动电源）、smartphone（智能手机）、tablet（平板计算机）、search engine（搜索引擎）、social media（社交媒体）和 cloud computing（云计算）等。

以下是一些英文产品说明书中常见的复合词及其举例：

（1）Waterproof（防水）：This phone case is waterproof, so you don't have to worry about your phone getting wet.

这款手机壳是防水的，所以您不必担心手机受潮。

（2）Bidirectional（双向的）：This charger is bidirectional, which means it can charge your phone and power bank simultaneously.

这款充电器是双向的，意味着它可以同时给手机和移动电源充电。

（3）Wireless（无线的）：The mouse is wireless, so you can use it without being connected to the computer by a cable.

这款鼠标是无线的，所以您可以在不通过电缆连接电脑的情况下使用它。

（4）Rechargeable（可充电的）：This battery is rechargeable, so you can charge it and use it again and again.

这款电池是可充电的，所以您可以充电并反复使用。

（5）Portable（便携的）：This speaker is portable, so you can take it with you and enjoy music anywhere.

这款扬声器是便携的，所以您可以随身携带，无论身在何处都可以享受音乐。

（6）High-definition（高清的）：This monitor has a high-definition display, which provides you with a clear and vivid visual experience.

这款显示器具有高清显示，为您提供清晰、生动的视觉体验。

（7）Dust-proof（防尘）：This camera is dust-proof, so you don't have to worry about dust getting into the lens.

这款相机是防尘的，所以您不必担心灰尘进入镜头。

（8）User-friendly（用户友好的）：This software is user-friendly, so it's easy for anyone to learn and use.

这款软件是用户友好的，所以无论谁都可以轻松学习和使用。

Unit 2　Arts Technology

1. *Read the following paragraphs and then answer the questions.*

Google Glass Enterprise 2 Guide VREXPERT

Getting Started

Attach/detach device to frame

1. To attach the device to the frame, hook the round attachment on the frame to the device's bayonet hinge, then gently pull the frame forward to snap the device into place.

2. To detach the device, hold the front of the device (near the camera), and gently push the frame backwards to snap the hinge backwards, then lift it off the bayonet hinge.

Get the right fit

1. First, turn Glass on. Press the power button on the inner right side of the device. The power LED lights up and Glass Enterprise Edition 2 boots up.
2. To start, modify the nose pads to adjust the fit of your Glass as needed. Keep both your eyes open as you squeeze the nose stem to position the display just above your right eye, but not in front of it. Then, move the display hinge until you can see the whole screen. Adjust the nose pads so they're flush with your skin.

Common gestures

The flat area on Glass next to your right temple is called the touchpad. You need it to navigate around the different cards on your Glass display. Here's how:

1. Tap the touchpad to activate the display and select actions.
2. Slide your finger forward or backward across the touchpad to navigate your applications or swipe through menu options.
3. To cancel or back out of certain actions, slide your finger from the top to the bottom of your touchpad.

Connecting to Wifi

You can connect to Wifi networks from the settings by using the "Wifi" icon.
To enable Wifi:

1. Tap on the Wifi icon.
2. Tap again to enable Wifi.

You can connect to a Wi-Fi network by scanning a QR code or selecting a network from the list. To connect to a Wi-Fi network by scanning a QR code:

1. Generate the Wifi QR code for your network using a generator (qifi.org).
2. Tap on the Wifi icon to enter the Wifi settings.
3. Swipe forward on the touchpad to select the "Scan QR code" option.
4. Tap to start scanning for the Wifi QR code (a camera preview will appear in the Viewfinder).
5. Center the QR code in the box displayed on your Viewfinder.

Updating Firmware

To update your Google Glass:

1. Open settings.
2. Swipe forward until you see the System card.
3. Tap to confirm selection.
4. Swipe forward until you see the System update card.
5. Tap to confirm selection.

Perform a system update
To manually perform system updates:

1. Tap on the perform system update icon.
2. Tap to check for new updates.
3. If an update is available, tap to download and install it automatically.
4. After the update is installed, a message will appear instructing you to reboot the device.

(1) How to detach the device?
_____

(2) How to get the right fit?
_____

(3) What is touchpad ? And please tell us its function.
_____

(4) How to connect to Wi-Fi?
_____

(5) How to update your Goole glass?
_____

2. *Map reading and translation.*

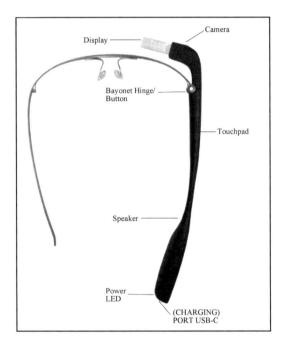

❶ Display_____   ❷ Camera _____
❸ Touchpad_____   ❹ Speaker _____
❺ Power LED_____

Workshop

Background

Digital art is growing into a new art form of cultural and creative industries in the 21st century, and the application of digital art has become the most important culture and creative, dynamic and creative emerging industries. We should pay attention to the research of digital art theory and the cultivation of talents, and face up to the continuous development of digital image technology.

We should reform the traditional mode of cultivating artistic talents in colleges and universities, and cultivate digital artistic talents across disciplines, so as to adapt to the development and change trend of digital technology and mainstream audiences as soon as possible.

With the rapid development of digital technology and information technology in the late 1980s, digital art began to appear. With computers and internet, the digital social space developed by Internet technology has created a new broad platform for artists who master digital technology and application ability to create digital art in all directions.

Task

Know more about digital arts through internet:

(1) The concept and development prospect of digital art.

(2) The impact of digital art on culture and society.

(3) The cultivation of Chinese and foreign digital art talents.

Process

Step 1. The whole class is divided into several groups, each group containing 3－4 students.

Step 2. Each group has a discussion on digital arts. Each member share his experiences as well as their thoughts with group members.

Step 3. Group members write a report about digital arts or show their work.

Step 4. Each group sends a representative to make a report.

Unit 3 E-commerce

Amazon Gets Physical

"The world wants you to be typical…Don't let it happen," Jeff Bezos warned in April in his last annual shareholder letter as CEO of Amazon. Hence bewilderment that his e-empire is to adopt a retail format that is very typical indeed: the department store. Having helped drive many chains out of business, it is now eyeing the format to boost its own retail fortunes.

As a company, Amazon is entering a more mature phase. Now with a new chief executive, Andy Jassy, it is being forced to recognize that pure e-commerce has limits. It is also facing fresh competition from conventional retailers like Walmart and Target that are belatedly showing that they, too, can do the internet well.

Amazon's high-street presence is small. Since 2015 it has opened 24 bookshops in America. Its 30 "4-star" shops, which stock items customers rate highly, function like a walk-in website. Whole Foods, an upmarket grocer it bought in 2017, contributes the bulk of its physical-store revenues, which accounted for just 4% of Amazon's total sales in the most recent quarter. Its new Amazon Fresh grocery chain and Amazon Go cashierless stores barely chip in.

So the new 30,000-square-foot (2,800-square-metre) retail spaces it is reportedly envisaging mark a departure. Amazon has neither confirmed nor denied its plans. But leaked details on the stores' size and locations suggest substance behind the reports. The first are to open in California and Ohio. If they go well, Amazon is expected to roll out more.

Why invest in the high street just as COVID-19 has lifted e-commerce? The growth rate of sales on Amazon's platforms, including third parties, had slowed before the crisis, from nearly 30% a year to below 20%. The trend reasserts itself as people return to shops. In the past quarter Amazon's own online sales grew by only 16%, short of investors' (muted) expectations.

In future customers will want "omni-channel" retail that combines online and physical shopping, says Mark Shmulik of Bernstein, a broker. As for Amazon's move into department stores, he has one question: "What took them so long?" The firm's motive is also defensive. Walmart has made omni-channel work well during the pandemic by melding its formidable physical network with its website and offering a same-day "click-and-collect" service.

Getting more physical may not be easy. Amazon's bricks-and-mortar performance has been ho-hum. Whereas most other big American grocers' sales have doubled or even tripled in the pandemic, those of Whole Foods have barely budged, notes Sucharita Kodali of Forrester, a research firm. Amazon's total physical-store revenues last year were 6% lower than in 2018.

Making Amazon marts appeal to shoppers may be harder than Amazon anticipates. It reportedly wants them to sell its cheap private-label garments and gadgets, which is at odds with its aspirations for the stores to offer high-end fashion, where it has struggled online. It is unclear if the outlets will mimic existing examples of the department-store canon, as Amazon Fresh shops resemble conventional grocers, or if Amazon plans to shake things up.

Another question is how the move will affect returns for shareholders. Amazon should be able to rent or buy locations cheaply — bankruptcies have left many department-store properties up for grabs. Yet investors may be disappointed that Amazon will devote ever more resources to retail. Many prefer its faster-growing, vastly more profitable and techier businesses: digital ads and cloud computing. "Why tackle a dying industry?" asks Ms. Kodali, suggesting that Amazon could have another crack at making smartphones.

Amazon's share price is down by 8% since its latest results. As well as posting slower online sales for the second quarter it forecast slowing total sales in the next. It also warned that costs will rise sharply in the future as it ramps up investing. Physical retail would claim some of the dosh. The irony would not be lost on Sears and other defunct department stores.

Words and Expressions

shareholder['ʃeəhəʊldə]/*n.* 股东；股票持有人
e-empire/*n.* 电子帝国
bewilderment/bɪ'wɪldəmənt/*n.* 困惑，迷惘
envisaging/ɪn'vɪzɪdʒ/*v.* 设想，展望；正视，面对
reassert/ˌriːə'sɜːt/*vt.* 重复主张；再断言
omni-channel/*n.* 全渠道
bricks-and-mortar/ˌbrɪks n'mɔːtə(r)/*n.* 传统的实体企业
ho-hum/həʊ'hʌm/*n.* 哈欠声；出口；*adj.* 无聊的
high-end/ˌhaɪ'end/*adj.* 高端的；高档的
shake up 摇匀；激励；使改组；重组
outlet/'aʊtlet/*n.* 商店，分销点；廉价经销店；从事大众媒体行业的公司
mimic/'mɪmɪk/*v.* 模仿（人的言行举止）；模拟（外观或效果）；*n.* 善于模仿的人；会模拟的动物（或植物）；*adj.* 模拟的，演习的
tackle/'tæk(ə)l/*v.* 应付，解决（难题或局面）；与…交涉；质问，责问；反对，反抗
crack/kræk/*n.* 尝试，试图；重击，猛击；好时光，友好愉快的交谈
ramps up 增加
dosh/dɒʃ/*n.* 钱
defunct/dɪ'fʌŋkt/*adj.* 已停业的；已倒闭的；停业的；已不存在的

Notes

1. Amazon：亚马逊公司，简称亚马逊，是美国最大的一家网络电子商务公司，位于华盛顿州的西雅图，是网络上最早开始经营电子商务的公司之一。亚马逊成立于1994年，一开始只经营书籍的网络销售业务，现在已扩展至其他产品，已成为全球商品品种最多的网上零售商和全球第二大互联网企业，其名下也包括了AlexaInternet、a9、lab126和互联网电影数据库（Internet Movie Database，IMDB）等子公司。亚马逊及其他销售商为客户提供数百万种独特的全新、翻新及二手商品，如图书、影视、音乐和游戏、数码下载、电子和计算机、家居园艺用品、玩具、婴幼儿用品、食品、服饰、鞋类和珠宝、健康和个人护理用品、体育及户外用品、玩具、汽车及工业产品等。

2. Walmart：沃尔玛是全球大型连锁零售企业之一，1962年在美国阿肯色州成立。目前，沃尔玛在全球开设了超过7000家商场，员工总数190多万人，分布在全球14个国家。沃尔玛在品牌经营策略上，选择了多种零售形式以针对不同档次的目标消费者。

3. Target：塔吉特百货，位于美国明尼苏达州明尼阿波利斯市（Minneapolis, Minnesota），在美国47个州设有1330家商店，提供时尚前沿的零售服务。塔吉特百货的市场定位是高级折扣零售店，是美国第四大零售商，在全球500强企业中排33名。

Exercises

I. Comprehension of the Text

Read the questions and complete the answers according to the text.

1. What has Alibaba recognized under its new chief executive, Andy Jassy?
_____

2. Why invest in the high street just as COVID-19 has lifted e-commerce?
_____

3. What will consumers look like in the future according to Mark Shmulik of Bernstein's broker?
_____

4. Where do investors prefer Amazon to put its resources?
_____

5. Where might Amazon again try to invest its resources?
_____

II. Languages Focus

A. *Match the following words in left with their explanations in right.*

1. Amazon   a. a rule or especially body of rules or principles generally established as valid and fundamental in a field or art or philosophy

2. bulk   b. the entire amount of income before any deductions are

	made
3. revenue	c. the property resulting from being or relating to the greater in number of two parts; the main part
4. mimic	d. having ceased to exist or live
5. defunct	e. constituting an imitation
6. departure	f. a businessman who buys or sells for another in exchange for a commission
7. broker	g. a variation that deviates from the standard or norm
8. pandemic	h. a device or control that is very useful for a particular job
9. gadget	i. an epidemic that is geographically widespread; occurring throughout a region or even throughout the world
10. canon	j. a major South American river; arises in the Andes and flows eastward into the South Atlantic; the world's 2nd longest river

B. *Fill in the blanks with the words or expressions given below. Change the form where necessary.*

ramp up	mimic	high-end	shake up	omni-channel
reassert	envisage	crack	defunct	tackle

1. Mrs.Daisy Wapshott would part with her _____ husband's inherited treasure.

2. He is a clever _____ who can take off most of the lectures in this college.

3. We've got to inspire all these people with old-fashioned ideas. The new chairman will _____ the company.

4. Nobody can _____ the consequences of total nuclear war.

5. His sense of humor was beginning to _____ itself.

6. More businesses are leveraging _____ retail, or the seamless approach of a retailer selling online, in a store and on the road.

7. That means better exercise equipment, _____ stuff, and classes，exercise classes, maybe aerobics.

8. Ecological groups say that nothing is being done to _____ the problem.

9. The aerodynamics involved are extremely complex and required a supercomputer to _____.

10. We needed to _____ our team with the appropriate application development tools quickly.

III. Translation

Translate the following sentences into Chinese.

1. Teachers are the bricks and mortar of the school system. If we don't look after them,

what hope do students have of getting the education they deserve?

2. Cusack was hired to ramp up growth and grab market share while the competition stumbled.

3. We know for example that if governments tackle the barriers that stop poor families accessing education, if they tackle the fees which many poor families often have to pay for education, they can encourage children to attend school.

4. We should also envisage taxing financial transactions and prohibition of products like hedge funds.

5. In addition, the company is busy developing an omni-channel program so that merchandise can be delivered to customers faster and with more certainty.

Ⅳ. Discussion

Directions: *With rapid development of informationization, global electronic commerce transaction has increased greatly within past decade years. Almost all kinds of industries are closely connected with electronic commerce. The trend towards promising e-commerce is an irresistible trend of times. It undoubtedly contributes to impayable prosperity of world economy. Please talk about the two sides of e-commerce.*

1. Why e-commerce is preferable to traditional commerce?
2. Why we should hold strong risk awareness to protect ourselves on e-commerce?

Part B

Autonomous deliveries

Although it is a business not many are aware of, sidewalk robots are set to become an industry with annual sales of $1 billion within a decade, reckons IDTechEx, a British firm of analysts. These four-or six-wheeled autonomous machines, usually the size of a suitcase, are already delivering groceries and other goods in America, China and Europe.

That puts them ahead of many driverless cars, vans and lorries being developed. Those bigger vehicles are held back not by technology but regulation, says Zehao Li of IDTechEx. This means having a "safety driver" on board ready to take over if there is a problem, which is hardly labor-saving.

For these larger contraptions regulators want to see safety systems thoroughly proved. But there are legal hurdles, too. In January Britain's Law Commission, which reviews legislation, recommended that it should not be the person in the driver's seat who faces prosecution if a vehicle in autonomous mode crashes, but the manufacturer or body that sought approval for its use.

Meanwhile, sidewalk robots are getting on with the job. Among them, Starship Technologies, based in San Francisco, reckons it has already clocked up more than 2.5 million deliveries with bots in a number of cities, university campuses and business parks in Europe and America. Amazon is carrying out trials with a similar sort of machine it calls Scout. Kiwibot, a Colombian startup, is making sidewalk deliveries in California.

Typically, these robots carry a few bags of groceries using a variety of sensors, including cameras, radar and GPS to navigate and avoid obstacles and people. Their progress can be monitored on a phone app, which also unlocks them for goods to be retrieved. As they are small, move slowly (Starship's bots might reach a heady 6kph) and are "telemonitored" by people in a control room who can take over, authorities seem more willing to give them a green light.

Such robots are also becoming more autonomous. In January Serve Robotics, another San Franciscan firm whose backers include Uber, a ride-hailing giant, said it had deployed a new sidewalk bot with "level 4" autonomy, which means it can operate without telemonitoring in some predesignated areas.

Robotic versions which operate on roads but have no driver's cab are also appearing. Nuro, a Silicon Valley firm, makes one about the size of a small car that can carry 24 bags of groceries. It has chilled and heated compartments for food and drinks. Udelv, also a Californian firm, is developing a larger type called Transporter to operate at highway speeds. Being much further along the road in earning their keep, these delivery bots are helping to pave the way for the time when bigger autonomous vehicles can join them.

Words and Expressions

contraption/kən'træpʃn/*n.* 奇妙的装置；精巧的设计
regulator/'regjuleɪtə(r)/*n.* 监管者，监管机构；调节器，校准器
hurdle/'hɜːd(ə)l/*n.* 障碍，难关；（供人或马在赛跑中跨越的）栏架，跨栏
legislation/ˌledʒɪs'leɪʃn/*n.* 法规，法律；立法，制定法律
prosecution/ˌprɒsɪ'kjuːʃ(ə)n/*n.* 起诉，诉讼；原告，控方；从事，进行
reckon/'rekən/*v.* 估算，计算；认为；把⋯看作
sensor/'sensə(r)/*n.* 传感器，敏感元件，探测设备
navigate/'nævɪɡeɪt/*v.* 导航，引路；航行于，横渡；穿过，穿越；驾驶
retrieve/rɪ'triːv/*v.* 找回，收回；检索
backers/'bækəz/*n.*（Backers）人名；（英）巴克斯
predesignate/priː'dezɪɡneɪt/*v.* 预先指示
telemonitor/ˌtelɪ'mɒnɪtə/*n.* 遥控
driver's cab 驾驶室

compartment/kəmˈpɑːtmənt/*n.* 隔层，分隔间；舱；区划；*v.* 分隔，划分

Notes

1. IDTechEx：咨询公司。为新兴技术及其市场提供值得信赖的独立研究。设立于 1999 年，帮助客户了解新技术、供应链和市场需求。

2. Starship Technologies：于 2014 年由 Ahti Heinla 和 Janus Friis 在爱沙尼亚成立，已经在全球多个城市推出无数个自动化交付试验，试验领域包括食物和其他小包裹。Starship Technologies 并没有像亚马逊等公司那样使用无人机，而是制造了很多地面机器人，能够自行在人行横道上行动。但是，在必要情况下，人们也可以对机器人进行远程监控和控制。

3. Udelv：它是第一个定制的公共道路自动送货车。Udelv 卡车配备了四级自动驾驶技术。卡车顶部安装了一系列激光雷达和摄像头传感器，可以感知其周围环境，自动实现站对站运输。

Exercises

I. Comprehension of the Text

Read the text and answer the following questions. Write the answers on the lines.

1. What equipment would these robots normally use to carry groceries?
_____

2. Why does IDTechEx, a British analytics firm, think sidewalk robots will be a $1 billion-a-year industry within a decade?
_____

3. What's holding these big cars back, says Mr. Li of IDTechEx?
_____

4. What are the advantages of a new sidewalk robot with "level 4" autonomy from San Francisco company Serve Robotics?
_____

5. Nuro, a Silicon Valley company, makes a car the size of a small car. Can it deliver frozen and heated food and drinks?
_____

II. Main Details Comprehension

Directions: *In this section, you are going to read a passage with ten statements attached to it. Each statement contains information given in one of the paragraphs. Identify the paragraph from which the information is derived. You may choose a paragraph more than once. Each paragraph is marked with a letter.*

The quiet heroism of mail delivery

A) On Wednesday, a polar wind brought bitter cold to the Midwest. Overnight, Chicago reached a low of 21 degrees Fahrenheit below zero, making it slightly colder than Antarctica (南极洲), Alaska, and the North Pole. Wind chills were 64 degrees below zero in Park Rapids, Minnesota, and 45 degrees below zero in Buffalo, North Dakota, according to the National Weather Service. Schools, restaurants, and businesses closed, and more than 1,000 flights were canceled.

B) Even the United States Postal Service (USPS) suspended mail delivery. "Due to this arctic outbreak and concerns for the safety of USPS employees," USPS announced Wednesday morning, "the Postal Service is suspending delivery Jan. 30 in some 3-digit ZIP Code locations." Twelve regions were listed as unsafe on Wednesday; on Thursday, eight remained.

C) As global surface temperatures increase, so does the likelihood of extreme weather. In 2018 alone, wildfires, volcanic eruptions, hurricanes, mudslides, and other natural disasters cost at least $49 billion in the United States. As my colleague Vann Newkirk reported, Puerto Rico is still confronting economic and structural destruction and resource scarcity from 2017's Hurricane Maria. Natural disasters can wreck a community's infrastructure, disrupting systems for months or years. Some services, however, remind us that life will eventually return, in some form, to normal.

D) Days after the deadly 2017 wildfires in Santa Rosa, California, a drone (无人机) caught footage (连续镜头) of a USPS worker, Trevor Smith, driving through burned homes in that familiar white van, collecting mail in an affected area. The video is striking: The operation is familiar, but the scene looks like the end of the world. According to Rae Ann Haight, the program manager for the national-preparedness office at USPS, Smith was fulfilling a request made by some of the home owners to pick up any mail that was left untouched. For Smith, this was just another day on the job. "I followed my route like I normally do," Smith told a reporter. "As I came across a box that was up but with no house, I checked, and there was mail — outgoing mail — in it. And so I picked those up and carried on".

E) USPS has sophisticated emergency plans for natural disasters. Across the country, 285 emergency-management teams are devoted to crisis control. These teams are trained annually using a framework known as the three Ps: people, property, product. After mail service stops due to weather, the agency's top priority is ensuring that employees are safe. Then it evaluates the health of infrastructure, such as the roads that mail carriers drive on. Finally, it decides when and how to re-open operations. If the destruction is extreme, mail addressed to the area will get sent elsewhere. In response to Hurricane Katrina in 2005, USPS redirected incoming New Orleans mail to existing mail facilities in Houston. Mail that was already processed in New Orleans facilities was moved to an upper floor so it would be protected from water damage.

F) As soon as it's safe enough to be outside, couriers (邮递员) start distributing accumulated mail on the still-accessible routes. USPS urges those without standing addresses to file change-of-address forms with their new location. After Hurricane Katrina hit in 2005, mail facilities were set up in dozens of locations across the country in the two weeks that USPS was unable to provide street delivery.

G) Every day, USPS processes, on average, 493.4 million pieces of mail — anything from postcards to Social Security checks to medicine. Spokespeople from both USPS and UPS told me all mail is important. But some mail can be extremely sensitive and timely. According to data released in January 2017, 56 percent of bills are paid online, which means that just under half of payments still rely on delivery services to be completed.

H) It can be hard to identify which parcels are carrying crucial items such as Social Security checks, but USPS and UPS try their best to prioritize sensitive material. They will coordinate with the Social Security Administration to make sure that Social Security checks reach the right people in a timely fashion. After Hurricane Florence and Hurricane Michael last fall, USPS worked with state and local election boards to make sure that absentee ballots were available and received on time.

I) Mail companies are logistics (物流) companies, which puts them in a special position to help when disaster strikes. In a 2011 USPS case study, the agency emphasized its massive infrastructure as a "unique federal asset" to be called upon in a disaster or terrorist attack. "I think we're unique as a federal agency," USPS official Mike Swigart told me, "because we're in literally every community in this country…We're obligated to deliver to that point on a daily basis".

J) Private courier companies, which have more dollars to spend, use their expertise in logistics to help revitalize damaged areas after a disaster. For more than a decade, FedEx has supported the American Red Cross in its effort to get emergency supplies to areas affected by disasters, both domestically and internationally. In 2012, the company distributed more than 1,200 MedPacks to Medical Reserve Corps groups in California. They also donated space for 3.1 million pounds of charitable shipping globally. Last October, the company pledged $1 million in cash and transportation support for Hurricanes Florence and Michael. UPS's charitable arm, the UPS Foundation, uses the company's logistics to help disaster-struck areas rebuild. "We realize that as a company with people, trucks, warehouses, we needed to play a larger role," said Eduardo Martinez, the president of the UPS Foundation. The company employs its trucks and planes to deliver food, medicine, and water. The day before I spoke to Martinez in November, he had been touring the damage from Hurricane Michael in Florida with the American Red Cross. "We have an obligation to make sure our communities are thriving," he said.

K) Rebuilding can take a long time, and even then, impressions of the disaster may still remain. Returning to a normal life can be difficult, but some small routines — mail delivery being one of them — may help residents remember that their communities are still their communities. "When they see that carrier back out on the street," Swigart said, "that's the first sign to them that life is starting to return to normal."

____1. The United States Postal Service has a system to ensure its employees' safety.

____2. One official says USPS is unique in that it has more direct reach to communities compared with other federal agencies.

____3. Natural disasters can have a long-lasting impact on community life.

____4. Mail delivery service is still responsible for the completion of almost half of payments.

____5. The sight of a mailman on the street is a reassuring sign of life becoming normal again.

____6. After Hurricane Katrina interrupted routine delivery, temporary mail service points were set up.

____7. Postal service in some regions in the U.S. was suspended due to extreme cold weather.

____8. Private postal companies also support disaster relief efforts by distributing urgent supplies.

____9. A dedicated USPS employee was on the job carrying out duties in spite of extreme conditions.

____10. Postal services work hard to identify items that require priority treatment.

Ⅲ. Translation

Translate the five following sentences into English, using the words or expressions given in brackets.

1. 在音乐中，我们必须注意的第二种节奏方式是经常遇到的三连音。（be aware of）
_____
2. 他的飞行让美国人觉得美国可以在太空竞赛中领先于苏联。（pull ahead of）
_____
3. 这位自行车传奇人物在领奖台上忍不住流下了眼泪，他知道这是他在本届奥运会上的最后一场个人比赛。（hold back）
_____
4. 在飞船上，最好的观察点是炮台状的圆顶，从那里的 6 个窗户可以俯瞰地球的全景。（on board）
_____
5. 自人工智能诞生之初，就有人担心有朝一日软件将接管世界，让人类的命运变得未知。（take over）
_____

Part C

Product Manual
信息类产品说明书语言特点

（一）名词化

产品说明书词汇的名词化是指其大量使用名词、名词短语和名词性前置修饰语结构，使其语言简洁、表意凝练。

名词化是把句中的动词或者形容词转换为名词或者名词性词组，从而使名词或名词词组获得动词或者形容词的意义而具有名词的语法功能。

产品说明书内容以客观介绍产品的组成部分、工作原理、操作使用、维护保养等为主，需要在上述各个部分里提及产品各部件名称，还要在附图上说明各部分名称，因此整个说明过程需要大量使用名词。

1．动词名词化

（1）"charging"（充电）变为"charging process"（充电过程）。

The charging process of this device is quick and efficient.

这款设备的充电过程快速且高效。

（2）control 名词化

The machine is equipped with a user-friendly control panel.

机器配备了用户友好的控制面板。

（3）"connecting to Wi-Fi"（连接 Wi-Fi）变为"Wi-Fi connection"（Wi-Fi 连接）。

The Wi-Fi connection of this device is stable and fast.

这款设备的 Wi-Fi 连接稳定且快速。

2．形容词名词化

（1）"waterproof"（防水的）变为"waterproof feature"（防水功能）。

This device has a waterproof feature, which allows it to be used in water.

这款设备具有防水功能，可在水中使用。

（2）flexibility 名词化

The machine has a high degree of flexibility in operation.

机器在操作方面具有很高的灵活性。

3．副词名词化

（1）efficiency 名词化

The machine has a high efficiency in operation.

机器在操作方面具有高效。

（2）precision 名词化

The machine can achieve high precision in its results.

机器可以在其结果中实现高精确度。

（3）safety 名词化

The machine is designed with safety in mind.

机器在设计时考虑了安全性。

在英文产品说明书中，名词化可以使描述更加准确、清晰和简洁，有助于用户更好地理解产品的特性和功能。

（二）非谓语动词

产品说明书承担着向消费者介绍产品的性能、作用、生产工艺和使用方法等多种信息的重要作用，其内容以客观描述、介绍产品的安全使用、工作原理、技术参数、结构、安装调试、操作和维护等为主，即内容一般为解释、说明、规定和建议等。所以，各种说明书体现在句子结构上的一个显著特点是:非谓语动词结构的使用普遍多于其他文体。

(1) Do not use this hair dryer near water contained the bath-tubs, basins or other vessels.

不要在盛水的浴缸、洗脸盆或其他器皿附近使用本电吹风。

本句中用过去分词 contained 作定语,代替定语从句。

(2) When pairing a new device, push the PAIR button again and repeat steps above.

配对新设备时,请再次轻按 PAIR(配对)按钮并重复以上步骤。

用于介绍操作流程时对消费者的实际操作有很强的指导性。

1. *Read the following paragraphs and then answer the questions.*

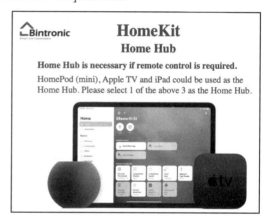

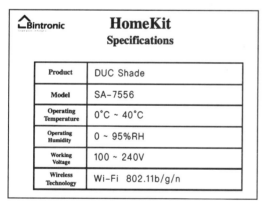

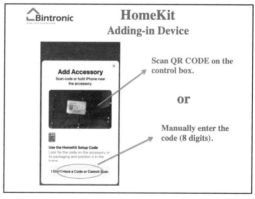

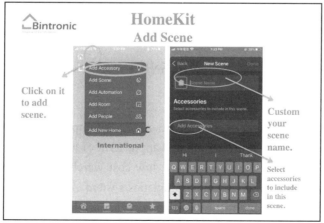

(1) What's Apple HomeKit for ?
_____

(2) What can we use as a Home Hub?
_____

(3) What's the Operating Temperature?
_____

(4) I want to add in device, then what should I do ?
_____

(5) Which button should I click, if I want to select accessories to include in this scene?
_____

2. *Map reading and translation.*

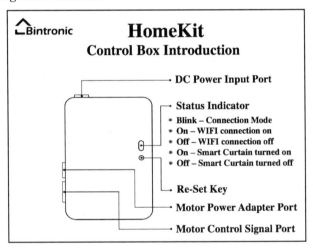

❶ DC Power Input Port_____
❷ Status Indicator_____
❸ Blink-Connection Mode_____
❹ Re-Set Key_____
❺ Motor Power Adapter Port_____

Workshop

Background

With the rapid development of social productivity, the improvement of scientific research and technology, the widespread promotion and application of automation technology, in order to adapt to the enterprise's efficient, accurate, low-cost warehousing, sorting, transportation and other logistics requirements, intelligent logistics system emerges at the historic moment, reduces the logistics industry and manufacturing costs in each link.

Task

How many aspects do you know about logistics industry? What is smart logistics? Find some information through internet and share your idea with other groups.

Process

Step 1. The whole class is divided into several groups, each group containing 3—4 students.

Step 2. Each group has a discussion on smart logistics. Each member shares his experiences as well as their thoughts with group members.

Step 3. Group members write a report about the development of logistics in our country.

Step 4. Each group sends a representative to make a report.

Unit 4 High-tech

How Can Big Data Save the World

Our ability to collect data far outpaces our ability to fully utilize it — yet those data may hold the key to solving some of the biggest global challenges facing us today.

Take, for instance, the frequent outbreaks of waterborne illnesses as a consequence of war or natural disasters. The most recent example can be found in Yemen, where roughly 10,000 new suspected cases of cholera are reported each week — and history is riddled with similar stories. What if we could better understand the environmental factors that contributed to the disease, predict which communities are at higher risk, and put in place protective measures to stem the spread?

Answers to these questions and others like them could potentially help us avert catastrophe.

We already collect data related to virtually everything, from birth and death rates to crop yields and traffic flows. IBM estimates that each day, 2.5 quintillion bytes of data are generated. To put that in perspective: that's the equivalent of all the data in the Library of Congress being produced more than 166,000 times per 24-hour period. Yet we don't really harness the power of all this information. It's time that changed — and thanks to recent advances in data analytics and computational services, we finally have the tools to do it.

As a data scientist for Los Alamos National Laboratory, I study data from wide-ranging, public sources to identify patterns in hopes of being able to predict trends that could be a threat to global security. Multiple data streams are critical because the ground-truth data (such as surveys) that we collect is often delayed, biased, sparse, incorrect or, sometimes, nonexistent.

For example, knowing mosquito incidence in communities would help us predict the risk of mosquito-transmitted disease such as dengue, the leading cause of illness and death in the tropics. However, mosquito data at a global (and even national) scale are not available.

To address this gap, we're using other sources such as satellite imagery, climate data and demographic information to estimate dengue risk. Specifically, we had success predicting the spread of dengue in Brazil at the regional, state and municipality level using these data streams as well as clinical surveillance data and Google search queries that used terms related to the disease. While our predictions aren't perfect, they show promise. Our goal is to combine information from each data stream to further refine our models and improve their predictive power.

Similarly, to forecast the flu season, we have found that Wikipedia and Google searches can complement clinical data. Because the rate of people searching the internet for flu symptoms often increases during their onset, we can predict a spike in cases where clinical data lags.

We're using these same concepts to expand our research beyond disease prediction to better understand public sentiment. In partnership with the University of California, we're conducting a three-year study using disparate data streams to understand whether opinions expressed on social media map to opinions expressed in surveys.

For example, in Colombia, we are conducting a study to see whether social media posts about the peace process between the government and FARC, the socialist guerilla movement, can be ground-truthed with survey data. A University of California, Berkeley researcher is conducting on-the-ground surveys throughout Colombia — including in isolated rural areas — to poll citizens about the peace process. Meanwhile, at Los Alamos, we're analyzing social media data and news sources from the same areas to determine if they align with the survey data.

If we can demonstrate that social media accurately captures a population's sentiment, it could be a more affordable, accessible and timely alternative to what are otherwise expensive and logistically challenging surveys. In the case of disease forecasting, if social media posts did indeed serve as a predictive tool for outbreaks, those data could be used in educational campaigns to inform citizens of the risk of an outbreak (due to vaccine exemptions, for example) and ultimately reduce that risk by promoting protective behaviors (such as washing hands, wearing masks, remaining indoors, etc.).

All of this illustrates the potential for big data to solve big problems. Los Alamos and other national laboratories that are home to some of the world's largest supercomputers have the computational power augmented by machine learning and data analysis to take this information and shape it into a story that tells us not only about one state or even nation, but the world as a whole. The information is there; now it's time to use it.

Words and Expressions

outpace /ˌaʊtˈpeɪs/ *vt.* 赶过；超过…速度
utilize /ˈjuːtəlaɪz/ *v.* 猜想，认为（某事有可能）
cholera /ˈkɒlərə/ *n.* ［内科］霍乱
suspect /səˈspekt/ *v.* 猜想，认为（某事有可能）; *n.* 嫌疑犯，可疑分子
riddle /ˈrɪd(ə)l/ *n.* 谜语；谜一般的人（或事）; *v.* 筛分
factor /ˈfæktə(r)/ *n.* 因素，要素
avert /əˈvɜːt/ *v.* 防止，避免；转移
virtually /ˈvɜːtʃuəli/ *adv.* 事实上，几乎；虚拟地，模拟地

quintillion/kwɪn'tɪljən/n. （美、法）百万的三次方，（英、德）百万的五次方
perspective/pə'spektɪv/n. 透镜，观点，洞察力
equivalent/ɪ'kwɪvələnt/adj. 相当的，等价的
harness/'hɑːnɪs/v. 控；n. 马具
pattern/'pætən/n. 方式，模式
bias/'baɪəs/n. 偏见
sparse/spɑːs/adj. 稀疏的
mosquito/mə'skiːtəʊ/n. 蚊子
incidence/'ɪnsɪdəns/n. 发生率；入射
tropics/'trɒpɪks/n. 热带地区
scale/skeɪl/n. 规模，测量
demographic/ˌdemə'græfɪk/adj. 人口的，人口统计的
regional/'riːdʒənl/adj. 区域性，地区的
municipality/mjuːˌnɪsɪ'pæləti/n. 市政当局，自治市
clinical/'klɪnɪk(ə)l/adj. 诊所的，医务室的；临床的
surveillance/sɜː'veɪləns/n. 监督，监视
query/'kwɪəri/n. 询问，查询
refine/rɪ'faɪn/v. 改善，提炼
complement/'kɒmplɪmənt/v. 补充，补足；n. 补足物
symptom/'sɪmptəm/n. 征兆，症状
onset/'ɒnset/n. 攻击，开端
spike/spaɪk/n. 猛增，尖状物
sentiment/'sentɪmənt/n. 感情，观点
conduct/kən'dʌkt/v. 传导，带领，引导
disparate/'dɪspərət/adj. 完全不同的
socialist/'səʊʃəlɪst/adj. 社会主义的
guerilla/gə'rɪlə/n. 游击队
throughout/θruː'aʊt/adv. 自始至终，遍及…地域，在…期间
poll/pəʊl/n. 民意调查
align/ə'laɪn/v. 使成一线
demonstrate/'demənstreɪt/v. 证明，游行
alternative/ɔːl'tɜːnətɪv/adj. 替代的，可供选择的
logistically/lə'dʒɪstɪkli/adv. 逻辑地
campaign/kæm'peɪn/n. 战役，运动
vaccine/'væksiːn/n. 疫苗
exemption/ɪg'zempʃn/n. 免除
augment/ɔːg'ment/v. 增强

Unit 4 High-tech 47

Notes

1. Big Data：一种规模大到在获取、存储、管理、分析方面大大超出了传统数据库软件工具能力范围的数据集合，具有海量的数据规模、快速的数据流转、多样的数据类型和价值密度低四大特征。

2. Dengue：登革热，是登革病毒经蚊媒传播引起的急性虫媒传染病。登革病毒感染后可导致隐性感染、登革热和登革出血热，登革出血热我国较为少见。典型的登革热临床表现为起病急骤，高热，头痛，肌肉、骨关节剧烈酸痛，部分患者出现皮疹、出血倾向，淋巴结肿大，白细胞计数减少和血小板减少等。本病主要在热带和亚热带地区流行，我国广东、香港和澳门等地是登革热流行区。本病系由伊蚊传播，故流行有一定的季节性，一般在每年的 5～11 月，高峰在 7～9 月。在新流行区，人群普遍易感，但发病以成人为主；在地方性流行区，发病以儿童为主。

3. FARC：哥伦比亚革命武装力量（Fuerzas Armadas Revolucionarias de Colombia，西语，FARC）成立于 20 世纪 60 年代，是拉丁美洲规模最大、历史最长的反政府游击队组织。领袖是曼努埃尔·马鲁兰达·贝莱斯，它是哥伦比亚一支自称为共产主义革命的游击队组织，是哥伦比亚共产党的一个武装分支。该组织原属于哥伦比亚共产党的军事机构，20 世纪 80 年代由于从事毒品交易，脱离哥伦比亚共产党成为独立组织。他们的行为不仅威胁政府，还危及平民、自然环境和基础设施，因此被哥伦比亚政府、美国和欧盟等认为是恐怖组织。它曾经是哥伦比亚境内组织最大、装备最完善、战斗力也最佳的游击队。现在已经解除武装，结束了持续半个多世纪的哥伦比亚内战。

Exercises

I. Getting the Message

There are 5 questions in this section. Read the questions and complete the answers according to the text.

1. What do the examples in paragraphs 2 and 6 show?
_____

2. According to the text, what are the features of survey data?
_____

3. What does "this gap" in paragraph 7 refer to? How to address it?
_____

4. To forecast the flu season, what can be used to complement clinical data?
_____

5. How will social media posts serve as a protective tool for disease outbreaks?
_____

II. Languages Focus

A. *Match the following words in left with their explanations in right.*

1. utilize   a. a thin object with a sharp point
2. spike   b. to go, rise, improve faster than sb./sth.
3. suspect   c. a feeling or an opinion, especially one based on emotions
4. municipality   d. official permission not to do sth. or pay sth. that you would normally have to do or pay
5. augment   e. to use sth.
6. outpace   f. a district with its own local government
7. alternative   g. to increase the amount, value, size
8. disparate   h. to be suspicious about sth.; to not trust sth.
9. sentiment   i. that can be used instead of sth. else
10. exemption   j. so different from each other that they cannot be compared

B. *Fill in the blanks with the words or expressions given below. Change the form where necessary.*

| riddle | outpace | factor | virtual | avert |
| bias | onset | refine | conduct | alternative |

1. The author considers himself usually good at _____ conversations.

2. Scientists claimed yesterday to have solved the _____ of the birth of the universe.

3. This technique is really a _____ of the previous technique.

4. _____, you can transfer money via a French bank in London.

5. The sound is _____ undetectable to the human ear.

6. For the moment, a potential crisis appears to have been _____.

7. The Chinese economy will continue to _____ its foreign rivals for years to come.

8. We are not born with an innate understanding of our _____.

9. Physical activity is an important _____ in maintaining fitness.

10. Most of the passes have been closed with the _____ of winter.

III. Translation

Translate the following sentences into Chinese.

1. Our ability to collect data far outpaces our ability to fully utilize it — yet those data may hold the key to solving some of the biggest global challenges facing us today.

2. Answers to these questions and others like them could potentially help us avert

catastrophe.

3. It's time that changed-and thanks to recent advances in data analytics and computational services, we finally have the tools to do it.

4. Our goal is to combine information from each data stream to further refine our models and improve their predictive power.

5. Similarly, to forecast the flu season, we have found that Wikipedia and Google searches can complement clinical data.

Ⅳ. Discussion

Advances in new technologies have long been closely linked to the increased carbon footprint and other environmental issues. In that regard, big data is changing the rules of the game. Many experts believe that big data will play a key role in tackling climate change in the coming years.

Work in pairs and discuss about your opinions on the role of big data in the world, and then write down your opinions.

High Technology at the Beijing Winter Olympics Venues

Halfway through the Beijing 2022 Winter Olympics, athletes from all over the world have gone on and on renewing their personal records, breaking and setting new Olympic records and world records in various venues in China. Behind such faithful practices of the Olympic motto of "Faster, Higher, Stronger — Together," Beijing's high-tech venues have played a crucial role in the athletes' pursuit of career ambitions.

In short track speed skating in the Capital Indoor Stadium, eight Olympic records have been set, including for the Women's 500 meters by Dutch skater Suzanne Schulting and one for the Men's 1,000 meters by South Korean legend Hwang Dae-heon. Schulting also set a world record in the Women's 1,000 meters quarter-final Stage 1.

Likewise, the National Speed Skating Oval, also known as the Ice Ribbon, witnessed the birth of even more Olympic and world records. Athletes from the Netherlands, Sweden, China, Japan and the Russian Olympic Committee set 12 Olympic records and one world record.

Gao Tingyu of China claimed the gold in the Men's 500 meters with a new Olympic record of 34.32 seconds, bagging the first ever gold in China's men's speed skating history, creating one of the most memorable moments.

Fastest Ice

Yang Shu'an, vice president of the Beijing Organizing Committee for the 2022 Olympic Winter Games (BOCOG), hailed the 12,000-square-meter rink of Ice Ribbon as the "fastest ice" in the world for its contribution to the athletes' amazing performances.

In speed skating, in which athletes achieve the fastest speed without assistance, the less the difference in temperature and the evener and flatter the ice surface would get contributed to better performances, according to insiders.

To help athletes achieve their best performances in Beijing with another technological leap, the Ice Ribbon has, for the first time, advanced carbon dioxide trans-critical direct cooling ice-making technology.

In addition to the ice technology, the design of the arena enhanced the performance of the athletes. The ring-shaped auditorium completely wraps around the track to help keep athletes excited. At the same time, the hyperbolic roof creates a better sense of space and helps athletes focus more on the track.

"It's one of the best speed skating rinks in the world, and I can get a good result here to stand on the podium, I am very happy," said Japanese speed skater Miho Takagi, who won three medals at the Beijing Winter Games.

Xu Qiang, director of the Beijing Science and Technology Commission, said at a Wednesday press conference in Beijing that the Ice Ribbon has won praise from the International Olympic Committee as well as the International Skating Union.

According to Xu, more than 200 technologies have been tested and used for Beijing 2022 in over 60 disciplines, making the event safer from the pandemic, more environmental friendly and more spectacular.

Chinese observers said that the great performance of athletes has not only delivered Beijing's promise of making the Beijing 2022 a "spectacular" one, but also showcased the strength of China's innovation.

Apart from the "fastest ice", high-tech elements are everywhere in the Beijing 2022 Winter Olympics, ranging from the robotic chef in the Olympic village, the hydrogen fueled shuttles, the bullet train connecting Beijing and Zhangjiakou competition zones, to the referee system camera.

More Than Speed

Records aside, many of the venues in Beijing have been praised by visiting Olympians and officials.

Thomas Bach, president of the International Olympic Committee, told the media that the Beijing venues are so outstanding that all athletes are content and some of them compared the venues to heaven.

Yuzuru Hanyu, world-renowned Japanese figure skater, spoke highly of the venues of the

Beijing Winter Olympics, saying both "the stadium and the ice are brilliant" and "I like it here", according to the Xinhua News Agency.

American Samoa's skeleton athlete Nathan Crumpton said the Yanqing National Sliding Center is one of the most beautiful tracks he has seen in the world, wrapped around the mountains, with great facilities and easy access.

The high-tech construction of venues for the Beijing Winter Olympics is an important part of the event, laying the foundation for its success, observers noted.

Words and Expressions

renew/rɪ'njuː/*v.* 重新开始，中止后继续；恢复
venue/'venjuː/*n.* （事件的）发生地点，（活动的）场所
witness/'wɪtnəs/*v.* 目击，目睹；见证，经历
claim/kleɪm/*v.* 赢得，获得
bag/bæɡ/*v.* 把…装进袋子；抢占，占有；捕获，猎杀；进球，得分
hail/heɪl/*v.* 赞扬，欢呼；呼喊，招呼
even/'iːv(ə)n/*adj.* 平坦的，水平的；平静的，平和的
technological leap 技术飞跃
trans-critical direct cooling ice-making technology 二氧化碳跨临界直冷制冰技术
arena/ə'riːnə/*n.* 竞技场，圆形剧场；斗争场所，活动舞台
auditorium/ˌɔːdɪ'tɔːriəm/*n.* 观众席；礼堂，会堂
wrap around 缠绕
hyperbolic/ˌhaɪpə'bɒlɪk/*adj.* 双曲线的；夸张的
podium/'pəʊdiəm/*n.* 讲台，乐队指挥台，领奖台
press conference 新闻发布会
discipline/'dɪsəplɪn/*n.* 纪律，风纪；训练，锻炼
pandemic/pæn'demɪk/*adj.* （疾病）大规模流行的
spectacular/spek'tækjələ(r)/*adj.* 壮观的，令人惊叹的；惊人的，突如其来的
showcase/'ʃəʊkeɪs/*n.* 展示（本领、优点等）的场合；玻璃陈列柜；*v.* 展示，展现
shuttle/'ʃʌt(ə)l/*n.* 往返于两地的交通工具，摆渡车
referee/ˌrefə'riː/*n.* （比赛的）裁判员；仲裁员，调解人
skeleton/'skelɪt(ə)n/*n.* 骨骼，骨架；钢架雪车

Notes

1. The National Speed Skating Oval：国家速滑馆，又称为"冰丝带"，位于北京市朝阳区林萃路2号，是2022年北京冬奥会北京主赛区标志性场馆，也是唯一新建的冰上竞赛场馆，北京冬奥会速度滑冰项目所设的14个小项的全部比赛都在这里进行。"冰丝带"的设计理念来自一个冰和速度结合的创意，22条丝带就像运动员滑过的痕迹，象

征速度和激情。国家速滑馆作为北京冬奥会大道速滑比赛场地，拥有亚洲最大的全冰面设计，冰面面积达 1.2 万平方米。平时可接待超过 2000 人同时开展冰球、速度滑冰、花样滑冰、冰壶等所有冰上运动。

2．The Fastest Ice：国家速滑馆致力于打造"最快的冰"，为各国选手提供更好展现自己的舞台。"最快的冰"采用了先进的二氧化碳跨临界直冷制冰技术，这项技术不仅环保，还能让整个冰面温差控制在 0.5℃。在速度滑冰场地，温差越小，冰面的硬度就越均匀，冰面就越平整，通俗来说就越"丝滑"。这样的冰面更利于选手滑行，使不同区域的软硬度感受保持一致，速度不会受到冰面的影响。这项技术作为北京冬奥会冰雪世界的坚实保障，成功打造了造雪温度和冰面温差的极限，让温室气体化身高效资源在赛场上实现环保节能最大化，助力打造了"冬奥历史上最快的一块冰"。

Exercises

Ⅰ. Comprehension of the Text

Read the text and answer the following questions. Write the answers on the lines.

1. What is the Olympic motto?
   _____

2. Which oval is also known as the Ice Ribbon?
   _____

3. Who got the first ever gold in China's men's speed skating history?
   _____

4. What kinds of high-tech elements were adopted in the Beijing 2022 Winter Olympics?
   _____

5. Who spoke highly of the venues of the Beijing Winter Olympics?
   _____

Ⅱ. Main Details Comprehension

Directions: *In this section, you are going to read a passage with ten statements attached to it. Each statement contains information given in one of the paragraphs. Identify the paragraph from which the information is derived. You may choose a paragraph more than once. Each paragraph is marked with a letter.*

The future of personal satellite technology is here — are we ready for it?

A) Satellites used to be the exclusive playthings of rich governments and wealthy corporations. But increasingly, as space becomes more democratized, they are coming within reach of ordinary people. Just like drones (无人机) before them, miniature satellites are beginning to fundamentally transform our conceptions of who gets to do what up above our heads.

B) As a recent report from the National Academy of Sciences highlights, these satellites hold tremendous potential for making satellite-based science more accessible than ever before. However, as the cost of getting your own satellite in orbit drops sharply, the risks of irresponsible use grow. The question here is no longer "Can we?" but "Should we?" What are the potential downsides of having a slice of space densely populated by equipment built by people not traditionally labeled as "professionals"? And what would the responsible and beneficial development and use of this technology actually look like? Some of the answers may come from a nonprofit organization that has been building and launching amateur satellites for nearly 50 years.

C) Having your personal satellite launched into orbit might sound like an idea straight out of science fiction. But over the past few decades a unique class of satellites has been created that fits the bill: CubeSats. The "Cube" here simply refers to the satellite's shape. The most common CubeSat is a 10cm cube, so small that a single CubeSat could easily be mistaken for a paperweight on your desk. These mini-satellites can fit in a launch vehicle's formerly "wasted space". Multiples can be deployed in combination for more complex missions than could be achieved by one CubeSat alone.

D) Within their compact bodies these minute satellites are able to house sensors and communications receivers/transmitters that enable operators to study Earth from space, as well as space around Earth. They're primarily designed for Low Earth Orbit (LEO)—an easily accessible region of space from around 200 to 800 miles above Earth, where human-tended missions like the Hubble Space Telescope and the International Space Station (ISS) hang out. But they can attain more distant orbits; NASA plans for most of its future Earth-escaping payloads (to the moon and Mars especially) to carry CubeSats.

E) Because they're so small and light, it costs much less to get a CubeSat into Earth's orbit than a traditional communications or GPS satellite. For instance, a research group here at Arizona State University recently claimed their developmental small CubeSats could cost as little as $3,000 to put in orbit. This decrease in cost allows researchers, hobbyists and even elementary school groups to put simple instruments into LEO or even having them deployed from the ISS.

F) The first CubeSat was created in the early 2000s, as a way of enabling Stanford graduate students to design, build, test and operate a spacecraft with similar capabilities to the USSR's Sputnik (前苏联的人造卫星). Since then, NASA, the National Reconnaissance Office and even Boeing have all launched and operated CubeSats. There are more than 130 currently in operation. The NASA Educational Launch of Nano Satellite program, which offers free launches for educational groups and science missions, is now open to U.S. nonprofit corporations as well. Clearly, satellites are not just for rocket scientists anymore.

G) The National Academy of Sciences report emphasizes CubeSats' importance in scientific discovery and the training of future space scientists and engineers. Yet it also acknowledges that widespread deployment of LEO CubeSats isn't risk-flee. The greatest concern the authors raise is space debris — pieces of "junk" that orbit the earth, with the potential to cause serious damage if they collide with operational units, including the ISS.

H) Currently, there aren't many CubeSats and they're tracked closely. Yet as LEO opens up to more amateur satellites, they may pose an increasing threat. As the report authors point out, even near-misses might lead to the "creation of a burdensome regulatory framework and affect the future disposition of science CubeSats".

I) CubeSat researchers suggest that now's the time to ponder unexpected and unintended possible consequences of more people than ever having access to their own small slice of space. In an era when you can simply buy a CubeSat kit off the shelf, how can we trust the satellites over our heads were developed with good intentions by people who knew what they were doing? Some "expert amateurs" in the satellite game could provide some inspiration for how to proceed responsibly.

J) In 1969, the Radio Amateur Satellite Corporation (AMSAT) was created in order to foster ham radio enthusiasts' (业余无线电爱好者) participation in space research and communication. It continued the efforts, begun in 1961, by Project OSCAR — a U.S.-based group that built and launched the very first nongovernmental satellite just four years after Sputnik. As an organization of volunteers, AMSAT was putting "amateur" satellites in orbit decades before the current CubeSat craze. And over time, its members have learned a thing or two about responsibility. Here, open-source development has been a central principle, Within the organization, AMSAT has a philosophy of open sourcing everything making technical data on all aspects of their satellites fully available to everyone in the organization, and when possible, the public. According to a member of the team responsible for FOX 1-A, AMSAT's first CubeSat, this means that there's no way to sneak something like explosives or an energy emitter into an amateur satellite when everyone has access to the designs and implementation.

K) However, they're more cautious about sharing information with nonmembers, as the organization guards against others developing the ability to hijack and take control of their satellites. This form of "self-governance" is possible within long-standing amateur organizations that, over time, are able to build a sense of responsibility to community members, as well as society in general. But what happens when new players emerge, who don't have deep roots within the existing culture?

L) Hobbyists and students are gaining access to technologies without being part of a long-standing amateur establishment. They're still constrained by funders, launch providers and a series of regulations — all of which rein in what CubeSat developers can and cannot do. But there's a danger they're ill-equipped to think through potential unintended consequences. What these unintended consequences might be is admittedly far from clear. Yet we know innovators can be remarkably creative with taking technologies in unexpected directions. Think of something as seemingly benign as the cellphone — we have microfinance and text-based social networking at one end of the spectrum, and improvised (临时制作的) explosive devices at the other.

M) This is where a culture of social responsibility around CubeSats becomes important — not simply to ensure that physical risks are minimized, but to engage with a much larger community in anticipating and managing less obvious consequences of the technology. This is not an easy task. Yet the evidence from AMSAT and other areas of technology development suggests that responsible amateur communities can and do emerge around novel technologies. The challenge here, of course, is ensuring that what an amateur communities considers to be responsible, actually is. Here's where there needs to be a much wider public conversation that extends beyond government agencies and scientific communities to include students, hobbyists, and anyone who may potentially stand to be affected by the use of CubeSat technology.

_____1. Given the easier accessibility to space, it is time to think about how to prevent misuse of satellites.

_____2. A group of mini-satellites can work together to accomplish more complex tasks.

_____3. The greater accessibility of mini-satellites increases the risks of their irresponsible use.

_____4. Even school pupils can have their CubeSats put in orbit owing to the lowered launching cost.

_____5. AMSAT is careful about sharing information with outsiders to prevent hijacking of their satellites.

_____6. NASA offers to launch CubeSats free of charge for educational and research purposes.

_____7. Even with constraints, it is possible for some creative developers to take the CubeSat technology in directions that result in harmful outcomes.

_____8. While making significant contributions to space science, CubeSats may pose hazards to other space vehicles.

_____9. Mini-satellites enable operators to study Earth from LEO and space around it.

_____10. AMSAT operates on the principle of having all its technical data accessible to its members, preventing the abuse of amateur satellites.

III. Translation

Translate the five following sentences into English, using the words or expressions given in brackets.

1. 也许你可以做到，但是不要试着创记录。(set records)

2. 突然，我感到两条细小的胳膊抱住了我的肚子。(wrap around)

3. 他把儿童比作年轻的树，它们都还在成长，而且可以被塑造成型。(compare to)

4. 一些人对于改编自小说的电影评价很高。(speak highly of)

5．我们在学校学到的将为我们的将来打下基础。（lay the foundation for）

Product Manual
英文产品说明书的若干常用句型

掌握好英文产品说明书的常用句型，进行产品说明书的翻译实践工作时就会思路清晰、事半功倍。英文产品说明书的若干常用句型如下：

（一）（情态动词）be＋形容词（或过去分词）＋目的状语

(1) The screen will be protected from scratches with the provided screen protector.
使用提供的屏幕保护膜，屏幕将受到保护，防止划痕。
(2) The product will be suitable for home use, office use, or outdoor activities.
该产品适用于家庭使用、办公使用或户外活动。

类似的常见语句类型还有：is used for …；is used to …；is used as …；is designed to …；is suitable to be used in …；is available for（to）…；may be applicable to …；may be used to …；can be used as …；can be designed as …；is adapted for（to）…；is designed to be …；so as to …；is capable of …．

（二）（情态动词）＋be＋介词短语

产品说明书中，情态动词（如 can, could, may, might, must, should, will, would, shall, should）与 be 动词搭配的介词短语常用于描述产品的功能、性能、操作方法等，例如：

(1) The product can be easily assembled following the instructions provided.
产品可以根据提供的说明书轻松组装。
(2) This device must be used with the included power adapter.
此设备必须使用随附的电源适配器。

（三）情态动词＋be＋名词：描述产品的用途或适用场景

(1) The fan must be quiet and energy-efficient to meet our requirements.
风扇必须安静且节能，以满足我们的要求。
(2) The camera should be high-resolution and equipped with a wide-angle lens for better performance.
摄像头应具有高分辨率，并配备广角镜头以获得更好的性能。

（四）be＋形容词＋介词短语

It's reliable in usage, convenient in maintenance and able to work under very bad conditions.

该机器操作时安全可靠，便于维修，能在恶劣条件下工作。

（五）现在分词＋名词

现在分词＋名词句型用于说明维修或操作程序及说明有关技术要求，例如：

(1) When operating, don't put your foot on the pedal switch board constantly, so as not to accidently stop on the switch, causing an accident.

工作时请注意不要经常把脚放在踏板上，以免不慎踏动，引起事故。

(2) When doing shallow drawings, care must be taken to ensure cleanness of the sheet and it is well lubricated.

浅拉伸时，要注意材料的清洁，并加油润滑。

（六）名词＋过去分词（或形容词）

在产品说明书中，名词+过去分词（形容词）结构通常用于描述产品的特性、功能和性能。这种结构可以帮助读者更好地理解产品，同时使描述更加生动和具体，例如：

（1）high-quality performance 高品质性能
（2）user-friendly interface 用户友好界面
（3）adjustable settings 可调节设置
（4）energy-efficient system 节能系统
（5）heat-resistant materials 耐热材料
（6）waterproof housing 防水外壳

这些例子中，名词和过去分词共同构成了形容词，用来描述产品的各个方面。通过使用这种结构，产品说明书可以更清晰地向读者传达产品的关键特性。

1. *Read the following paragraphs and then answer the questions.*

4 Assembling

1 Insert the steering bar into the steering socket at the back of the mainframe.

2 Install the two screws. Tighten securely with the included hex wrench.

3 Snap the lid securely with hearing the sound of "click".

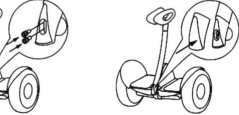

Check the Power ON/OFF status after assembly.

⚠ For your safety, your Ninebot S is not activated at this time and will beep occasionally after Power ON. Until activated, the Ninebot S maintains a very low riding speed and steering sensitivity, and should not be ridden. Install the Segway-Ninebot App on your mobile device (with Bluetooth 4.2 or above), connect to the Ninebot S with Bluetooth, and follow the App instructions to activate your Ninebot S and follow the training procedures.

5 Charging

⚠ Do not connect the charger if the charge port or charge cable is wet. The battery pack is only to be charged by adults.

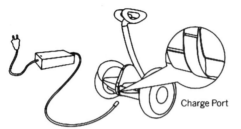

Charge Port Lift up the cover Open the rubber cap Insert the plug into the socket

- Your Ninebot S is fully charged when the LED on the charger changes from red (charging) to green (trickle charge). Close the rubber cap when not charging.

6 First Ride

 There are safety risks when learning to ride the Ninebot S. You must read the Safety Instructions and follow the New Rider Tutorial in the App before your first ride.

For your safety, your Ninebot S is not activated at this time and will beep occasionally after Power ON.

Until activated, the Ninebot S maintains a very low riding speed and steering sensitivity, and should not be ridden. Install the App on your mobile device (with Bluetooth 4.2 or above), connect to the Ninebot S with Bluetooth, and follow the App instructions to activate your Ninebot S and follow the training procedures.

 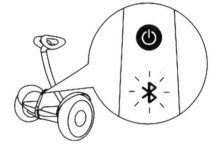

1 Install App and register/login.

2 Power ON the Ninebot S. The Bluetooth icon blinking indicates the Ninebot S is waiting for a connection.

3 In the APP, click Vehicle, scan and select your Ninebot S. The Ninebot S will beep when the connection is successful. The Bluetooth icon will stop blinking and remain illuminated.

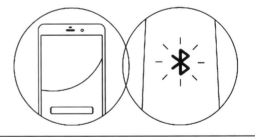

(1) How should you secure the screws during the assembly process?

(2) What is the indication that the lid is securely snapped into place?

(3) How can you tell that the Nine bot S is fully charged?

(4) What should you do with the rubber cap when the Nine bot S is not charging?

(5) What safety risks are mentioned when learning to ride the Nine bot S?

Unit 4 High-tech   59

2. Map reading and translation.

| Always wear a helmet when riding. Use an approved bicycle or skateboard helmet that fits properly with the chin strap in place, and provides protection for the back of your head. |

 ❶ _____

| Do not attempt your first ride in any area where you might encounter children, pedestrians, pets, vehicles, bicycles, or other obstacles and potential hazards. |

 ❷ _____

| In places without laws and regulations governing self-balancing electric vehicles, comply with the safety guidelines outlined in this manual. Neither Ninebot nor Segway Inc. is responsible for any property damage, personal injury/death, accidents, or legal disputes caused by violations of the safety instructions. |

 ❸ _____

| Be alert! Scan both far ahead and in front of your Ninebot S — your eyes are your best tool for safely avoiding obstacles and low traction surfaces (including, but not limited to, wet ground, loose sand, loose gravel, and ice). |

 ❹ _____

| As with any electronic device, use a surge protector when charging to help protect your Ninebot S from damage due to power surges and voltage spikes. Only use the Ninebot supplied charger. Do not use a charger from any other product. |

 ❺ _____

Workshop

Background

As is known to all, we live in a world that is rapidly developing. Looking back to the history, we are always astonished to find there have been many changes in our lives. For example, people aren't troubled with height any more, because they can reach to the top of a high building by a lift within few minutes; people aren't troubled with distance any more, because they can talk with their family or friends by telephone whenever and wherever possible; people aren't troubled with the hard work any more, because robots can supersede human beings for heavy or dangerous work…There is no doubt that they are all due to scientific and technological innovation.

Task

1. Interview some classmates and your families on this topic.
2. Search more information online.

Process

Step 1. Complete the task in groups. Form small groups with 5－6 students respectively.

Step 2. Interview your parents and search information online.

Step 3. Have a discussion with your classmates on the relation between high-tech and our life.

Step 4. Make an oral presentation in class.

Unit 5 Artificial Intelligence

Technology in Science Fiction

Facts are pieces of information we can show to be true. When we read history, we want to know the facts — what really happened. Fiction is the opposite. Writers of fiction make up stories, telling of people and events that come from the writer's imagination. Science fiction writers imagine not only people and events but, perhaps most importantly, technology. They often write about the effects of that technology on a person, a group, or society. These writers usually set their stories in the future. Some of them have predicted technology that seemed impossible at the time but really does exist today.

An Englishwoman, Mary Shelly, was one of the first writers of science fiction. In 1818, she wrote the book *Frankenstein*, which tells the story of a young scientist, Dr. Frankenstein, who wants to create a human life. He puts together parts of dead people's bodies, including — by mistake — the brain of a criminal, and then uses electricity to bring the creature to life. However, he cannot control the creature, and it kills him. Since then, the idea of a "mad scientist" (someone who tries to use science and technology to gain power) has been very popular in science fiction, especially in the movies.

In 1863, the French writer Jules Verne wrote the first of his many great science fiction adventure stories, *Cinq Semaines en Ballon* (*Five Weeks in a Balloon*). It is the story of three men traveling across Africa by hot-air balloon. Readers loved it, but many were confused: Was it fact or fiction? The story sounded unlikely, but the writer's style and the scientific details made it seem true.

Later, Jules Verne wrote *Paris au Vingtième Siècle* (*Paris in the Twentieth Century*), a story he set in the 1960's, 100 years into the future. This story has descriptions of high-speed trains, gas-powered cars, calculators, skyscrapers, and modern methods of communication. Verne imagined all these things at a time when neither he nor anyone in Paris had even a radio! In another book, *De la Terre à la Lune* (*From the Earth to the Moon*), he predicted that people would travel in outer space and walk on the moon, a prediction that came true on July 20, 1969. Verne even got some of the details right. Both in his book and in real life, there were Florida, and they came down in the Pacific Ocean on their return.

Space travel continued to be a popular subject for science fiction in the twentieth century. The best writers based the science and technology in their stories on a real understanding of the science and technology of their time. Computers, robots, and genetic engineering all appeared in the pages of science fiction long before they appeared in the news.

The following quotation comes from a story by the great science fiction writer Isaac Asimov. He wrote these words in 1954. When you read them remember that at that time, people had no computers in their homes. In fact, the few computers that existed were as big as some people's homes. In *The Fun They Had*, Asimov describes a child of the future using a personal computer to learn math:

Margie went into the schoolroom. It was right next to her bedroom, and the mechanical teacher was on and waiting for her...

The screen was lit up, and it said, "Today's arithmetic lesson is on the addition of proper fractions. Please insert yesterday's homework in the proper slot".

Margie did so with a sigh. She was thinking about the old schools they had when her grandfather's grandfather was a little boy. All the kids from the whole neighborhood came, laughing and shouting in the schoolyard, sitting together in the schoolroom...

And the teachers were people...

Back in 1954, readers probably found Asimov's story hard to believe. Today, his ideas do not seem so strange, do they? Maybe we should pay more attention to what science fiction writers are saying today about the world of tomorrow. But we should also remember that their predictions have been wrong more often than right. Here we are in the 21st century without flying cars, vacations on the moon, or robots cooking our dinner. And in spite of computers, people still do go to school.

Words and Expressions

fiction/ˈfɪkʃ(ə)n/*n*. 小说；虚构的事，谎言；杜撰，编造

create/kriˈeɪt/*v*. 创造，创建；设计，创作；造成，引起；授予，册封

criminal/ˈkrɪmɪn(ə)l/*n*. 罪犯；*adj*.犯法的，犯罪的；刑事的；应受责备的，可耻的；罪犯的，犯人的

confuse/kənˈfjuːz/*v*. 使糊涂，使迷惑；混淆，弄错；使复杂化

skyscraper/ˈskaɪskreɪpə(r)/*n*. 摩天大楼

genetic/dʒəˈnetɪk/*adj*. 基因的，遗传学的；有共同起源的

fraction/ˈfrækʃn/*n*. 分数，小数；小部分，微量；持不同意见的小集团；分离；（基督教用语）分切圣餐面包

Notes

1. Frankenstein: 弗兰肯斯坦（英国女作家 Mary W. Shelly 所著同名小说中的主角）；人形怪物。

2. Jules Gabriel Verne： 儒勒·凡尔纳（1828—1905 年），19 世纪法国小说家、剧作家及诗人。凡尔纳一生创作了大量优秀的文学作品，以《在已知和未知的世界中的奇

Unit 5 Artificial Intelligence   63

异旅行》为总名,代表作为《格兰特船长的儿女》《海底两万里》《神秘岛》三部曲,还著有《气球上的五星期》《地心游记》等。他的作品对科幻文学流派有着重要的影响,因此他与赫伯特·乔治·威尔斯都被称作"科幻小说之父",还被誉为"科学时代的预言家"。

　　3. Isaac Asimov:艾萨克·阿西莫夫(1920—1992 年),美国著名科幻小说家、科普作家、文学评论家,是美国科幻小说黄金时代的代表人物之一。与儒勒·凡尔纳、赫伯特·乔治·威尔斯并称为科幻历史上的三巨头,同时还与罗伯特·海因莱因、亚瑟·克拉克并列为科幻小说的三巨头。其作品中的《基地系列》《银河帝国三部曲》和《机器人系列》三大系列被誉为"科幻圣经"。

 Exercises

I. Getting the Message

Read the questions and complete the answers according to the text.

1. What famous character did the author Mary Shelly create?
_____

2. In which novel did Jules Verne predict the invention of the calculator?
_____

3. What world changing prediction did Jules Verne make? And when did it occur in real life?
_____

4. What was the teacher in Isaac Asimov's *The Fun They Had*?
_____

5. What was the popular subject for science fiction in the 20th century?
_____

II. Languages Focus

A. *Match the following words in left with their explanations in right.*

　　1. imagine　　　　　　　　a. a living thing, real or imaginary, that can move around, such as an animal

　　2. appear　　　　　　　　 b. a type of literature that describe imaginary people and events, not real ones

　　3. sigh　　　　　　　　　 c. to take in and let out a long, deep, audible breath

　　4. simulation　　　　　　　d. a small electronic device for calculating with numbers

　　5. algorithm　　　　　　　 e. a set of rules that must be followed when solving a particular problem

　　6. calculator　　　　　　　f. the act of pretending that something is real when it is not

7. predict   g. to say that something will happen in the future
8. unlikely   h. to form an idea or notion of
9. creature   i. not probable
10. fiction   j. to come into sight or view

B. *Fill in the blanks with the words or expressions given below. Change the form where necessary.*

| confuse | predict | include | in spite of…imagination |
| communication | sigh | insert…quotation… | subject |

1. The cabin was so remote that _____ back home would be difficult.
2. The fortune-teller was somehow able to _____ the future.
3. The students wanted to be _____ in every part of the decision-making process.
4. Children tell the best stories, because they have the wildest _____.
5. Juliet let out a _____, as she would not be allowed to go out tonight.
6. The scientist _____ the needle into the patient's arm.
7. The students were _____ as to what would be on the test.
8. _____ everything he had seen, John refused to turn back.
9. This is a famous _____ from Martin Luther King.
10. Philosophy is often described as a difficult _____.

Ⅲ. Translation

Translate the following sentences into Chinese.

1. Facts are pieces of information we can show to be true.

_____

2. When we read history, we want to know the facts — what really happened.

_____

3. This story has descriptions of high-speed trains, gas-powered cars, calculators, skyscrapers, and modern methods of communication.

_____

4. The best writers based the science and technology in their stories on a real understanding of the science and technology of their time.

_____

5. Maybe we should pay more attention to what science fiction writers are saying today about the world of tomorrow.

_____

Ⅳ. Discussion

Directions: *The topic for us to discuss today is "Rise of the Machines: The Rapid Growth* *of Artificial Intelligence in Our Everyday Lives".*

Robot-proof: Higher Education in the Age of Artificial Intelligence

Thousands of years ago, the Agricultural Revolution transformed our foraging ancestors into farmers. Hundreds of years ago, the Industrial Revolution turned farmers into factory workers. Dozens of years ago, the Digital Revolution changed factory workers into knowledge workers.

Today, a new technological leap — the Artificial Intelligence (AI) Revolution — is again upending previous certainties about employment.

That is because smart machines are getting smarter. Several studies — including from the University of Oxford, McKinsey and Price-waterhouse Coopers — predict that up to half of all jobs performed by humans could disappear within the next 20 years. At the same time, new jobs will emerge, including ones that we can't even imagine today.

Learning has always been the surest antidote to technological redundancy. This remains true today; it is now the obligation of educators to ensure that our learners become "robot-proof".

This will present both a mandate, and an opportunity, for higher education to change. A robot-proof education will prepare learners to perform those jobs that only humans can do.

What is needed to meet this challenge is a new blueprint for higher education, which must include three important components.

First, we need a new curriculum involving the integration of technical literacies, such as coding and data analytics, with uniquely human literacies, such as creativity, entrepreneurship, ethics and cultural agility. This integration will develop a creative mindset and the mental elasticity to invent, discover and produce original ideas in the AI age.

Second, we must allow students to hone their uniquely human attributes. They will learn to collaborate better with other people (and machines) while performing the complex, highly skilled work of tomorrow. We can also teach students to recognize when technology is not the answer, when we must rely on human qualities such as empathy and teamwork. In other words, we can give them the tools to succeed at any situation.

To fully master this curriculum, however, classroom learning is not enough. Unlike machines, human beings don't improve simply through exposure to ever greater volumes of information. Ideally, we learn by putting knowledge into use in different living contexts. Experiential learning transforms theory into real knowledge. Co-ops, internships, research and global experiences help students to deepen their understanding beyond "what" into "why".

Integrating classroom learning and real-world experience bridges the abstract and the tangible, teaching students to transfer knowledge to unexpected situations — a talent lacking in even the most brilliant machines.

A robot-proof model must also account for the fact that learning cannot end on the day a person graduates. No one is set for life. As machines continue to improve, people must follow suit, honing their mental capacities, skills and technological knowledge. Lifelong learning is no longer optional, which means that universities should promote it from the sidelines of higher education to the center of the educational enterprise.

To reach lifelong learners — many of whom work full-time — universities will need to meet people where they are. The idea that a mid-career professional can take one or two years out of the workplace to pursue an advanced degree is increasingly unrealistic.

Universities should, therefore, seize the opportunity to partner with employers, keeping content relevant to workforce needs. They can embed educational programs directly into workplaces, reaching employees in the conference room and on the factory floor. They can organize content in flexible ways, shedding the constraints of traditional degree programs by offering learning in modular blocks, stacked according to demand.

For centuries, the great universities of the world have played a leading role in creating knowledge and preparing students for active and engaged lives within society. For learners to master the economic and social challenges brought on by smart machines, higher education will need to adapt.

The solutions necessary to make our citizens robot-proof are clear. All we need now is the courage to make them a reality.

Words and Expressions

forage/'fɒrɪdʒ/*n.* 饲料；草料；搜索；*vi.* 觅食；搜寻

leap/liːp/*v.* 猛冲，突然而迅速地移动；剧增，猛涨；赶紧抓住（机会）；（心）猛跳；跳，跳跃；*n.* 跳跃，跳高；骤变，激增；（对新事物的）认真尝试

upend/ʌp'end/*v.* 使颠倒，倒放；（水中的鸭或其他鸟捕食时头部与前腹部潜入水中，尾部翘起）倒栽葱；（使某人）跌倒，翻转；（足球赛中）故意绊倒，铲倒（对方队员）

emerge/ɪ'mɜːdʒ/*v.* 浮现，出现；显露，知悉；恢复过来，幸存下来；形成，兴起

antidote/'æntidəʊt/*n.* 解毒药，解毒剂；矫正方法，对策

redundancy/rɪ'dʌndənsi/*n.* 裁员，解雇；多余，累赘；复置装置，冗余（机器、系统等某部件发生故障后的替代装置

integration/ˌɪntɪ'greɪʃ(ə)n/*n.* 结合，融合；取消种族隔离；（数）积分法，求积分；（心理分析）整合

literacy/'lɪtərəsi/*n.* 识字，读写能力；专业知识；精通文学

entrepreneurship/ˌɒntrəprə'nɜːʃɪp/*n.* 企业家精神

elasticity/iːlæ'stɪsəti/*n.* 弹性，弹力；灵活性

hone/həʊn/*v.* 磨练，训练（尤指技艺）；磨（刀、剑等）；导向，朝向（honeinon）；渴望；发牢骚；*n.* 磨刀石

tangible/'tændʒəb(ə)l/*adj.* 明确的，真实的；可触摸的，可感知的；*n.* 可触知的东西
modular/'mɒdjələ(r)/*adj.* （尤指英国大学里的课程）分单元的（由独立单元组成，学生可选修）；组合式的；模块化的；模数的；有标准组件的

Notes

1. the Agricultural Revolution：农业革命。农业的产生是人类历史上的一次巨大革命。这场革命被称为第一次农业革命或新石器革命。

2. the Industrial Revolution：工业革命是指18世纪60年代起在世界范围内的系列生产与科技革命，其发源于英格兰中部地区，是指资本主义工业化的早期历程，由于蒸汽机的发明及运用成为了这个时代的标志，因此历史学家称这个时代为"蒸汽时代"。随后向英国乃至整个欧洲大陆传播，19世纪传至北美，促进了经济的发展，人类进入了"电气时代"，开始了第二次工业革命。到20世纪四五十年代，科学理论出现重大突破，一定的物质、技术基础的形成，也是由于社会发展的需要，开始的新科学技术革命，这次科技革命被称为"第三次科技革命"。而第四次工业革命则是利用信息化技术促进产业变革的时代，也就是智能化时代。

3. McKinsey：麦肯锡公司（McKinsey & Company）是由James O'McKinsey于1926年创建的，是全球最著名的管理咨询公司之一。

4. Price-waterhouse Coopers：普华永道，即普华永道会计师事务所（Price-waterhouse Coopers，PwC），是一家会计师事务所公司。1998年，它的两个前身——普华会计师事务所和永道会计师事务所在英国伦敦合并成为了如今的普华永道。普华永道在2008财年获利约280亿美元，它的雇员约146 000人，遍布150个国家或地区。

Exercises

I. Comprehension of the Text

Read the text and answer the following questions. Write the answers on the lines.

1. Today, what is again upending previous certainties about employment?
___
2. Who can ensure that our learners become "robot-proof"?
___
3. What is needed to meet the challenge of a robot-proof education?
___
4. How can human beings put knowledge into use in different living contexts?
___
5. How can universities help students to achieve lifelong learning?
___

II. Main Details Comprehension

Directions: *In this section, you are going to read a passage with ten statements attached to it. Each statement contains information given in one of the paragraphs. Identify the paragraph from which the information is derived. You may choose a paragraph more than once. Each paragraph is marked with a letter.*

Fake holiday villa websites prompt warning

A) During the British winter, the thought of two weeks in a coastal villa(别墅)with soul-stirring views of the sea and a huge pool to enjoy is enough to offset(抵消) the labor until the holidays start. For a growing number of people, however, their yearly break is turning into a nightmare as they find that the property they have paid thousands for does not exist and the website through which they booked it has disappeared.

B) Consumers have been warned to be aware of the potential for deception in this market, which is far from uncommon. In 2017 there were 1,632 cases of reported "villa fraud (诈骗)", with victims losing an average of £2,052 according to Action Fraud. the national center for reporting such frauds. "Millions of pounds are lost each year by holidaymakers," says Sean Tipton of the Association of British Travel A gents (ABTA).

C) The problem has ballooned in the last 10 years, with frauds becoming more and more sophisticated. The fake websites have authentic-sounding names involving a mix of keywords, typically including the place name, "summer", "villas" or "rentals". Details of legitimate (合法) villas are often stolen from other sites. "When the fraudsters first started it was unsophisticated — the websites looked amateur and there wasn't a lot of effort," says Tipton. "Now they are clever. They extensively rip off legitimate websites and use a different website name. They'll have pictures of a sales team and it might be a poor actor in New York that is down as their head of sales".

D) Fraudsters target popular seaside destinations for British tourists visiting Spain where prices can soar if demand exceeds supply. Prices are kept within reasonable ranges to avoid arousing suspicion. "A villa might cost 5,000 elsewhere and they will offer it at say 3,500. But a bit of a giveaway is that the villa will be cheaper than on other websites and there's unlimited availability," says Tipton. Fraudsters also invest in pay-per-click advertising to feature at the top of search engines when people type in phrases such as "Spanish seaside villas".

E) With such a degree of professionalism, how can consumers find out if the website they're looking to book with is trustworthy? "When people book holiday villas they are doing so through rose-colored glasses," says Tony Neate, chief executive of Get Safe Online. "They should be Googling the property, and looking on websites like Google Maps and Street View to see if it's there. Also, speak to the person you're booking the villa with on a landline phone, as fraudsters tend to only use mobiles." He also suggests asking someone not going on the holiday to have a look at the website. "They might spot problems you don't spot." Another potential red flag is being asked to pay by bank transfer. "The problem is that when the money leaves your account it's in theirs straightaway and it's very hard to track it," says Barclays' head of digital safety, Jodie Gilbert. "We generally recommend other forms of payment, like credit card".

F) Little seems to be known about these fraudsters. "There is no way to definitely know who they are," says Neate. "It could be anyone. It could be your next-door neighbor or organized crime in Russia." Action Fraud says people should ensure the company renting the villa is a member of a recognized trade body such as ABTA.

G) "By working with industry partners such as ABTA and Get Safe Online, we are able to issue alerts about the latest threats they should be aware of. If you believe you have fallen victim to fraud or cyber-crime, please report it to Action Fraud," it adds. ABTA says it is trying to combat the issue by running public awareness campaigns. "It's a growing problem and people can't stop fraudsters being dishonest," says Tipton. "They're still going to do it. It's not impossible to stop but as it's internet-based it's harder to pursue".

H) Nick Cooper, the founder and co-owner of villa booking company Villa Plus, estimates his company has uncovered more than 200 fake villa websites over the past two years, and doesn't believe enough is being done. "It is hopeless to report fake villa websites to the internet giants who host them," he says. "I found it impossible to speak to anyone. Also, once one bank account gets reported, they simply use another."

I) For now, the only way to stop fraudsters appears ultimately to lie in the hands of the consumer. "When people book their holidays, they get so emotionally involved, and when they find that villa at a good price with availability in peak season, they are an easy target," says Cooper. "The public has to learn to be far more aware they are a target for these sort of frauds." But it's not just the financial cost. "A family will turn up at villa and find out it doesn't exist or the owner doesn't know who you are," says Tipton. "The problem then is you have to find accommodation at short notice. It can be incredibly expensive but it's the emotional cost, too".

J) Carla O'Shaughnessy from Sydenham was searching last year for a good deal to book a villa in Majorca for a summer break for the family. "I was comparing prices online and found one on that came in a bit cheaper than others," says O'Shaughnessy. She emailed the company via its website, asking how far the villa was from the airport and about local restaurants. "They came back with plausible answers; it was all very friendly and professional," she says. Happy with the responses, O'Shaughnessy paid the full amount of 3,000 via bank transfer into the travel agent's account and then forgot about it until a month before the booking.

K) "I tried logging on to the website and couldn't," she recalls. "I Googled the agent's name and there were lots of complaints about him being a fraudster. If only I'd Googled before but I never thought of it." Although she found another villa in time for their holiday, she admits she was much more cautious. "I paid through a secure third-party site and had phone conversations with the agent. But I wasn't able to relax until we turned up and I had the keys".

_____1. Fraudsters often steal villa-booking information from authentic holiday websites.

_____2. Fraudsters keep changing their bank accounts to avoid being tracked.

_____3. It is suggested that people not going on the holiday might help detect website frauds.

_____4. More and more British holidaymakers find the seaside villas they booked online actually nonexistent.

_____5. By checking an agent's name online before booking a villa holidaymakers can avoid falling into traps.

_____6. Fraudsters are difficult to identify according to an online safety expert.

_____7. Holidaymakers have been alerted to the frequent occurrence of online villa-booking frauds.

_____8. It is holidaymakers that can protect themselves from falling victim to frauds.

_____9. Holidaymakers are advised not to make payments by bank transfer.

_____10. Fraudsters advertise their villas at reasonable prices so as not to be suspected.

Ⅲ. Translation

Translate the five following sentences into English, using the words or expressions given in brackets.

1．数十年前，数字革命将工厂工人转变为知识工作者。（Digital Revolution）

_____

2．对抗机器人的教育将会帮助学习者做好准备，执行那些只有人类才能完成的工作。（robot-proof education, prepare）

_____

3．一直以来，学习是解决技术性失业的最可靠方案。（antidote，technological redundancy）

_____

4．合作教育项目、实习机会、研究和全球经验帮助学生深化理解"为什么"，而不仅是"是什么"。（Co-ops，internships，global experiences）

_____

5．几个世纪以来，世界知名大学在创造知识和培养学生积极投入社会生活方面发挥了主导作用。（play a leading role）

_____

Part C

Product Manual
信息类产品说明书中简单句的使用

产品说明书的目的在于用准确简单的语言把产品的情况解说清楚，其要求说明书作者用最短的篇幅、最明白的语言、最直观的手段将信息准确充分地传达给读者，具有提

Unit 5　Artificial Intelligence 71

供信息的功能。产品说明书还兼具广告的特征，具有用词准确简洁、句式简单明了、逻辑清楚等特点。产品说明书的最主要的功能是介绍产品的有关信息，指导消费者正确合理地使用产品。因此，产品说明书的表达较少用复合句和并列句，多使用简单句，使句子结构简化，语言简洁清晰，结构层次明了，易于理解。例如：

(1) A laser is a device for light amplification by stimulated emission of radiation.
激光器是一种光受激辐射的放大器。

(2) Air bubble engraved lid, prevents spill and keeps warm effectively.
气泡雕刻盖，防止溢出，并有效地保暖。

(3) This device is a high-quality camera.
这款设备是一款高品质的相机。

(4) Press the power button to turn on the camera.
按下电源按钮来打开相机。

(5) Adjust the focus ring to achieve a clear image.
调整对焦环以获得清晰的图像。

(6) Insert the memory card into the card slot.
将内存卡插入卡槽。

(7) Connect the camera to your computer using a USB cable.
使用 USB 数据线将相机连接到计算机。

(8) Download the latest software update from our website.
从我们的网站下载最新的软件更新。

(9) Charge the battery using th included charger.
使用随附的充电器给电池充电。

(10) Press the shutter button to take a photo.
按下快门按钮来拍摄照片。

(11) Review your photos and videos on the built-in display.
在内置显示屏上查看您的照片和视频。

(12) Use the included strap to secure the camera to your wrist.
使用随附的腕带将相机固定在手腕上。

通过使用简单句，产品说明书可以更加简洁明了地传达信息，使读者更容易理解操作步骤和产品功能。

1. *Read the following paragraphs and then answer the questions.*

> **Product features**
> The **Alienware AW3420DW** monitor has an active matrix, Thin-Film Transistor (TFT), Liquid Crystal Display (LCD) and LED backlight. The monitor features include:
> - 86.72 cm (34.14 inch) viewable area (measured diagonally). Resolution: Up to 3440 x 1440 through DisplayPort and HDMI, with full-screen support or lower resolutions, supporting a high refresh rate of 120 Hz.
> - Nvidia G-SYNC-enabled monitor with a rapid response time of 2 ms gray to gray in **Extreme** mode *.
> - Color gamut of 134.5% sRGB and DCI P3 98%.
> - Tilt, swivel, and height adjustment capabilities.
> - Removable stand and Video Electronics Standards Association (VESA™) 100 mm mounting holes for flexible mounting solutions.
> - Digital connectivity via 1 DisplayPort and 1 HDMI port.
> - Equipped with 1 USB upstream port and 4 USB downstream ports.

- Plug and play capability if supported by your system.
- On-Screen Display (OSD) adjustments for ease of setup and screen optimization.
- AW3420DW offers a couple of preset modes, including FPS (First-Person Shooter), MOBA/RTS (Real-Time Strategy), RPG (Role-Playing Game), SPORTS (Racing) and three customizable game modes for user's own preference. In addition, key enhanced gaming features such as Timer, Frame Rate, and Display Alignment are provided to help improve gamer's performance and provide best-in game advantage.
- 0.5 W standby power when in sleep mode.
- Optimize eye comfort with a flicker-free screen.

⚠ **WARNING: The possible long-term effects of blue light emission from the monitor may cause damage to the eyes, including eye fatigue, digital eye strain, and so on. ComfortView feature is designed to reduce the amount of blue light emitted from the monitor to optimize eye comfort.**

* The 2 ms gray-to-gray mode is achievable in the **Extreme** mode to reduce visible motion blur and increased image responsiveness. However, this may introduce some slight and noticeable visual artifacts into the image. As every system setup and every gamer's needs are different, Alienware recommends that users experiment with the different modes to find the setting that is right for them.

(1) How many parts does The Alienware AW3420DW monitor have?

(2) How much is the resolution of the monitor?

(3) How many modes does AW3420DW offers?

(4) How many USB ports does AW3420DW equip?

(5) What is the function of Comfort View feature?

2. *Map reading and translation.*

(1) Front view

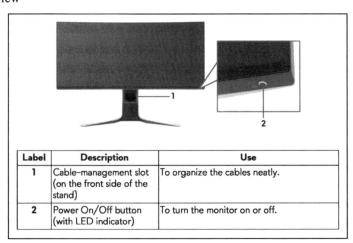

Label	Description	Use
1	Cable-management slot (on the front side of the stand)	To organize the cables neatly.
2	Power On/Off button (with LED indicator)	To turn the monitor on or off.

(2) Back view

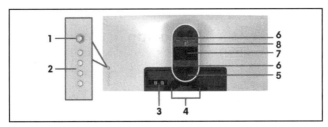

Back view without monitor stand

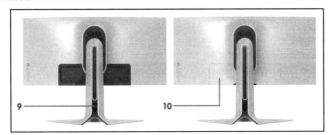

Back view with monitor stand

Label	Description	Use
1	Joystick	Use it to control the OSD menu.
2	Function buttons	For more information, see Operating the monitor.
3	Barcode, serial number, and Service Tag label	Refer to this label if you need to contact Dell for technical support.
4	Cable-management clip	To organize the cables neatly.
5	Stand release button	Releases stand from the monitor.
6	VESA mounting holes (100 mm x 100 mm - behind VESA Cover)	Wall mount monitor using VESA-compatible wall mount kit (100 mm x 100 mm).
7	Regulatory label	Lists the regulatory approvals.
8	Lighting dock connector	When the stand riser is attached to the monitor, the dock supplies power to the light on the stand.
9	Cable-management slot (at the back of the stand)	To organize cables by routing them through this slot.
10	I/O cover	Protects the I/O ports.

❶ Joystick _____

❷ Function buttons _____

❸ Barcode, serial number, and Service Tag label _____

❹ Cable-management clip _____

❺ Stand release button _____

❻ VESA mounting holes _____

❼ Regulatory label _____

❽ Lighting dock connector _____

❾ Cable-management slot _____

❿ I/O cover _____

Workshop

Background

Through the Internet, information can be spread so fast that the whole world would be astonished. To understand the real meaning of "Information Age", students are required to investigate one big event that originated from the Internet.

Task

Read this month's newspaper, news magazine or online news to see whether there are big news which originated from Internet information source. Discuss with classmates to decide on the news to be investigated. Search on the Internet to understand the whole process of the event.

Process

Step 1. Decide the event to be investigated through discussion.

Step 2. Use search engine such as GOOGLE and BAIDU to search the related news, comments and pictures or videos.

Step 3. Report to the whole class the big event that your group has investigated.

Step 4. Have a discussion on the power of information age.

Unit 6 Energy Technology

Energy and Public Safety

As is well known, the energy crisis has been with us for a longtime, and will be with us for an even longer time. It has become evident in the past few years that the amount of fossil fuel in the earth's substrata is not an infinite source of energy. Due to a steady increase in industrial and technological demand, an energy shortage is highly probable if the industrialized nations do not conserve existing resources and establish alternative ones. The fossil fuels, coal, oil and natural gas, are rapidly diminishing in supply as consumption increase.

Clearly, a replacement for these natural sources of energy is required. Several possible alternatives have been suggested, such as solar, geothermal and nuclear energy. Solar energy has the obvious advantage that the sun is an inexhaustible and abundant source which is free of both pollution and radioactivity. A lot of research is currently directed at discovering ways of harnessing solar power cheaply and efficiently, and of storing solar energy in reasonably small spaces. Geothermal energy, which involves stored underground reservoirs of steam, is also pollution free. Nuclear fission , a process whereby a uranium nucleus absorbs a neutron, is not. The reaction causes the nucleus to split into lighter elements, producing a large amount of heat. The by-product of this reaction is dangerously radioactive.

One of the major problems of nuclear energy is the inability of scientists to discover a safe way to dispose of the radioactive wastes that occur throughout the nuclear process. Many of these wastes remain dangerously active for tens of thousands of years. While others have a life span closer to a quarter of a million years. Various methods have been used to date, but all have revealed weaknesses, forcing scientists to continue their search.

The nuclear process involves several stages, with the danger of radioactivity constantly present. Fuel for nuclear reactors comes from uranium ore, which, when mined, spontaneously produces radioactive substances as by-products. This characteristic of uranium ore went undetected for a long time, resulting in the deaths, due to cancer, of hundreds of uranium miners.

Extraction of the uranium follows mining of the ore. The ore is crushed to the consistency of fine sand and the uranium is removed. In Canada and the United States, millions of tons of residue containing radioactive by-products remain uncovered in massive piles. The result is that some of it is washed into rivers contaminating entire river systems.

The ore having been extracted, the uranium is sent to a chemical plant. There, it is transformed into uranium hexafluoride, which in turn is sent to a gas diffusion plant to be enriched. The enriched uranium is sent to other plants, where it is transformed into uranium oxide in the form of small pellets. These are enclosed in long metal tubes, which become the fuel rods for nuclear reactors. The rods are then installed in reactors, where they remain until the accumulation of waste becomes such that the fuel is no longer usable. The "used" fuel is then sent to a reprocessing plant, where the radioactive wastes are removed. The remaining uranium is sent to a chemical plant to start the fuel cycle over again. The radioactive wastes are sent to be stored or buried. The nature of these wastes together with their lengthy life span has made it extremely difficult for scientists to find a way of disposing of them safely and permanently.

The United States attempted to bury much of its radioactive wastes material in containers made of steel covered in concrete, and capable of holding a million gallons. For a long time it was believed that the nuclear waste problem had been solved until some of these tanks leaked, allowing the radioactive wastes to seep into the environment. Canada presently stores its nuclear waste in underwater tanks with the long-term effects largely unknown.

However, plans are under consideration for above-ground storage of spent fuel from reactors. These plans include the building of three vast concrete containers, which would be two stories high, and approximately the length and width of two football fields. Other suggestions include enclosing the waste in glass blocks and storing them in underground caverns, or placing hot containers in the Antarctic region, where they would melt the ice, thereby sinking down about a mile. This idea has since been abandoned because of the possible adverse effect on the ice sheets.

Words & Expressions

evident/'evɪdənt/*adj.* 清楚的，显然的
fossilfuel/'fɒs(ə)lfjuːəl/*n.* 矿物燃料，化石燃料
substrata/ˌsʌb'streɪtə/*n.* 根基；下层；地层内段（substratum 的复数）
infinite/'ɪnfɪnət/*adj.* 无限的，无穷尽的；（数量或程度上）极大的，无穷大的；非限定的
diminish/dɪ'mɪnɪʃ/*v.* 减弱，降低，减少；贬低，轻视
consumption/kən'sʌmpʃ(ə)n/*n.* 消费，消耗
geothermal/ˌdʒiːəʊ'θɜːml/*adj.* 地热的；地温的
radioactivity/ˌreɪdɪəʊæk'tɪvəti/*n.* 放射性，放射现象；放射物（或其辐射）
reservoir/'rezəvwɑː(r)/*n.* 水库，蓄水池；储藏，蓄积
fission/'fɪʃ(ə)n/*n.* 裂变；分裂；分体；分裂生殖法
neutron/'njuːtrɒn/*n.* 中子
by-product/'baɪprɒdʌkt/*n.* 副产品；附带产生的结果；意外收获

inability/ˌɪnə'bɪləti/*n.* 无能，无力，不能
dispose of 处理；转让；解决
uranium ore 铀矿石，铀矿
spontaneously/spɒn'teɪnɪəsli/*adv.* 自发地，不由自主地；自然地
crush/krʌʃ/*v.* 压坏，压碎；捣碎
residue/'rezɪdjuː/*n.* 剩余物，残留物
contaminate/kən'tæmɪneɪt/*v.* 污染，弄脏；毒害，腐蚀（人的思想或品德）
extract/'ekstrækt/*v.* 提取，提炼
plant/plɑːnt/*n.* 工厂，发电厂
uranium hexafluoride 六氟化铀
uranium oxide 氧化铀
pellet/'pelɪt/*n.* 小球；（军）小子弹（枪用）；（生科）沉淀物
reactor/rɪ'æktə(r)/*n.* 反应器；[核]反应堆
permanently/'pɜːmənəntli/*adv.* 永久地；（问题或困难）不断发生地，一直存在地
concrete/'kɒŋkriːt/*adj.* 确实的，具体的；混凝土的；物质的；*n.* 混凝土
tank/tæŋk/*n.*（储存液体或气体的）箱，罐，缸
seep into 渗入；影响到；流入
enclose/ɪn'kləʊz/*v.* 包围，围住；随信附上，随信装入
cavern/'kævən/*n.* 洞穴；凹处；*vt.* 挖空；置…于洞穴中
thereby/ˌðeə'baɪ/*adv.* 因此，从而
adverse/'ædvɜːs/*adj.* 不利的，有害的；相反的；敌对的

Notes

1. Nuclear Fission：核裂变，又称核分裂，是指由重的原子核（主要是指铀核或钍核）分裂成两个或多个质量较小的原子的一种核反应形式。原子弹或核能发电厂的能量来源就是核裂变。

2. Nuclear Waste：核废料泛指在核燃料生产、加工和核反应堆用过的不再需要的并具有放射性的废料。核废料按物理状态可分为固体、液体和气体 3 种。

Exercises

I. Getting the Message

There are 5 questions in this section. Read the questions and complete the answers according to the text.

1. What is the situation of fossil fuel today?
_____

2. What is the advantage of solar energy?

3. What is one of the major problems of nuclear energy?

4. Why did hundreds of uranium miners die?

5. What did the United States and Canada do to deal with radioactive wastes?

II. Languages Focus

A. *Match the following words in left with their explanations in right.*

1. evident   a. to remove or obtain a substance from sth.
2. infinite   b. therefore
3. diminish   c. to break sth. into small pieces or into a powder by pressing hard
4. inability   d. clear; easily seen
5. crush   e. a factory or place where power is produced
6. thereby   f. without limits; without end
7. extract   g. to surround sth.
8. plant   h. the fact of not being able to do sth.
9. enclose   i. negative and unpleasant
10. adverse   j. to become or to make sth. become smaller or weaker

B. *Fill in the blanks with the words or expressions given below. Change the form where necessary.*

| evident | infinite | able | crush | adverse |
| permanent | concrete | seep into | enclose | thereby |

1. An immigrant is a person who comes to live _____ in a foreign country.
2. This drug is known to have _____ side effects.
3. Via the Internet, we are exposed to _____ information.
4. The posts have to be set in _____.
5. She walked slowly down the road, _____ in pain.
6. Radioactive water had _____ underground reservoirs.
7. Some families go without medical treatment because of their _____ to pay.
8. Regular exercise strengthens the heart, _____ reducing the risk of heart attack.
9. Bread is _____ and blended in like everything else.
10. The yard had been _____ with iron railings.

III. Translation

Translate the following sentences into Chinese.

1. Due to a steady increase in industrial and technological demand, an energy shortage is highly probable if the industrialized nations do not conserve existing resources and establish alternative ones.

2. Solar energy has the obvious advantage that the sun is an inexhaustible and abundant source which is free of both pollution and radioactivity.

3. Various methods have been used to date, but all have revealed weaknesses, forcing scientists to continue their search.

4. The nature of these wastes together with their lengthy life span has made it extremely difficult for scientists to find a way of disposing of them safely and permanently.

5. This idea has since been abandoned because of the possible adverse effect on the ice sheets.

IV. Discussion

Green and low-carbon transition is the overwhelming trend that all countries should work together for. Low-carbon energy development concerns the future of humanity. China attaches great importance to low-carbon energy development and actively promotes energy consumption, supply, technology and institutional transformation. China is ready to work with the international community to strengthen energy cooperation in all aspects, safeguard energy security, address climate change, protect the ecology and environment, promote sustainable development and bring more benefits to people around the world.

Work in pairs and discuss about your opinions on the low-carbon energy development, and then write down your opinions.

Earth Resources Technology Satellites

The first earth resources technology satellite, Landsat, was launched in 1972. Since then this and several other Landsat satellites have taken thousands of pictures of the earth's surface.

These pictures are helping us learn more about the earth, its mountains, vegetation, and bodies of water.

The Landsat spacecraft orbits the polar regions of the earth at a height of 920 kilometers. Once every 103 minutes the satellite makes a complete orbit of the earth. At this speed the satellite passes over the entire surface of the rotating earth in only eighteen days. The satellite is powered by photovoltaic cells in two solar panels, which provide 500 watts of electrical energy for the orbiting craft, taking pictures of earth.

The orbiting spacecraft is equipped with special instruments. These are used to produce sequential, overlapping pictures of the surface of the earth. One of these instruments is called a multi-spectral scanner. This instrument is able to sense a wide variety of wavelengths emitted by reflected sunlight from the earth. Some of the wavelengths are from the bands of the visible spectrum. That included red, yellow and blue. The invisible infrared spectrum is also sensed by the multi-spectral scanner. Since water, vegetation, and minerals each have unique identifying patterns in multi-spectral light. The scanner can identify different features of the earth. As an example, the longer infrared waves indicate temperature. And, therefore, the possibility of life. One set of unchanging wavelengths is characteristic of water, another is indicative of vegetation, and so on. Particular combinations of wavelengths identify everything from streams and rivers to plains and mountains.

Multi-spectral Scanner Data Transmission

During its eighteen-day orbit Landsat records more than 30,000 scenes. Each scene is made up of 32 million tiny squares called picture elements, or "pixels". These satellite picture elements are transmitted to earth. In somewhat the same way that a television station sends "pictures" to your home. The receiving stations on earth convert the emerging picture elements into images in a method. Similar to the way your television converts electrical signals into a picture. The images are turned into black-and-white or color pictures. The color pictures are in "false" colors other than their natural ones. As an example, bare ground appears white or light gray. Water is black or dark blue. Vegetation appears in varying shades of red. This standardized coloring system was developed to assist scientists in image interpretation.

Uses of Landsat Imagery

More than 130 countries are currently receiving pictures from the Landsat satellites. The pictures can be very valuable and can be used to make more accurate maps.

Geologists study lineaments in the pictures. Lineaments are land structures that form raised or depressed areas. One example of a lineament is a geological fault in the earth's crust. The Landsat satellite detects lineaments on the earth's surface very clearly. Studying lineaments is important because mineral deposits such as uranium and petroleum are located on or near the lineaments. Agronomists and farmers use the pictures to study crops. Each crop has slightly different colors detectable by the satellite. Viewers sort out the different colors and determine the name of the crop, where it is, and how many hectares of it there are. In addition, the pictures can indicate which crops are ready for harvest, or they can serve as an early warning system of potential damage to these renewable resources. Some examples of potentially damaging conditions are insect infestation and corn blight. Landsat pictures are also being used to monitor water pollution, analyze droughts, and study soil conditions. Scientists predict the expanding use of earth resource technology satellites for future natural resource surveillance .

Words & Expressions

vegetation/ˌvedʒə'teɪʃ(ə)n/*n*.（总称）植物，植被；（植物的）生长；呆板单调的生活

orbit/'ɔːbɪt/*n*.（环绕地球、太阳等运行的）轨道；势力范围，影响范围；眼眶，眼窝；*v*. 沿轨道运行，环绕…运行；使（卫星）进入轨道

polar/'pəʊlə(r)/*adj*. 极地的，来自极地的；（固体）离子的；（几何）（球体）轴极的；*n*.（几何）极线；极光双子星

rotate/rəʊ'teɪt/*v*.（使）旋转，（使）转动；（人员）轮换，轮值；轮种，轮作；定期调换地点（或位置）；*adj*.（植）辐状的

photovoltaic/ˌfəʊtəʊˌvɒl'teɪɪk/*adj*. 光电伏打的，光电的

photovoltaic cell 光电池

solar panel 太阳能板；太阳能电池板

be equipped with 配备有…；装有…；装备有

sequential/sɪ'kwenʃ(ə)l/*adj*. 连续的，按顺序的；依次发生的，相继发生的；（主计算机）顺序的

overlap/ˌəʊvə'læp/*v*.（与…）复叠；（在关注的问题、承担的责任等方面）部分地重叠，部分相同；（与…）同时发生；*n*.（物体的）重叠部分，重叠量

multi-spectral scanner 多光谱扫描器

spectrum/'spektrəm/*n*. 范围，幅度；光谱；波谱，频谱；余象

infrared/ˌɪnfrə'red/*adj*. 红外线的；（设备，技术）使用红外的，涉及红外的；*n*. 红外区，红外线，红外辐射

indicative/ɪn'dɪkətɪv/*adj*. 指示的，表明的，象征的；陈述（语气）的

pixel/'pɪksl/*n*. 像素

convert into 使转变；把…转化成；折合

lineament/'lɪnɪəmənt/*n*. 容貌；相貌；面部轮廓

geological/ˌdʒiːə'lɒdʒɪkl/*adj*. 地质的，地质学的

geological fault 地质断层

crust/krʌst/*n*. 面包皮；（馅饼或比萨饼等的）酥皮；硬外皮，硬外壳；地壳；*v*. 形成（或结成）硬皮（或硬壳）

deposit/dɪ'pɒzɪt/*v*. 放下，放置；储蓄；存放，寄存；沉积，沉淀；支付（押金、订金或预缴费用）；*n*. 沉积物，沉积层；订金；押金；存款；竞选保证金

mineral deposit 矿床，矿产资源

agronomist/ə'grɒnəmɪst/*n.* 农学家
blight/blaɪt/*n.* 枯萎病；荒芜；*vt.* 破坏；使…枯萎；*vi.* 枯萎
surveillance/sɜː'veɪləns/*n.* 监视，监察

Notes

1. Landsat：美国 NASA 的陆地卫星计划。自 1972 年 7 月 23 日以来，已发射 8 颗（第 6 颗发射失败）。Landsat 1～4 均相继失效，Landsat 5 于 2013 年 6 月退役。Landsat 7 于 1999 年 4 月 15 日发射升空。Landsat 8 于 2013 年 2 月 11 日发射升空，经过 100 天测试运行后开始获取影像。陆地卫星计划是运行时间最长的地球观测计划，1972 年 7 月 23 日地球资源卫星（Earth Resources Technology Satellite）发射，后来此卫星被改称为陆地卫星。陆地卫星上所装备的仪器已获得数以百万计的珍贵图像，这些图像被储存在美国和全球各地的接收站中。这一独特资源用于全球变化的相关研究，并应用在农业、制图、林业、区域规划、监控和教育等领域中。Landsat 7 拥有 7 个光谱波段，空间分辨率为 15～60 米不等，时间分辨率为 16 天。

2. Multispectral Scanner：对同一地区、在同一瞬间摄取多个波段影像的摄影机，称为多光谱摄影机。采用多光谱摄影是为了充分利用地物在不同光谱区有不同的反射这一特征，来获取目标更多的信息量，以便提高影像几何关系的判读和识别能力。多光谱扫描仪安装在飞行器上。扫描仪的扫描镜旋转，使接收的瞬时视场作垂直于飞行方向的运动，从而实现行扫描。飞行器的向前运动，扫描仪遂完成二维扫描。地物景像被逐点扫过，并逐点分波段测量，从而获得多光谱的遥感图像信息。

Exercises

I. Comprehension of the Text

Read the text and answer the following questions. Write the answers on the lines.

1. What do scientists use resources satellites for?
_____

2. How does a multi-spectral scanner identify different features of the earth?
_____

3. What will happen to the satellite if there is much vegetation?
_____

4. How do Agronomists and farmers use the pictures to study crops?
_____

5. What is the author's purpose to write the article?
_____

II. Main Details Comprehension

Directions: *In this section, you are going to read a passage with ten statements attached to it. Each statement contains information given in one of the paragraphs. Identify the paragraph from which the information is derived. You may choose a paragraph more than once. Each paragraph is marked with a letter.*

Astrology

A) Astrology is the study of how the sun, the moon, planets, and stars are supposedly related to life and events on the earth. It is based on the belief that the heavenly bodies form patterns that can reveal a person's character or future. Many people throughout the world believe in astrology. These people base important decisions on the advice of an astrologer (a person who tells fortunes by studying the stars). Other people declare there is no scientific basis for astrology, and they consider it a form of entertainment.

B) Astrology differs from astronomy. Astrology developed from a set of principles that originated more than 2, 000 years ago. At that time, astronomy was also based on those same principles. But during the 1500's and 1600's, several astronomers, including Nicolaus Copernicus of Poland and Tycho Brahe of Denmark, made discoveries about the heavenly bodies that conflicted with the principles of astrology. As a result, astrology and astronomy became widely different in their methods and purposes. Today, astrologers observe the heavenly bodies to understand things that happen on the earth. Astronomers seek scientific knowledge about the various objects in space.

C) The basic principle of astrology is that the heavenly bodies influence what happens on the earth. Astrologers learn about this influence by casting (drawing) a circular chart called a horoscope or birth chart. A horoscope shows the position of the planets in relation to both the earth and the stars at a certain time. In most cases, it shows the position of these bodies at the time of a person's birth. The system used by astrologers to cast a horoscope is based on a special view of the universe. This view involves four elements (1) the earth; (2) the planets; (3) the zodiac(黄道), and (4) the houses.

D) In casting a horoscope, astrologers place the earth at the center of the solar system. Therefore, all heavenly bodies-revolve around the earth rather than around the sun. Astrologers use this arrangement to determine the positions of the heavenly bodies in relation to the earth. They believe that the study of the positions of the heavenly bodies can reveal a person's character and future. In astrology, the moon and the sun are considered planets, along with Jupiter, Mars, Neptune, Pluto, Saturn, Uranus, and Venus. Each planet supposedly represents a force that affects people in a certain way. Astrologers believe the planets influence a person more than do any other heavenly bodies.

E) The zodiac is a band of stars that appear to encircle the earth. It is divided into 12 equal parts, called signs. Each sign of the zodiac has certain characteristics, which are determined by a particular planet and other factors. Astrologers believe the signs determine how the planets affect a person's character. The houses. Like the zodiac, the earth's surface is divided into 12 parts. Each of these parts, called houses, represents certain characteristics of an individual's life. Astrologers believe the houses determine how the planets and the signs influence a person's daily life.

F) Astrology began sometime before 2000 BC in Babylonia(now southeastern Iraq). Astrologers of that time knew of five planets — Jupiter, Mars, Mercury, Saturn and Venus. They believed that the sun, the moon, and planets sent out different forces, which had certain characteristics. For example, one of the planets — now known as Mars — appeared to be red. Astrologers linked it with anger, aggression and war.

G) The zodiac was probably developed in ancient Egypt, and the Babylonians adopted it sometime after 1000 BC Astrologers gradually developed a system that linked seasonal changes with specific group of stars called constellations (星座). At that time, for example, heavy rainfall occurred in Babylonia when the sun was in a certain constellation. As a result, astrologers named the constellation Aquarius, the water bearer.

H) At first, astrologers studied the heavenly bodies in making general predictions about the future. But between 600 BC and 200 BC, they developed the system of casting individual horoscopes (以占星术算命). The ancient Greeks and Romans practiced astrology and greatly influenced its development. The Roman names for the planets and the signs of the zodiac are still used today.

I) Interest in astrology declined in Europe with the coming of Christianity as people sought guidance from religious leaders rather than from astrologers. Astrology regained popularity during the AD 1100's. By the 1600's, it was particularly strong in England. Several astrological almanacs (历书) were published, and many other books either defended or attacked astrology. The number of followers of astrology fell in England during the 1700's, but the subject's popularity returned again in the early 1800's. By the late 1800's and early 1900's, interest in astrology had spread to many other nations. Newspapers in England began publishing horoscope columns during the 1930's. Such columns soon appeared in newspapers throughout the world, and people became increasingly interested in astrology. Today, astrology is followed more widely than ever before.

J) Many people believe astrology is simply a superstition, and scientists declare that its whole basis is unscientific. Scientists point out that the earth's position has changed in space since ancient times. As a result, the signs of the zodiac used by astrologers no longer match the constellations for which they were named. Some people who believe in astrology support it in terms of magnetic fields, solar storms and other natural occurrences. Others, though they also believe in astrology, claim that it cannot be supposed scientifically. They consider it a set of powerful symbols that can provide a deep understanding of human beings. They defend astrology by pointing out that, in many cases, it works.

_____1. Astrologers hold the belief that the planets exert more influence on a person than other heavenly bodies do.

____2. Publishing horoscope columns in newspapers helped to make astrology spread across the world widely.

____3. Whenever the sun was in the constellation Aquarius, it rained heavily in Babylonia.

____4. The discoveries of heavenly bodies that were against the principles of astrology led to great differences between astrology and astronomy in their methods and purposes.

____5. Astrology is based on the conviction that the patterns the heavenly bodies form can tell a person's character or future.

____6. Some people still believe in astrology, though they know it is unscientific, by claiming that it works in many cases.

____7. During the 1700's in England, astrology gained less popularity than before.

____8. In astrology, the earth is regarded as the center of the solar system.

____9. Since Mars appeared to be red, astrologers believed that it represented anger, aggression and war.

____10. It's believed by the astrologers that the houses determine how the planets and the signs influence a person's daily life.

III. Translation

Translate the five following sentences into English, using the words or expressions given in brackets.

1. 我们学校的每间课室将来都会装备平板计算机。（be equipped with）

_____

2. 头衔通常表示级别和身份。（indicative）

_____

3. 我们想把阁楼改造成又一间卧室。（convert into）

_____

4. 我们敦促他们及早解决那个问题。（sort out）

_____

5. 让我们医治世界，让伤痛枯萎。（blight）

_____

Part C

Product Manual
信息类产品说明书中祈使句的使用

  信息类产品说明书句式的另一个突出特点是多使用祈使句。由于祈使句简洁有力，且说明书编纂者相对于读者来说属于权威信息源，这就要求说明书中的陈述和指导尽量清楚、直截了当、表意明确。祈使句常常用来表示强调、命令、警告，用在说明书的警告、注意事项、操作要点等要求消费者特别注意的事项。例如 PHILIPS 显示器安装指南的译文：

Turn off your computer and unplug its power cable.

Connect the blue connector of the video cable to the blue video connector on the back of your computer.

Connect your monitor's power cable to the power port on the back of the monitor.

Plug your computer's power cord and your monitor into a nearby outlet.

Turn on your computer and monitor. If the monitor displays an image, installation is complete.

If you are using BNC connectors (not available on all models), please remember to switch to "Input B" from "Input A" by simultaneously pressing the "OK" and "UP" knobs on front control panel.

以上 7 句译句中有 6 句是祈使句，可见祈使句在电器、电子产品说明书英译时使用之广泛。说明书与其他句子不同，祈使句不使用含有动作名词的名词化结构，大都使用平易的表意明确的动词。如 install...，open...，check...等后直接加宾语。

信息类产品说明书都属 The-D's-and-Don'ts Style（"注意事项"文体）。因为没有主语的表述显得准确客观而又简洁明了。常用的祈使句型包括：

（一）肯定祈使句

肯定祈使句表示对用户的建议，以"动词原型＋宾语"结构为主，例如：

(1) Lift the Kilburn active loudspeaker by the carry strap.
请使用手提带提携 Kilburn 有源音箱。

(2) Be sure to turn off the high voltage power supply, and disconnect the electric cable before working on the unit.
在使用本机前，务必关闭高压电源，并断开电源线。

(3) Fully charge the Kilburn battery be-fore it is used for the first time.
初次使用前，请将 Kilburn 的电池充满电。

原文本中的祈使句一般是对用户的操作提出建议，以保证用户正确使用该产品，具有非常强的呼唤功能。

（二）否定祈使句

常见的也有少量否定祈使句，表示"禁止"，结构一般为"Do not＋动词原形＋宾语"，例如：

(1) Don't open the box if you are not an authorized repairman.
非专业修理人员请勿拆开机盖。

(2) Do not disassemble, install backward, or expose batteries to liquid，moisture, fire or extreme temperature．
不要拆卸、反向安装电池，不要将电池暴露在液体、潮湿或极端温度之下。

(3) Do not use an old and a new battery together, also never use an alkaline battery with a manganese battery.

请不要将新电池和旧电池混合使用，且绝不能将碱性电池和锰电池混合使用。

(4) Don't confuse adiabatic methods with today's power-saving features on laptops, however.

但是，不要把绝热方法同现在手提计算机的节能特点混淆。

祈使句主要指导产品的使用方法，注意事项和在特殊情况下应采取的必要措施。祈使句的使用增加了句式的权威性，使阅读者更加重视语句的内容。

1. *Read the following paragraphs and then answer the questions.*

Highlighted Features Huawei Share OneHop

With Huawei Share OneHop, you can quickly transfer images, videos, and documents, as well as share clipboards and documents between your computer and phone, all without the need of a data cable.

• Multi-Screen Collaboration: Once your phone is connected to the laptop, the phone screen will automatically pop up on the laptop. Easily maneuver around your phone with a larger screen!

• OneHop File Sharing: Transfers images, videos, and documents between your phone and computer at high speeds.

• OneHop Screen Recording: Shake your phone and tap to record your PC screen automatically for 60s. The recording will be saved to your phone for quick sharing.

Currently, OneHop Screen Recording feature is only available on computers with the Intel chip.

• OneHop Clipboard Sharing: Allows you to copy content from your phone and paste it on your computer, and vice versa.

For more details, please visit the official Huawei Share OneHop website.

Eye Comfort mode

When reading for prolonged periods, enable Eye Comfort mode on your computer to reduce blue light output and prevent eye strain and fatigue.

Right-click any blank area on the desktop and select Display Manager. Enable Eye Comfort.

Eye Comfort mode reduces the amount of blue light emitted from the screen, which may give the screen a slightly yellow hue.

F10 system reset/factory reset

If your computer system encounters a serious problem as a result of a virus, malware, etc., the built-in F10 system reset/factory reset feature can quickly restore your computer to its initial or factory state.

Before restoring the factory settings, back up all files on the drive C.

Connect your computer to the charger. Press and hold F10 when powering on your computer to access the restore screen.

Follow the onscreen instructions to restore your computer to the factory settings.

(1) Can you find some imperative sentences in this passage? Please underline them.

(2) What is Huawei Share OneHop?

(3) How to set OneHop Screen Recording?

(4) How to set the Eye Comfort mode?

(5) Before restoring the factory settings, what should you do?

2. *Map reading and translation.*

| ☼ F1 | Decrease the screen brightness. |

❶

| ☼ F3 | Enable or disable the keyboard backlight, and adjust the backlight brightness. |

❷

| | **Tap with one finger**: Click the left mouse button. |

❸

| | **Tap and drag with one finger**: Move the mouse cursor. |

❹

| · Click 👤 to change, lock, or log out of the current user account. |

❺

Workshop

Background

Energy resources are closely related to the stable development of world economy and the well-being of all people. It is reported that many traditional energy resources, such as the fossil fuels, coal, oil and natural gas, are rapidly diminishing. Due to a steady increase in industrial and technological demand, an energy shortage is highly probable if the industrialized nations do not conserve existing resources and establish alternative ones.

Therefore, it's time for us to take advantage of technology to exploit and utilize new energy, such as Nuclear energy, Solar energy, Geothermal energy, Wind energy, Ocean energy, Bio-energy, Hydrogen energy and so on.

Task

1. Interview some classmates and your friends on this topic.
2. Search more information online.

Process

Step 1. Complete the task in groups. Form small groups with 5—6 students respectively.

Step 2. Interview your friends and search information online.

Step 3. Have a discussion with your classmates on the technology of energy exploitation and utilization, and make a list of those technologies.

Step 4. Make an oral presentation and introduce those technologies in class.

Unit 7　Technology and Future

"Iron Man" Armor Might Actually Come into Our Lives

Imagine wearing high-tech body armour that makes you super strong and tireless. Such technology, more specifically called an exoskeleton, sounds like the preserve of the Iron Man series of superhero movies.

Yet the equipment is increasingly being worn in real life around the world. And one manufacturer — California's SuitX — expects it to go mainstream.

"There is no doubt in my mind that these devices will eventually be sold at hardware stores," says SuitX's founder Homayoon Kazerooni.

In simple terms, an exoskeleton is an external device that supports, covers and protects its user, giving greater levels of strength and endurance.

Sometimes also referred to as "wearable robots", they can be battery-powered and computer-operated, incorporating motors and hydraulics. Or they can be more simple, passive designs that use springs and dampeners.

"Integrating humans and machines into one system opens up a new realm of opportunity," says Adrian Spragg, an expert on the technology at management consultancy Accenture. "Many of the early applications have been focused on military and medical applications, but in the last several years there's been an explosion of use in a range of cases".

This expansion, which has come together with rapid advances in the technology, has seen exoskeletons increasingly used by manufacturing workers. Versions for consumers are also now being developed to help people more easily do everything from DIY, to walking, climbing stairs, and other daily activities.

One report says sales are now due to rocket as a result. Global exoskeleton revenues are expected to rise from $392 million in 2020 to $6.8 billion in 2030, according to a study by ABI Research.

SuitX's "suits" are now being tested by car manufacturers General Motors and Fiat. Prof Kazerooni, who is also the director of the University of California's Berkeley Robotics and Human Engineering Laboratory, says that the primary benefit of the firm's exoskeletons is to prevent muscle fatigue.

"We've shown that muscle activity in the back, shoulder and knees drops by 50%," he says. "If muscle activities drop, that means the risk of muscle injury is less".

"This means that factory or plant managers get more productivity, their insurance costs are lower, and there are less workdays lost to injury. There's less cost and more productivity".

General Motors is also looking at a battery-powered exoskeleton glove developed by Bioservo.

This glove, called the Iron Hand, has sensors and motors in each finger, which automatically respond to the level of force that the wearer applies to his or her hand when lifting or gripping something. The glove therefore takes up some of the strain.

BioServo says it can increase the wearer's hand strength by 20% for extended periods.

The most advanced exoskeletons use artificial intelligence (AI) computer systems — software that can to a certain extent learn and adapt by itself.

At the moment, however, more widespread adoption of exoskeleton technology is still held back by a number of factors, including battery capacity, limited range of motion, and cost.

"The average cost (of a full-body exoskeleton) is around $45,000," says Accenture's Mr Spragg. "However, with economies of scale and technological maturity, prices will come down".

SuitX's Prof Kazerooni says that falling prices will also open up the possibility to tap into a potentially huge market — recreational exoskeletons. His firm is now working on such a device that supports the wearer's knee.

"It's not only for people who are going climbing and hiking, or younger people who want to be more adventurous, or for people who want to do more walking and climbing but not hurt their knees," he says. "It'll be for all ages. It's simply giving you a little boost".

Words & Expressions

armour/'ɑːmə(r)/*n.* 盔甲；装甲；护面
exoskeleton/'eksəʊskelɪt(ə)n/*n.* 外骨骼
preserve/prɪ'zɜːv/*v.* 保护，维护；保持，维持；*n.*（某人或某个团体的）专属领域，独有活动；动物保护区，外人禁入的猎地
manufacturer/ˌmænju'fæktʃərə(r)/*n.* 生产商，制造商
mainstream/'meɪnstriːm/*n.* 主流；*adj.* 主流的；*v.* 使主流化，使成为主流
hardware/'hɑːdweə(r)/*n.*（计算机）硬件；五金制品；装备，设备
hardware stores 五金店
external device 外部设备
endurance/ɪn'djʊərəns/*n.* 持久力，忍耐力；耐久性，耐用度
battery/'bætri/*n.* 电池，蓄电池；一组，一系列
battery-powered 电池供能的
hydraulics/haɪ'drɒlɪks/*n.* 水力学
passive/'pæsɪv/*adj.* 消极的，被动的
dampener/'dæmpnə(r)/*n.* 令人扫兴的人；[机] 阻尼器，减震器（等于 damper）

realm/relm/*n*. （知识、活动、思想的）领域，范围；王国；（动物学）界

military/'mɪlətri/*adj*. 军事的，军队的；陆军的；军人般的，军人作风的；*n*. 军人，军方

explosion/ɪk'spləʊʒ(ə)n/*n*. 爆破，爆炸（声）；激增；爆发，迸发

revenue/'revənju/*n*. （企业、组织的）收入，收益；（政府的）税收；税务局，税务署

fatigue/fə'ti:g/*n*. 疲乏，厌倦；（金属部件的）疲劳；*v*. 使疲劳，使劳累；*adj*. 疲劳的

productivity/ˌprɒdʌk'tɪvəti/*n*. 生产率，生产力

insurance/ɪn'ʃʊərəns/*n*. 保险；保险费；保险业；预防措施，安全保障

sensor/'sensə(r)/*n*. （探测光、热、压力等的）传感器，敏感元件，探测设备

automatically/ˌɔ:tə'mætɪkli/*adv*. 自然地，必然地；不假思索地，无意识地；自动地

strain/streɪn/*n*. 焦虑，紧张；负担，紧张；张力，压力；*v*. 拉伤，扭伤；使紧张；拉紧

maturity/mə'tʃʊərəti/*n*. 成熟；发育成熟，长大成人；到期

tap into 挖掘；接进

recreational/ˌrekri'eɪʃn(ə)l/*adj*. 娱乐的，消遣的

tireless/'taɪələs/*adj*. 不知疲倦的，孜孜不倦的

incorporate/ɪn'kɔ:pəreɪt/*v*. 包含，合并；组成公司；掺和，混合（成分）；使具体化，体现；*adj*. 合成一体的，合并的；具体化的；组成公司（或社团）的

consultancy/kən'sʌltənsi/*n*. 咨询公司；咨询意见，顾问工作

application/ˌæplɪ'keɪʃ(ə)n/*n*. 申请书，申请表；应用，实施

expansion/ɪk'spænʃ(ə)n/*n*. 扩大，扩张；扩充，展开；扩张物；膨胀

respond to 响应

adventurous/əd'ventʃərəs/*adj*. 勇于冒险的，敢于创新的；新奇的，令人兴奋的

Notes

1. SuitX：SuitX 是从加州大学伯克利分校机器人与人类工程实验室分拆出来的，专业从事职业和医疗外骨骼研发的公司。2021 年 11 月，SuitX 被 Ottobock（奥托博克）收购，Ottobock 和 SuitX 正在结合他们的专业知识和产品，将外骨骼市场提升到一个新的水平，并促进外骨骼在全球范围内的采用。SuitX 主要面向行动不便或行动障碍的用户。产品分为医疗外骨骼与工业外骨骼，可以支撑体重，减少整个行程的工作量，并减轻工人的疲劳感，还可以矫正站姿远离并发症。整套外骨骼的重量仅为 12.25kg，并且其能够按照个人不同的需求来进行私人定制。

2. Exoskeleton：外骨骼机器人技术是融合传感、控制、信息、融合、移动计算，为作为操作者的人提供一种可穿戴的机械机构的综合技术。外骨骼机器人是指套在人体外面的机器人，也称"可穿戴的机器人"。它是一种支撑、遮盖和保护使用者的外部设备，为其提供更高水平的力量和耐力。按用途，外骨骼机器人分为 3 种类型：第一类是助力型外骨骼机器人，主要面向健康人群，提高人的负载能力，用于军事领域，可增强士兵负重能力；第二类是步态训练康复型外骨骼机器人。主要面向下肢运动能力受损患者的康复治疗中，使患者通过训练以达到逐渐恢复下肢运动的能力，实现自主行走；第

三类是下肢运动辅助型外骨骼机器人。这类机器人主要面向丧失下肢运动能力的残疾人，以帮助他们能够像正常人那样站立以及行走。外骨骼可以通过多种方式驱动，但最常见的是液压驱动，气压驱动和电机驱动3种方式。

Exercises

I. Getting the Message

There are 5 questions in this section. Read the questions and complete the answers according to the text.

1. What is exoskeleton?
_____

2. What can exoskeleton do for people?
_____

3. What benefits can SuitX's exoskeletons bring to factory or plant managers?
_____

4. How does the battery-powered exoskeleton glove work?
_____

5. What will open up the possibility of exoskeleton to tap into the potentially huge recreational market?
_____

II. Languages Focus

A. *Match the following words in left with their explanations in right.*

1. military	a. an area of activity, interest, or knowledge
2. preserve	b. accepting what happens or what people do without trying to change anything or oppose them
3. manufacturer	c. a person or company that produces goods in large quantities
4. mainstream	d. to make sure that sth. is kept
5. hardware	e. connected with soldiers or the armed forces
6. passive	f. a feeling of being extremely tired
7. realm	g. pressure on sb./sth. because they have too much to do or manage
8. fatigue	h. tools and equipment that are used in the house and garden/yard
9. strain	i. willing to take risks and try new ideas
10. adventurous	j. the ideas and opinions that are thought to be normal because they are shared by most people

B. *Fill in the blanks with the words or expressions given below. Change the form where necessary.*

| preserve | manufacture | mainstream | hardware | passive |
| strain | adventure | consult | apply | expand |

1. He set up several adverting_____ business in the UK.
2. The components are readily available in_____ stores.
3. The transport service cannot cope with the _____ of so many additional passengers.
4. That was great for the consumer, not so much for the_____.
5. The _____ of Western capitalism incorporated the Third World into an exploitative world system.
6. The damaged church was _____ as a constant reminder of the horrors of war.
7. Animation has stopped being eye-candy for kids and geeks and become _____ enter-tainment.
8. For the more _____ tourists, there are trips into the mountains with a local guide.
9. It's a sad truth that children are the biggest victims of _____ smoking.
10. The service works as a software _____ that is accessed via the internet.

Ⅲ. Translation

Translate the following sentences into Chinese.

1. Such technology, more specifically called an exoskeleton, sounds like the preserve of the Iron Man series of superhero movies.

_____

2. Versions for consumers are also now being developed to help people more easily do everything from DIY, to walking, climbing stairs, and other daily activities.

_____

3. This means that factory or plant managers get more productivity, their insurance costs are lower, and there are less workdays lost to injury.

_____

4. This glove, called the Iron Hand, has sensors and motors in each finger, which automatically respond to the level of force that the wearer applies to his or her hand when lifting or gripping something.

_____

5. At the moment, however, more widespread adoption of exoskeleton technology is still held back by a number of factors, including battery capacity, limited range of motion, and

cost.

Ⅳ. Discussion

With the development of science and technology, great changes have taken place in people's lives. There is no doubt that we have benefited greatly from many different scientific advances. For example, the invention of computers has greatly improved work efficiency, helped to complete many difficult tasks that could not have been accomplished in the past, and new medical discoveries and technologies have improved people's health and enabled them to enjoy a longer life span.

Due to the development of science and technology, the ability of human beings to explore the world around them has also been enhanced. From space to the deep sea, human society is booming and more convenient. However, science is like a double-edged sword, which will bring problems.

As we all know, nuclear energy, an environmentally friendly energy, can also be developed into weapons of mass destruction. In addition, human cloning is expected to cure serious disease, may bring about social moral disaster. In fact, scientific progress is mostly at the cost of our precious natural resources, so it has caused great harm to our living environment.

How to correctly treat the progress of science and technology is a problem worthy of our serious consideration. Work in pairs and discuss this topic.

Building Better Ultralight Computers

The Holy Grail of mobile computing is a portable device that has the power of a desktop computer, lasts more than a day on a single battery charge, and weighs next to nothing.

Right now, such a computer is still a myth. But computer makers are pushing the limits of weight and power.

Today's so-called ultralight computers, which retail from about $1,800 to more than $3,000, are less than an inch thick, weigh less than three pounds, and have the computing power of a typical year-old desktop.

Yet many of the smallest, lightest computers are studded with tradeoffs. They, for example, won't last more than a few hours on a single battery, don't come with built-in CD or DVD drives, and have less powerful processors than "normal" PCs. "Right now, people do see that you have to compromise to get to the form factor," that is, the ideal size and weight, says Michael Abary, senior product marketing manager for Sony's Vaio line of notebook PCs. "But we're making plans to offset them (the compromises)." One of the most promising new technologies to help achieve that goal is a new breed of low-powered microprocessors that can vary the speeds at which they operate.

During complex computing tasks — such as crunching a large amount of numerical data in a spreadsheet — the processors might run at their top rate, or "clock speed." But for less demanding tasks — running a word processor or playing music, for instance — the chip can slow way down.

The chief advantage of these processors, including Intel's Mobile Pentium III-M and Transmeta Corp. 's Crusoe, is the power they save. At slow speeds, for example, they typically require less than 1 watt, which means a computer's rechargeable batteries will last much longer between charges. Meanwhile, labs are testing new battery technologies.

For now, most rechargeable batteries, made of lithium, provide portable computers about four or five hours before they need to be recharged. But research into different, lighter materials — such as zinc combined with air — could produce batteries with greater "energy densities." If more power can be packed into less space, portable computers can be made even lighter than the current crop of ultralights.

"Unfortunately, unlike a lot of electronic technology which sees a doubling in capabilities every 18 months, battery technology growth is only linear," says Tom Bernhard, director of product marketing for Fujitsu. By Bernhard's estimates, really interesting developments won't happen for another three to five years.

While they wait for the battery improvements, computer makers are touting a new type of portable computer called the tablet PC, which they hope to offer for sale by next year. Compaq, NEC and Toshiba all showed off models at this week's Comdex computer trade show in Las Vegas.

These computers — typically the size and shape of a 1.5-inch-thick stack of typing paper — feature a screen that users can "write" on using a plastic stylus. The software, a special version of Microsoft's new Windows XP operating system, can interpret those pen strokes. And, instead of using a computer mouse to click on icons, users will merely tap on the screen to access the Internet or start programs.

Ted Clark, vice president for Compaq's Tablet PC, says such pen-based computers will have all the power, memory and features of an ordinary notebook computer.

Such snazzy portables may not be as cheap as ordinary notebooks, however. Early tablet PCs were priced well above $3,000 because of expensive parts such as the touch-sensitive screen.

Words & Expressions

ultralight/ˈʌltrəlaɪt/*adj*. 超轻型的；*n.* 超轻型飞机
ultralight computer 超轻型计算机

Unit 7　Technology and Future

portable/'pɔ:təb(ə)l/*adj.* 便携式的，轻便的；（变更工作或情景时）可转移的，可随带的；*n.* 手提式电器
compute/kəm'pju:t/*v.* 估算，计算；用计算机计算；*n.* 计算，估计
stud/stʌd/*v.* 用饰钉（或类似物）装饰；散布于，密布于，（零星地）点缀
be studded with 被镶上
tradeoff/'treɪdɒf/*n.* 权衡；折衷；（公平）交易（同 trade-off）
processor/'prəʊsesə(r)/*n.* （计算机的）处理器（机）；处理程序；文件经办人
offset/'ɒfset/*v.* 补偿，抵销；衬托出；使偏离直线方向；*n.* 抵消物，补偿
breed/bri:d/*v.* 饲养，培育；养育，培养；引起，酿成；（通过核反应）增殖可裂变物质；*n.* 品种；（人的）类型，种类
crunch/krʌntʃ/*v.* （大量地）处理（数字）；*n.* 压碎声，碎裂声
numerical/nju:'merɪk(ə)l/*adj.* 数字的，用数字表示的
chip/tʃɪp/*n.* 芯片；碎块，碎屑
rechargeable/ˌri:'tʃɑ:dʒəbl/*adj.* 可再充电的；收费的
lithium/'lɪθiəm/*n.* 锂（符号 Li）
zinc/zɪŋk/*n.* 锌
pack/pæk/*v.* 把…打包，收拾（行李）；包装，装箱；（用柔软材料）把…裹
crop/krɒp/*n.* 产量；（同时涌现的）一批，一帮
linear/'lɪniə(r)/*adj.* 直线的，线性的；连续的，连贯的；（关系）直接的，明显的
improvement/ɪm'pru:vmənt/*n.* 改善；改进之处
tout/taʊt/*vt.* 兜售；*vi.* 兜售；招徕顾客；拉选票
stack/stæk/*n.* （整齐的）一堆；垛，堆；大量，许多
stylus/'staɪləs/*n.* 铁笔；唱针；尖笔；药笔剂
stroke/strəʊk/*v.* 轻抚，抚摸；轻挪，轻触，轻拭；击球
icon/'aɪkɒn/*n.* 图标；偶像，代表；画像
tap/tæp/*v.* 轻拍，轻扣，轻敲
snazzy/'snæzi/*adj.* 时髦的；漂亮的；新潮的
touch-sensitive screen 触敏视屏

Notes

1. Holy Grail：圣杯是在公元 33 年，犹太历尼散月十四日，也就是耶稣受难前的逾越节晚餐上，耶稣遣走加略人犹大后和 11 个门徒所使用的一个葡萄酒杯子。耶稣曾经拿起这个杯子吩咐门徒喝下里面象征他的血的红葡萄酒，借此创立了受难纪念仪式。后来有些人认为这个杯子因为这个特殊的场合而具有某种神奇的能力。相传彼世安温的魔法炉则是圣杯的前身，中世纪传说它被带到英国，然后就成为骑士们追求的目标，而只有思想、言辞和行为纯洁高尚的人才能获得。

2. The Pentium Ⅲ：Intel Pentium Ⅲ 处理器出产在 1999 年。一般常见的有 800 MHz、1.0 GHz、1.3 GHz 等主频的 CPU 型号，每种型号又分盒装和散装 2 种形式。奔腾Ⅲ处理器在 PⅣ 处理器出现后被迅速淘汰，仅偶见于少数老旧家用机。

3. Crusoe：Crusoe 是一个具有强大实力运用于笔记本计算机和 Internet 设备的处理器，由 Transmeta 公司于 2000 年发布。Transmeta 公司在研发过程中采用了一种革命性的微处理器设计方案，与主流的 x86 处理器完全使用硬件设计不同，Crusoe 处理器的解决方案采用软硬兼施办法，即硬件引擎核心和软件核心的合成结构。

Exercises

I. Comprehension of the Text

Read the text and answer the following questions. Write the answers on the lines.

1. What are the disadvantages of many of the smallest, lightest computers?

2. What is the chief advantage of these processors, including Intel's Mobile Pentium III-M and Transmeta Corp. 's Crusoe?

3. How often should Lithium battery be recharged?

4. What is the most promising technology to make an ultralight computer?

5. How can the scientist make a lighter computer?

II. Main Details Comprehension

Directions: *In this section, you are going to read a passage with ten statements attached to it. Each statement contains information given in one of the paragraphs. Identify the paragraph from which the information is derived. You may choose a paragraph more than once. Each paragraph is marked with a letter.*

Are we ready for the library of the future?

A) Librarians today will tell you their job is not so much to take care of books but to give people access to information in all forms. Since librarians, like so many people, believe that the entire universe of commerce, communication and information is moving to digital form, they are on a reform to give people access to the Internet — to prevent them from becoming second-class citizens in an all-digital world. Something funny happened on the road to the digital library of the future, though. Far from becoming keepers of the keys to the Grand Database of Universal Knowledge, today's librarians are increasingly finding themselves in an unexpected, overloaded role: They have become the general public's last-resort providers of tech support.

B) It wasn't supposed to be this way. Today's libraries offer a variety of media and social-cultural events — they are "blended libraries." to use a term created by Kathleen Imhoff, assistant director of the Broward County Library of Fort Lauderdale, Florida. At the newly remodeled San Francisco Public Library, the computers are prominently displayed in the center of the library building while the books are all but hidden on the periphery (外围). Imhoff's own library has word processing and other types of software for visitors to use, Internet access, audio CDs, videotapes, concerts, lectures, books and periodicals in three forms (print, microfiche and digital). Many libraries have found that this kind of "blending" is hugely popular in their communities, and librarians explain the changes in their institutions' roles by pointing to the public demand for these new services. But other trends are at work, too.

C) For some time, libraries have been automating their back-end, behind-the-desk functions for reasons of cost and convenience, just like any other business. Now, the computers have moved out from behind librarians' desks and onto the floor where the visitors are. This means that, suddenly, library-goers will have to know how to use those computers. This sounds reasonable enough until you take a close look. Unfortunately, the same technology that cuts costs and relieves librarians of work behind the scenes increases it for the public — and for the librarians at the front desk who have to help the public figure out how to use the technology. The unhappy result: People are simply not finding the information they seek.

D) If you are just coming to the library to read a book for pleasure and you know what a card catalog is and you have some basic computer skills, then you are going to be OK. But if you are trying to find some specific information — say, whether software in the classroom helps kids learn better or the causes of lung cancer or the basic procedure for doing a cost-benefit analysis of computer systems (three topics I have actually tried to look up in the San Francisco library) — then you're in trouble.

E) To begin with, library visitors must now be able to type, to use a mouse and a menu and to understand the various types of computer interfaces (terminal text, windows and browsers). It's also nice if you know 17 different ways to quit a program, which electronic databases you should look in for what kinds of information, the grammar necessary to define your search and the Library of Congress' controlled vocabulary. After I had been to the new San Francisco library three times, I started keeping a folder of instructions on how to do a keyword search (for an author, for example), since l would forget between visits.

F) Probably half the population has never used a computer, fewer know how to type and almost nobody knows anything about electronic databases or searching grammar. As a result, the public library is now engaged in a massive attempt to teach computer literacy to the entire country. Some librarians compare it to the adult literacy programs the library also sponsors, but this is on a far larger scale — and less closely tied to the library's traditional mission. The response at each library system has been different. Some libraries actually give courses in word processing, accounting program and so on. But even at libraries where the staff has resisted becoming computer trainers, they are still forced to devote significant resources to the problem.

G) Such has been the case in San Francisco, where people with disabilities can sign up to use the voice-recognition program Dragon Dictate — but only if they can prove they already know how to use the software. The librarians have neither the time nor the peculiar skill (nor the time to develop the skill) to teach it to them. At the reference desks, librarians try not to spend a lot of time teaching people the basics of how to use the computer, but sometimes it's unavoidable. "We try to get them started," says business librarian John Kenney. "We let them do as much as they call on their own and they come get us. It's certainly a big problem".

H) The San Francisco library offers classes on its own electronic catalog, commercial periodical indexes and the Internet twice a week as well as occasional lectures about the Internet. Although it seems odd to me that people now need to take a two-hour class before they can use the library, the classes are always full. But despite the excellent teachers, two hours is simply not enough to meet the needs of the students, many of whom have never used a computer before in their lives and many of whom simply can't type. When I took the class one Tuesday, the man sitting next to me said he has used the library's computer catalog many times, but he keeps making typing mistakes without knowing it. This unexpectedly throws him into the wrong screens and he doesn't know how to get back. On the floor, he repeatedly has to ask a librarian for help.

I) "Providing technology does not mean people can use the technology," says Marc Webb, a San Francisco librarian and one of the teachers. "Half the voters are still trying to read English." The library has also had to deal with the practical difficulties of making its catalog accessible via the Internet, a new service many libraries are starting to offer. "It's absolutely overwhelming," Webb says. "Everyone is getting to us with multiple transports, they're all using different software, they have Winsock or Telnet set up differently, and suddenly the library is forced to become a hardware and software help desk. When you're trying to tell someone over the telephone how to set up Winsock through AOL when this is the first time they've ever used a computer, it's very difficult".

_____1. Computers are more prominently displayed than books in San Francisco Public Library.

_____2. Libraries have been automating their back-end, behind-the-desk functions in consideration of cost and convenience.

_____3. Recently, many libraries are trying to provide the visitors with anew service: making their catalogs accessible via the Internet.

_____4. As 50% of the population may have never used a computer, the public library now has been engaged in computer literacy programs.

_____5. In today's libraries, the librarians are playing an unexpected roles a provider of tech support for the public.

_____6. Library visitors have to know how to type and use a mouse if they want to seek information in the modern library.

_____7. If you have some basic knowledge of card catalogue computer skills, you will be able to read a book for pleasure.

____8. The San Francisco library regularly provides classes on computers skills and the Internet.

____9. Blended libraries are hugely popular in communities at the present time.

____10. Dragon Dictate is the software which is used to help the disabled in library use.

III. Translation

Translate the five following sentences into English, using the words or expressions given in brackets.

1. 移动诊所将需要帮助的孩子们带去看医生。（portable）

_____

2. 你的耳坠也应镶有钻石。（be studded with）

_____

3. 为补偿原料成本的增加，价格被提高了。（offset）

_____

4. 不过也有一些例外，如充电式牙刷。（rechargeable）

_____

5. 我们期望来年会有更进一步的改善。（improvement）

_____

Product Manual
信息类产品说明书中条件句的使用

条件句在英文说明书中必不可少，是信息类产品使用说明书的另一个明显的特征。说明书不仅需要给出一般情况下的操作指南，也必须考虑用户可能出现的特殊情况，条件句恰好满足这一需求。条件句可以用来假设一些情况，主句则给出解决办法。例如，"If the appliance is damaged in any way, stop using it"，"If you have any medical concern, consult your doctors before you use this appliance"等。

句子时态以一般现在时为主，结构多为"If you＋动词"，对用户可能出现的特殊情况进行假设，并给出应对措施。

(1) If the internal battery is broken or worn out，you can replace it with a new one.
如果内置电池损坏或电量耗尽，您可以将其更换为新电池。

(2) If the battery contacts touch metal objects, the battery may short-circuit, discharge energy, become hot or leak.
若电池触点与金属接触，则电池可能短路、放电、变热或泄露。

(3) If you answer no to this message，you are prompted to terminate the AutoInstall.
如果对该提示输入了no，就要终止自动安装程序（AutoInstall）。

(4) If the needle points towards the minus(—)sign of the scale when the switch is turned on, the battery is being discharged.

点火开关转到通电位置时,指针指在"—"的一侧,表示蓄电池放电。

(5) Eventually it may be necessary to shut down the compressor, if there is inadequate cooling of the reactor effluent, if there is inadequate cooling of the auxiliaries due to loss of cooling water pumps, or if there is insufficient steam condensing capacity.

如果未充分冷却反应流出物,或因泵内冷却水流失导致辅助设备未获得充分冷却,又或蒸汽凝结量出现不足,则最终可能需要关闭压缩机。

(6) If the decoder is installed, it can support the following video formats: *.wmv; *.avi; *.mov; *.mpeg; *.mpg; *.dat; *.rm; *.rmvb; *.asf; *. mp4; *. flv; *.mkv; *.vob; *.swf; and following audio formats: *.mp3; *.wav; *.wma; *.mid.

如果安装解码器,它可以支持以下视频格式:*.wmv;*.avi;*.mov;*.mpeg;*.dat;*.rm *.rmvb;*. asf;*.mp4;*.flv;*.mkv;*.vob;*;音频格式同样支持:*.mp3;*.wav;*.wma;*.mid。

1. *Read the following paragraphs and then answer the questions.*

Flight Modes

DJI Air 2S has three flight modes, plus a fourth flight mode that the aircraft switches to in certain scenarios. Flight modes can be switched via the Flight Mode switch on the remote controller.

Normal Mode: The aircraft utilizes GNSS and the Forward, Backward, Upward and Downward Vision Systems and Infrared Sensing System to locate itself and stabilize. When the GNSS signal is strong, the aircraft uses GNSS to locate itself and stabilize. When the GNSS is weak but the lighting and other environment conditions are sufficient, the aircraft uses the vision systems to locate itself and stabilize. When the Forward, Backward, Upward and Downward Vision Systems are enabled and lighting and other environment conditions are sufficient, the maximum flight altitude angle is 35° and the maximum flight speed is 15 m/s.

Sport Mode: In Sport Mode, the aircraft uses GNSS for positioning and the aircraft responses are optimized for agility and speed making it more responsive to control stick movements. The maximum flight speed is 19 m/s. Obstacle sensing is disabled in Sport mode.

Cine Mode: Cine mode is based on Normal mode and the flight speed is limited, making the aircraft more stable during shooting.

The aircraft automatically changes to Attitude (ATTI) mode when the Vision Systems are unavailable or disabled and when the GNSS signal is weak or the compass experiences interference. In ATTI mode, the aircraft may be more easily affected by its surroundings. Environmental factors such as wind can result in horizontal shifting, which may present hazards, especially when flying in confined spaces.

⚠
- The Forward, Backward and Upward Vision Systems are disabled in Sport mode, which means the aircraft cannot sense obstacles on its route automatically.
- The maximum speed and braking distance of the aircraft significantly increase in Sport mode. A minimum braking distance of 30 m is required in windless conditions.
- A minimum braking distance of 10 m is required in windless conditions while the aircraft is ascending and descending.
- The responsiveness of the aircraft significantly increases in Sport mode, which means a small control stick movement on the remote controller translates into the aircraft moving a large distance. Make sure to maintain adequate maneuvering space during flight.

(1) How many flight modes do DJI Air 2S have?

___

(2) When the Forward, Backward, Upward and Downward Vision Systems are enabled

Unit 7　Technology and Future 　103

and lighting and other environment conditions are sufficient, what is the maximum flight altitude angle?

_____

(3) What is the advantage of Cine Mode?

_____

(4) When will the aircraft automatically change to Attitude(ATTI) mode?

_____

(5) In Sport mode, why can't the aircraft sense obstacles on its route automatically?

_____

2. *Map reading and translation.*

| | • If a USB connection prompt appears when using an Android mobile device, select the option to charge only. Otherwise, it may fail to connect. |

❶ _____

| …… | Alternating red, green, and yellow | Blinks | Turning on and performing self-diagnostic tests |

❷ _____

📖	GNSS	Description
Home Point	10	The default Home Point is the first location where the aircraft received a strong to moderately strong GNSS signal where the icon is white. The Home Point can be updated before takeoff as long as the aircraft receives a strong to moderately strong GNSS. If the GNSS signal is weak then the Home Point cannot be updated.

❸ _____

| | • If the RTH is triggered through DJI Fly and the aircraft is farther than 5 m from the Home Point, a prompt will appear in the app for users to select a landing option. |

❹ _____

> **Auto Landing**
> Use auto landing:
> 1. Tap . If conditions are safe to land, press and hold the button to confirm.
> 2. Auto landing can be cancelled by tapping ❌.
> 3. If the Vision System is working normally, Landing Protection will be enabled.
> 4. Motors stops after landing.

❺ _____

Workshop

Background

Looking forward to the future, there will be numerous potential breakthroughs and achievements in science and technology, solutions to current social and economic problems will be found. In the field of industry, agriculture and service industry, possible products and manufacturing methods might be realized, hi-tech industry could develop faster. The future generation will have the opportunities to create the kind of life, to have the kind of freedom, that all previous generations only dreamed of. It's hard to describe in detail the vision of a better life in the future. It's indeed like a riddle, some areas of which are beyond the reach of our imagination. Nevertheless, one thing is certain: the advancement of science and technology will characterize the future.

Task

1. Interview some classmates and your friends on their imagination of the future life.
2. Search more information online.

Process

Step 1. Complete the task in groups. Form small groups with 5－6 students respectively.

Step 2. Interview your friends and search information online.

Step 3. Have a discussion with your classmates on their imagination of the future life, and make a list.

Step 4. Make an oral presentation in class.

Unit 8   Technology and Communication

Facebook Wants to Emulate WeChat. Can it?

As Mark Zuckerberg begins shifting Facebook to private messaging and away from public sharing and open conversations, the vision he has sketched out for the future of social networking already exists — just not in the United States.

Instead, it is a reality in China through a messaging app called WeChat.

Developed by the Chinese internet giant Tencent in 2011, WeChat lets people message each other via one-on-one texts, audio or video calls. Users can also form groups of as many as 500 people on WeChat to discuss and debate the issues of the day.

While Facebook users constantly see ads in their News Feeds, WeChat users only see one or two ads a day in their Moment feeds. That's because WeChat isn't dependent on advertising for making money. It has a mobile payments system that has been widely adopted in China, which allows people to shop, play games, pay utility bills and order meal deliveries all from within the app. WeChat gets a commission from many of these services.

What is happening in China offers clues to not only how Facebook may carry out its shift, but how the internet more broadly might change. Many of Silicon Valley's tech giants are dependent today on online advertising to make enough money to keep growing and innovating on new services. Some call online ads the lifeblood of the internet.

But WeChat, which has 1.1 billion monthly active users, shows that other models — particularly those based on payments and commerce — can support massive digital businesses. That has implications for Google, Twitter and many others, as well as Facebook.

Mr. Zuckerberg didn't elaborate much this week on how the change toward private messaging would affect Facebook's business, which relies on people publicly sharing posts to be able to serve them targeted advertisements. In a blog post, he said Facebook would build more ways for people to interact on top of messaging, "including calls, video chats, groups, stories, businesses, payments, commerce, and ultimately a platform for many other kinds of private services".

Yet it's unclear whether Mr. Zuckerberg can pull all those features off with Facebook. On WeChat, those services are underpinned by its mobile payments system, WeChat Pay. Because payments are already tied into the messaging service, people can easily order meal deliveries, book hotels, hail ride-sharing cars and pay their bills. WeChat Pay itself has 900 million monthly active users.

People also use WeChat Pay to transfer money and to buy personal finance products. More than 100 million customers have purchased WeChat's personal finance products, which managed over 500 billion yuan, or $74 billion, by the end of last September, Tencent has said. Its users can buy everything from bonds and insurance to money market funds through the app.

Facebook lacks such a payments system. So to be more like WeChat, the Silicon Valley company could have to acquire banking and payment licenses in many countries. One sign that Facebook has been thinking about payments is its work on a new crypto coin that is meant to let people send money to contacts on their messaging systems.

To make Facebook a private messaging product, Mr. Zuckerberg may have a lot else to learn from Allen Zhang, the creator of WeChat. Mr. Zhang is famous for his perfectionist pursuit of a well-designed service.

Mr. Zhang fought many internal battles when Tencent's revenue department pushed to put more ads on WeChat. In a four-hour speech earlier this year, he pondered the question of why there were not more ads on the messaging service, especially the opening-page ads that are the norm in many other Chinese mobile apps.

Mr. Zhang's answer: Many Chinese spent a lot of time — about one third of their online time — on WeChat, he said. "If WeChat were a person, it would have to be your best friend so that you would be willing to spend so much time with it," he said. "How could I post an ad on the face of your best friend? Every time you see it, you'll have to watch an ad before you can talk to it".

"Zuck is clearly trying to address Facebook's problems of privacy and fake news, but it will greatly affect its monetization capability," said Ivy Li, a venture capitalist at Seven Seas Partners in Menlo Park, Calif. "How comprehensive the surgery is going to be and whether the implementation will be twisted by all kinds of compromises is a big question".

She added: "Facebook is trying to seek a balance between a public square and a private space in an increasingly polarizing society. The final result could be it will be abandoned by both".

Words & Expressions

emulate/'emjuleɪt/v. 努力赶上，同…竞争

sketch out 概述；简述

giant/'dʒaɪənt/n. 巨人；大公司，强大的组织；伟人，卓越人物；adj. 巨大的；特大的；伟大的

utility/juː'tɪləti/n. 公用事业；实用，效用；［计算机］实用程序；adj.［只用于名词前］多用途的，多效用的，多功能的

commission/kə'mɪʃn/n. 委员会；佣金，回扣；手续费；做出（错事），犯下（罪行）

clue/kluː/n. 线索，迹象；提示；v. 给（某人）提供最新信息

Unit 8　Technology and Communication

carry out　实行
lifeblood/'laɪfblʌd/ n. （事物的）命脉，生命线；（人的）命脉，生命必需的血液
implication/ˌɪmplɪ'keɪʃn/ n. 可能的影响（或作用、结果）；含意，暗示；（被）牵连，牵涉
elaborate/ɪ'læbərət/ v. 详尽阐述；精心制作；adj. 复杂的；详尽的；精心制作的
pull off　做成（某件难事）；停靠路边
underpin/ˌʌndə'pɪn/ v. 加强，巩固，构成…的基础等；加固（墙）基
hail/heɪl/ v. ［常用被动］赞扬（或称颂）…为…；招手（请车停下）；跟…打招呼，向…喊；下雹；n. 冰雹；一阵像冰雹般袭来的事物
bond/bɒnd/ n. 纽带，联系，契合；债券，公债；[律] 保释金；v. 使牢固结合，把…仅仅连接到；增强（与某人的）信任关系
crypto/'krɪptəʊ/ n. 加密货币；加密
revenue/'revənjuː/ n. 财政收入，税收收入；受益
ponder/'pɒndə(r)/ v. 沉思，考虑，琢磨
norm/nɔːm/ n. 常态，正常行为；规范，行为标准；定额，定量
monetization/ˌmʌnɪtaɪ'zeɪʃn/ n. 货币化
venture/'ventʃə(r)/ n. （尤指有风险的）企业，投机活动，经营项目；v. 敢于去（危险或令人不快的地方）；小心地说，谨慎地做；冒着（失去贵重或重要的东西）的危险
comprehensive/ˌkɒmprɪ'hensɪv/ adj. 全部的，所有的，（几乎）无所不包的，详尽的
implementation/ˌɪmplɪmen'teɪʃ(ə)n/ n. 实施，执行
compromise/'kɒmprəmaɪz/ n. 妥协，折中，互让，和解；v. （为达成协议而）妥协，折中，让步；违背（原则），达不到（标准）
polarize/'pəʊləraɪz/ v. （使）两极化，截然对立；使（物体）极化

Notes

1. Facebook & Mark Zuckerberg：Facebook 是源于美国的社交网络服务及社会化媒体网站，总部位于美国加州圣马特奥县门洛帕克市。成立初期名为"the Facebook"，名称的灵感来自美国高中提供给学生通讯录的昵称"face book"。Facebook 用户除了文字消息之外，还可发送图片、视频、文档、贴图和声音媒体消息给其他用户，以及透过集成的地图功能分享用户的所在位置。Facebook 的会员最初仅限哈佛学生加入，但后来逐渐扩展，其他在波士顿区域的同学也能使用，包括一些常春藤名校、麻省理工学院、纽约大学、斯坦福大学等，接着逐渐支持让其他大学和高中学生加入，并在最后开放给任何 13 岁或以上的人使用。现在 Facebook 允许任何声明自己年满 13 岁的用户注册。Mark Zuckerberg（马克·扎克伯格）出生于美国纽约州白原市，Facebook 创始人、Meta 董事长兼首席执行官，同时也是一名软件设计师，被誉为 Facebook 教主。Facebook 是由他和哈佛大学的同学们于 2004 年共同创立。

2. Silicon Valley：硅谷。硅谷是高科技事业云集的美国加利福尼亚州圣克拉拉谷的别称，位于加州北部、旧金山湾区南部。硅谷这个词最早是由加利福尼亚企业家瓦尔斯特创造的，但却是由其朋友唐·霍弗勒在一系列关于电子新闻的标题中第一次使用的。

1971 年的 1 月 11 日开始被用于《每周商业》报纸电子新闻的一系列文章的题目——美国硅谷。之所以名字当中有一个"硅"字，是因为当地企业多数是从事加工制造高精度硅的半导体行业和计算机工业。而"谷"则是从圣克拉拉谷中得到的。

3. **Allen Zhang**：张小龙，1969 年生于湖南省邵阳市洞口县，Foxmail 创始人，微信创始人，腾讯公司高级副总裁。张小龙毕业于华中科技大学电信系，分别获得学士、硕士学位。曾开发国产电子邮件客户端——Foxmail，加盟腾讯公司后开发微信，被誉为"微信之父"，被《华尔街日报》评为"2012 中国创新人物"。2022 年，张小龙以 130 亿财富位列《2022 衡昌烧坊·胡润百富榜》第 473 位。

4. **Seven Seas Partners**：七海资本由腾讯前 CTO 熊明华于 2014 年 9 月创立，其总部位于美国硅谷，在中国上海有分部。"七海"是古阿拉伯书籍中记载的从西方到中国的贸易路线的 7 个水体，在英语中是"全世界"的意思。七海资本致力通过对中美两国创业企业的投资，搭建连接大洋两岸创业者与市场之间的桥梁。七海资本专注于互联网、物联网及高科技领域的初创及成长期企业的投资。

Exercises

I. Getting the Message

Read the questions and complete the answers according to the text.

1. Why isn't WeChat dependent on advertising for making money?
   _____
2. What are the possible functions of Facebook on top of messaging in the future?
   _____
3. What can people do with WeChat's mobile payments system?
   _____
4. How does Facebook deal with the problem that it lacks a payments system?
   _____
5. According to Ivy, what might be the result of Facebook's attempt?
   _____

II. Languages Focus

A. *Match the following words in left with their explanations in right.*

1. giant   a. to support or form the basis of an argument, a claim, etc.
2. utility   b. an amount of money that is paid to sb. for selling goods and which increases with the amount of goods that are sold
3. commission   c. an agreement made between two people or groups in which each side gives up some of the things they want so that both sides are happy at the end

4. implication	d. a very large and powerful organization
5. elaborate	e. including all, or almost all, the items, details, facts, information, etc., that may be concerned
6. underpin	f. a possible effect or result of an action or a decision
7. ponder	g. a service provided for the public, for example an electricity, water or gas supply
8. comprehensive	h. to separate or make people separate into two groups with completely opposite opinions
9. compromise	i. to explain or describe sth. in a more detailed way
10. polarize	j. to think about sth. carefully for a period of time

B. *Fill in the blanks with the words or expressions given below. Change the form where necessary.*

norm	underpin	compromise	ponder	commission
comprehensive	clue	polarize	elaborate	implication

1. She concocted some _____ story to explain her absence.
2. The two sides eventually reached an uneasy _____.
3. Am I alone in recognizing that these two statistics have quite different _____?
4. I found myself constantly _____ the question: "How could anyone do these things?"
5. Public opinion has _____ on this issue.
6. You get a 10% _____ on everything you sell.
7. Deviation from the _____ is not tolerated.
8. The report is _____ by extensive research.
9. The police think the videotape may hold some vital _____ to the identity of the killer.
10. They were _____ beaten in the final.

III. Translation

Translate the following sentences into Chinese.

1. Some call online ads the lifeblood of the internet.

2. He didn't elaborate much on how the change toward private messaging would affect Facebook's business.

3. Yet it's unclear whether he can pull all those features off with Facebook.

4. He pondered the question of why there were not more ads on the messaging service.

5. Facebook is trying to seek a balance between a public square and a private space in an increasingly polarizing society.

Ⅳ. Discussion

Directions: *The founder and CEO of Facebook, Mark Zuckerberg, once infamously said that privacy is no longer a "social norm" — and he stays true to his word. From its ever-changing privacy settings to collecting personal data via third-party apps, Facebook seems to constantly be lurking in the background, with many people unaware of the various ways it invades our privacy on a daily basis. For example, on Facebook, people can follow you without your knowledge.*

Work in pairs and discuss the following questions:
1. How can social network invade your privacy?
2. What can you do to prevent it from doing so?
3. Do the advantages of having social network outweigh its disadvantage?

Challenges for a Webbed Society

There are subtle, complex changes taking place in human communication, thought, and relationships within online communication and information communities. The Web is part of these changes, enabling new forms of communication and information delivery, and bringing up new associations among people. One challenge for our society is to find a solution to the questions raised by these changes. How might our culture, society, and communication patterns change as a result of widespread Web use?

Vannevar Bush, in an article called "As We Think" in the July, 1945 issue of *The Atlantic Monthly*, described his vision of a device for helping the human mind cope with information. Bush observed that previous inventions expanded human abilities to deal with the physical world, but not floods of information and knowledge. Bush's vision was for a system of information, which could link documents in "trials" that could be saved and shared with others.

The Web fulfills Bush's dream in many respects. It can link information in useful ways, giving rise to new insights — transformation of information to knowledge that Bush described in terms of applications in law, medicine, chemistry, and history.

In addition to fulfilling many needs of human intellectual activities identified by Bush, it can also fill the "media gap" which is defined by Tetsuro Tomita. In his essay, "The New Electronic Media and Their Place in the Information Market of the Future," Tomita observed a pattern in the way traditional communications methods were used to reach audience. Methods such as letters, telegrams, and conversation reach a very small audience in amounts of time ranging from immediate (telegram, telephone) to days (letters). The mass media such as radio, television, newspapers, books, and movies reach a large audience in amounts of time ranging from immediate (radio, television) to weeks (magazines) to months (books). But the middle range — audiences of 10 to 10,000 people reached within times ranging from immediate to a day — is a gap filled by few traditional media. This is too small an audience for mass media and too large an audience for personally controlled (traditional) media. Yet this is the audience and time delay gap that many forms of computer-mediated communication fill, including the Web.

The Web offers immediate delivery of information to specialized audiences. Before the invention of computer networks, an individual could not easily seek out several hundred others interested in a specialized hobby or area of interest, when those people were spread worldwide. No traditional media offered a personally available means to accomplish this. But the Web does fill this "media gap", and this feature is certainly a contributor to the Web's popularity and growth.

Associative linking promotes relationships among people in addition to relationships among information. Experts in a particular field create pools of knowledge on their home page, when other people link to these pages, groups of expert's form. These groups might be based on information or on hobbies, interests, culture, or political leanings. The result is that "electronic tribe" can form that gather people in associations that could not be possible any other way.

As the Web alters communication and information patterns, the resulting change raises issues our society must face for individual, group, and societal responsibility. Moral and legal issues will arise in the areas of individual behavior, societal responsibility for issues of access and information literacy, and the new relationships, communications, and thought patterns the Web promotes.

Words & Expressions

subtle/ˈsʌtl/*adj.* 不易察觉的，微妙的；机智的，狡猾的；巧妙的；敏锐的，头脑灵活的

bring up 提出；养育

issue/ˈɪʃuː/*n.* 重要议题；（有关某事的）问题，担忧；一期，期号；发行，分发；*v.* 宣布，公布；［常用被动］发给，供给；出版，发表

device/dɪˈvaɪs/*n.* 装置，仪器，器具；炸弹，爆炸装置；手段，策略，技巧；花招，诡计

trial/ˈtraɪəl/*n.* （法院的）审判，审理；（对能力、质量、性能等）试验，试用；预赛；考验

fulfill/fʊl'fɪl/v. 实现；履行，执行，符合；起…作用；使高兴，使满意
give rise to 引起
in terms of 在…方面；依据，按照
telegram/'telɪɡræm/n. 电报
mass media 大众传媒
mediate/'miːdieɪt/v. 调停，调节，斡旋；促成（协议）；影响…的发生，使…可能发生
associative/ə'səʊʃiətɪv/adj. 联想的；[数] 结合的
tribe/traɪb/n. 部落；一伙（人），一帮（人）；（动物或植物的）群，族；大群，大批（人）
literacy/'lɪtərəsi/n. 读写能力

Notes

1. Vannevar Bush：美国工程师，发明家和科学行政人员，在第二次世界大战期间担任美国科学研究与开发办公室的负责人，几乎所有的战时军事研发都是通过该办公室进行的，包括雷达的重要发展以及曼哈顿计划的启动和早期管理。他强调了科学研究对国家安全和经济福祉的重要性，并敦促建立国家科学基金会。

2. *The Atlantic Monthly*：《大西洋月刊》，创刊于1857年的美国马萨诸塞州波士顿，是一本文学和文化评论杂志，发表关于废除当代政治事务中的奴隶制、教育及其他重大问题的著名作家评论。首期大西洋杂志出版于1857年11月1日，它因出版著名作家的文学作品而闻名，现更名为《大西洋》（*The Atlantic*）。

Exercises

I. Comprehension of the Text

Read the text and answer the following questions. Write the answers on the lines.

1. How does Web change people's communication, thought and relationships?
_____
2. What does Bush's vision really mean?
_____
3. What does the media gap mean?
_____
4. How can we form an expert group on the Internet?
_____
5. What is the purpose of this article?
_____

II. Main Details Comprehension

Directions: *In this section, you are going to read a passage with ten statements attached to it. Each statement contains information given in one of the paragraphs. Identify the paragraph from which the information is derived. You may choose a paragraph more than once. Each paragraph is marked with a letter.*

How to Fix the Internet

A) We have to fix the internet. After 40 years, it has begun to corrode, both itself and us. It is still a marvelous and miraculous invention, but now there are bugs in the foundation, bats in the belfry, and trolls in the basement.

B) I do not mean this to be one of those technophobic rants insulting the internet for rewiring our brains to give us the nervous attention span of Donald Trump on Twitter or pontificating about how we have to log off and smell the flowers. Those worries about new technologies have existed ever since Plato was concerned that the technology of writing would threaten memorization and oratory (演讲术). I love the internet and all of its digital offshoots. What I feel sad for is its decline.

C) There is a bug in its original design that at first seemed like a feature but has gradually, and now rapidly, been exploited by hackers and trolls and malevolent actors: Its packets are encoded with the address of their destination but not of their authentic origin. With a circuit-switched network, you can track or trace back the origins of the information, but that's not true with the packet-switched design of the internet.

D) Compounding this was the architecture that Tim Berners-Lee and the inventors of the early browsers created for the World Wide Web. It brilliantly allowed the whole of the earth's computers to be webbed together and navigated through hyperlinks. But the links were one-way. You knew where the links took you. But if you had a webpage or piece of content, you didn't exactly know who was linking to you or coming to use your content.

E) All of that protected the potential for anonymity. You could make comments anonymously. Go to a webpage anonymously. Consume content anonymously. With a little effort, send email anonymously. And if you figured out a way to get into someone's servers or databases, you could do it anonymously.

F) For years, the benefits of anonymity on the net outweighed its drawbacks. People felt more free to express themselves, which was especially valuable if they were holding different opinions or hiding a personal secret. This was celebrated in the famous 1993 *New Yorker* cartoon, "On the Internet, nobody knows you're a dog".

G) Now the problem is nobody can tell if you're a troll. Or a hacker. Or a bot .Or a Macedonian (马其顿的) teenager publishing a story that the Pope has supported Trump. This has poisoned civil discourse, enabled hacking, permitted cyberbullying, and made email a risk.

H) The lack of secure identification and authentication (身份认证) inherent in the internet's genetic code had also prevented easy transactions, obstructed financial inclusion, destroyed the business models of content creators, unleashed the overflow of spam (垃圾邮件), and forced us to use passwords and two-factor authentication schemes that would have confused Houdini. The trillions being spent and the IQ points of computer science talent being allocated to tackle security issues make it a drag, rather than a spur, to productivity in some sectors.

I) It Plato's *Republic*, we learn the tale of the Ring of Gyges. Put it on, and you're invisible and anonymous. The question that Plato asks is whether those who put on the ring will be civil and moral. He thinks not. The internet has proven him correct. The web is no longer a place of community, no longer a marketplace. Every day more sites are eliminating comments sections.

J) If we could start from scratch, here's what I think we would do: Create a system that enables content producers to negotiate with aggregators (整合者) and search engines to get a royalty whenever their content is used, like ASCAP has negotiated for public performances and radio airings of its members' works. Embed (嵌入) a simple digital wallet and currency for quick and easy small payments for songs, blogs, articles, and whatever other digital content is for sale. Encode emails with an authenticated return or originating address. Enforce critical properties and security at the lowest levels of the system possible, such as in the hardware or in the programming language, instead of leaving it to programmers to incorporate security into every line of code they write. Build chips and machines that update the notion of an internet packet. For those who want, their packets could been coded or tagged with metadata (元数据) that describe what they contain and give the rules for how it can be used.

K) Most internet engineers think that these reforms are possible, from Vint Cerf, the original TCP/IP coauthor, to Milo Medin of Google, to Howard Shrobe, the director of cybersecurity at MIT. "We don't need to live in cyber hell," Shrobe has argued. Implementing them is less a matter of technology than of cost and social will. Some people, understandably, will resist any reduction of anonymity, which they sometimes label privacy.

L) So the best approach, I think, would be to try to create a voluntary system, for those who want to use it, to have verified identification and authentication. People would not be forced to use such a system. If they wanted to communicate and surf anonymously, they could. But those of us who choose, at times, not to be anonymous and not to deal with people who are anonymous should have that right as well. That's the way it works in the real world.

M) The benefits would be many. Easy and secure ways to deal with your finances and medical records. Small payment systems that could reward valued content rather than the current incentive to concentrate on clickbait for advertising. Less hacking, spamming, cyberbullying, trolling, and spewing of anonymous hate. And the possibility of a more civil discourse.

_____ 1. The one-way hyperlinks enable users to do many things online anonymously.

_____ 2. Although anonymity can make people conceal their identity online, now it has poisoned their online life.

_____ 3. To adopt the voluntary system would be advantageous to our online life in a number of aspects.

_____ 4. There are several ways to reduce anonymity if we can rebuild the internet from the very beginning.

_____ 5. The author suggested inventing a system to let people go online anonymously or not as they wish.

_____ 6. The author thinks the internet should be fixed not because he is afraid of new technologies but because problems arise in it.

_____ 7. Public opposition could become one of the biggest obstacles to carrying out the reforms.

_____ 8. The hazard of anonymity mentioned by Plato has been shown on the internet.

_____ 9. People used to think that anonymity online did more good than harm.

_____ 10. It is the design of the internet that makes it impossible to find out where the information comes from.

III. Translation

Translate the five following sentences into English, using the words or expressions given in brackets.

1. 幼儿园应该起到为儿童进小学做准备的作用。(fulfill)
_____

2. 他提出了一个在以往交谈中很少被提及的话题。(bring up)
_____

3. 由一个独立机构介入,在劳资之间进行调解。(mediate)
_____

4. 大雨引起了大面积的洪水。(give rise to)
_____

5. 这些度假胜地在价格上仍是无可匹敌的。(in terms of)
_____

Product Manual
信息类产品说明书时态特点

在时态方面,英文说明书的句子结构通常比较严谨,条理清晰,逻辑性强,不会有含糊不清的情况。所以,在信息类产品的说明书中,一般现在时和将来时的使用都非常频繁。

（一）一般现在时

信息类产品英文说明书中常用一般现在时表述客观事实。一般现在时一般描述的是客观事实，表示客观的存在，如客观真理、自然现象等事实，可以体现出产品说明书内容的客观性、形式的简单化，从而使用者能够读懂使用方法。例如：

(1) The Kilburn is equipped with an internal battery supporting a playing time for up to 20 hours at mid volume.

Kilburn 配有内置电池，中等音量播放可持续长达 20 小时。

(2) If the battery LED starts to flash when the loudspeaker is on battery power, the battery has less than 20% charge left.

当音箱使用电池供电时，如果电池 LED 灯开始闪烁，则表明电池所剩电量不足 20%。

(3) Apple takes the security of your personal information very seriously.

苹果手机始终非常重视用户的个人信息的安全。

一般现在时是产品说明文中最常用的时态之一，是一种表示通常性、规律性、真理性的动作或状态。这个句子要向用户传达的是苹果公司对用户信息安全的重视态度，这是从始至终一贯的行为，不是暂时个别的现象，因此在翻译这个句子时应该注意该信息的传达，如果用别的动词时态就没有现在时态的这种表达效果，也不符合英文产品说明书的惯例。

（二）将来时

在英文说明书中，若要陈述对未来指令或后果的预测时，通常采用一般将来时。

(1) Once your phone is connected to the laptop, the phone screen will automatically pop up on the laptop.

一旦您的手机连接到笔记本计算机，手机屏幕将自动在笔记本计算机上弹出。

(2) This will cause the compressor efficiency to decrease and may result in the need for a feed rate reduction to the unit to match the available recycle gas.

这将导致压缩机效率下降，因而可能需要根据装置内可用循环气的含量，相应地降低装置的进料率。

(3) During the instrument air failure emergency, the spillback control valve(s) on the hydrogen make-up compressor(s) will fail safe to the open position. This action will prevent make-up hydrogen from flowing to the reactor section. Shutdown, isolate and purge the compressors.

在仪表空气系统突发故障时，新氢压缩机上的回流控制阀将应急开启以防新氢进入反应器，接着，操作员需关闭新氢压缩机，将其隔离并进行清洁。

(4) Fresh feed will be lost if the reactor charge pump shuts down or the supply of feed is stopped. Two things will happen that can cause difficulty in controlling the hydrocracking reactions.

如果反应器加料泵停机或原料停止供应，则新鲜原料的含量将减少，由此将引发两个导致加氢裂化反应难以控制的问题。

(5) There is no material but will deform more or less under the action of forces.

没有哪一种材料在力的作用下不或多或少地变形的。

通过上述例句可以看出，在条件句中，从句时态以一般现在时为主，对用户可能出现的特殊情况进行假设，但主句常用将来时给出应对措施。

(6) After it is released, the stretched rubber band will return to its original state.

松开后，被拉伸的橡皮筋会恢复到原来的状态。

(7) If the current is sufficiently strong, the coil will noticeably attract iron objects.

如果电流足够强，线圈将吸引铁质地物体。

(8) Under this condition, there will be a current flow in the circuit.

在这种情况下，电路中会有电流流动。

(9) Iron or steel parts will rust, if they are unprotected.

铁件或钢件是会生锈的，如果不加以保护的话。

1. *Read the following paragraphs and then answer the questions.*

Kindle User's Guide

3.1 Types of Content

There are many types of reading material available for your Kindle, such as books, audiobooks, newspapers, magazines, and blogs. If you want to begin purchasing and downloading reading material, you can learn more in Chapter 5. You can even have Amazon convert and deliver personal documents to your Kindle. The different types of supported content are described below.

Books

Thousands of books in different categories—both popular and hard-to-find—are available in the Kindle Store. Once you buy a book, it usually arrives wirelessly in under a minute. Because you can't always judge a book by its cover, you can download and read a sample of most Kindle books for free. If you like it, simply buy it from within the sample and continue reading. You can learn more about this feature in Chapter 5.

Newspapers

The Kindle Store offers a selection of U.S. and international newspapers. Subscriptions are delivered wirelessly to your Kindle so that the latest edition arrives as soon as it is available, and every newspaper subscription starts with a free trial.

Magazines

The Kindle Store offers an expanding selection of magazines to meet every interest. As with newspapers, all magazine subscriptions are delivered wirelessly and start with a free trial.

Blogs

The Kindle Store offers thousands of Kindle blogs, including up-to-the-minute news feeds and topical blogs. Blog categories include business, technology, sports, politics, culture, entertainment, humor, and science. Kindle blogs are sent to you wirelessly throughout the day, allowing you to keep current. Unlike traditional feeds, which often only provide headlines, Kindle downloads the complete feed onto the device so you can read them even when you are not wirelessly connected.

Personal Documents

In addition to purchased content, you can read your personal documents on Kindle.

> Kindle can display a PDF document without losing the formatting of the original file. You can either drag PDF files over USB to your device or e-mail them to your dedicated Kindle e-mail address (found on the Settings page on Kindle or the Manage Your Kindle page on Amazon). You can rotate your device sideways for widescreen viewing. For more information on the unique aspects of reading PDF files on Kindle, see "Reading PDF Files."
>
> If you have PDF files, or files formatted as text, Microsoft Word, HTML, or image files like GIF or JPEG, you can e-mail the files as attachments to your Kindle e-mail address. Amazon will convert the files if necessary and send them back to your computer for free or via Whispernet to your Kindle (fees may apply). For more information on transferring, converting, and e-mailing your personal documents, see Chapter 8.

(1) What types of reading materials are available for Kindle?

_____

(2) How quickly does a purchased book typically arrive on your Kindle?

_____

(3) How can you preview a Kindle book before purchasing it?

_____

(4) What options do you have for transferring personal documents to your Kindle?

_____

(5) If you have files formatted as text, Microsoft Word, HTML, or image files, how can you send them to your Kindle? What conversion options are available?

_____

2. *Map reading and translation.*

> **Enter URL** — takes you directly to the URL field where you can enter a web address to visit.

❶ _____

> **History** — displays your History page, which keeps track of the sites you have visited.

❷ _____

> **Browser Settings** — displays your list of settings where you can change the options for Web Browser.

❸ _____

> **Tip:** Your Kindle will also go to sleep by itself after ten minutes if you are not using it. If your Kindle had wireless on prior to going to sleep, it will continue to receive your regularly scheduled subscriptions while in sleep.

❹ _____

> The Whispernet service is active and your Kindle has a strong signal. The more bars that are filled in with black, the stronger the wireless signal. Note that a weak signal can increase power consumption.

❺ _____

Workshop

Background

Social media experience a rapid rise in recent years and steep into almost every aspect of people's lives by altering their lifestyles and creating an impact on their wellbeing, which is also not rare to see in university students' daily life. According to researches, the need for maintaining interpersonal interconnectivity, entertainment value and social enhancement value derives the students' participation in social networking sites.

Indeed, social media has made it possible for students to connect more than ever, especially in these trying times when they are geographically separated from their friends, family, and classmates. However, social media may have a harmful effect on students' physical and mental health, even if it offers numerous advantages, like the opportunity for creative expression, learning possibilities, and the possibility to interact with others. It is simple to develop an addiction, and studies have shown that students who use social media excessively may have a variety of problems, including poor sleep, eye fatigue, negative body image, depression, anxiety, cyberbullying, and more.

Task

Interview your classmates, friends or other acquaintances about:
1. What kinds of social network applications/websites do they use every day?
2. How much time do they spend in social network applications/websites every day?
3. What are the pros and cons of spending time in social network applications/websites?

Process

Step 1. The whole class is divided into several groups, with each group containing 3—4 students.

Step 2. Group members collect information based on interview questions.

Step 3. Each group analyzes the data (Interview Question 1—2) and write a report about how to take advantage of social network (Interview Question 3).

Step 4. Each group delivers a presentation based on the interview and report.

Unit 9　Space Technology

The US Rover Perseverance Has Successfully Landed on Mars

NASA's Perseverance rover has successfully touched down on the surface of Mars after surviving a blazing seven-minute plunge through the Martian atmosphere. The rover's clean landing sets the stage for a years-long journey to scour the Red Planet's Jezero Crater for ancient signs of life.

"Touchdown confirmed," Swati Mohan, a member of NASA's Entry, Descent, and Landing team, said. "Perseverance is safely on the surface of Mars ready to begin seeking the signs of past life." The landing team of roughly 30 engineers at NASA's Jet Propulsion Laboratory in California jumped from their seats and cheered at the confirmation. Moments after touching down, Perseverance beamed back its first image from one of its 19 cameras.

Perseverance hit Mars' atmosphere on time at 3:48 PM ET at speeds of about 12,100 miles per hour, diving toward the surface in an infamously challenging sequence engineers call the "seven minutes of terror." With an 11-minute comms delay between Mars and Earth, the spacecraft had to carry out its seven-minute plunge at all by itself with a wickedly complex set of pre-programmed instructions.

Enduring blazing heat, the rover was shielded by a protective shell and parachute to help slow itself down. A descent stage with six rocket thrusters fired as it neared the surface, slowing Perseverance to a much calmer 2 mph. Clutching the rover, the descent stage hovered 66 feet above the surface to execute a "skycrane" maneuver, where it gently lowered Perseverance on a set of cables the rest of the way to the surface.

With its six wheels planted on the surface, the rover snipped the skycrane cables, prompting the rocket-powered descent stage to move itself far away from Perseverance.

The on-time landing at 3:55 PM ET marks NASA's sixth successful landing on the Red Planet. The $2.7 billion rover is essentially a 2,263-pound laboratory on wheels: for the next several years, Perseverance will traverse Mars' Jezero Crater to collect soil samples for a future retrieval mission, analyze the makeup of Martian rocks with a laser-beaming camera system, and deploy a helicopter named Ingenuity, a four-foot-on wide rotorcraft that will demonstrate the first powered flight on another planet.

Spirits were high during a post-landing press conference. Thomas Zurbuchen, NASA's top science official, was elated and began his remarks on Perseverance's landing victory by holding up a printout of the mission's contingency plan — a blueprint for the team in case the mission goes awry — and ripping it in half. "Here's for the contingency plan!" he said before tearing the paper apart and tossing it behind him, sparking applause in the JPL auditorium.

"Now the fun really starts," said Lori Glaze, director of NASA's Planetary Science Division. The science team is already analyzing the several low-res images the rover already beamed back to Earth, she said. More images will stream in throughout the week, with the first drop of audio coming as soon as Thursday night and the first high-definition video of Perseverance's landing expected on Monday.

The SUV-sized rover has traveled 293 million miles since launching last summer atop an Atlas V rocket from United Launch Alliance. It launched during a slim window of time as Earth and Mars closely aligned in their orbits around the Sun. That alignment only comes once every two years, and NASA launched its rover around the same time as China and UAE, whose Martian spacecraft also reached the planet earlier this month. China's Tianwen-1 probe, which arrived in Martian orbit on February 10th, will deploy a lander and rover in the coming months, joining Perseverance just over a thousand miles away on Mars' surface.

Perseverance's journey through space was even more uneventful than expected. Toward the end of its seven-month journey, Perseverance's cruise stage carried out fewer orbital correction maneuvers than originally planned, in part due to an ultra-precise insertion on its Mars trajectory when it launched. "When we hit the bullseye, that means they had a ton more propellant" that NASA didn't have to use on its journey to Mars, ULA CEO Tory Bruno told *The Verge*. Unlike Tianwen-1, which is hanging out in orbit before heading to the surface, Perseverance booked it straight for the surface upon reaching Mars.

The Jezero Crater posed the most challenging landing site NASA has faced. Perseverance had to steer clear of the crater's steep cliffs, massive boulders, and dangerously sandy pits to reach its landing spot. Scientists believe the 28-mile-wide hole was a river delta some 3.5 billion years ago — potentially a goldmine for fossilized microorganisms. Its mix of different rock formations offers researchers a smorgasb.ord of potential samples to collect during its mission.

Zurbuchen said Perseverance engineers are already moving forward with the next leg of NASA's Mars ambitions: the sample return mission, a joint effort with the European Space Agency to send a fleet of spacecraft to Mars and retrieve the soil samples Perseverance will scatter around the Jezero crater. That mission is slated to launch sometime in 2026.

"Many concrete steps are also happening towards another horizon goal, which is human exploration of Mars as well," Zurbuchen said, floating distant plans to send astronauts to the Red Planet sometime in the 2030s.

rover/'rəʊvə(r)/*n.* 漫游者，流浪者

perseverance/ˌpɜːsɪ'vɪərəns/n. 毅力，韧性，不屈不挠的精神

touch down 着陆

blazing/'bleɪzɪŋ/adj. 酷热的，炽热的；极其愤怒的；感情强烈的

plunge/plʌndʒ/n. 突然跌落，突然分离；（价格、数量的）骤减，暴跌，卷入，参与；跳水，快速有用；v. 使突然前冲/下落；暴跌，骤降；陡峭地向下倾斜；（剧烈）颠簸，震荡

Martian/'mɑːʃn/adj. 火星的，来自火星的

scour/'skaʊə(r)/v.（彻底）搜寻，翻找；（用粗糙的物体）擦净，擦亮；冲刷成；冲刷出

Red Planet 红色星球，指火星

crater/'kreɪtə(r)/n. 火山口；（由炸弹爆炸或巨物撞击形成的）坑

descent/dɪ'sent/n. 下降，下倾；斜坡，坡道；血统，祖籍，祖先

propulsion/prə'pʌlʃn/n. 推动力，推进

beam/biːm/v. 笑容满面，眉开眼笑；发射（电波），播送；照射；n. 光线，波束，（粒子的）束；（建筑物的）梁；笑容

comms/kɒmz/n. communications 的缩写

wickedly/'wɪkɪdli/adv. 邪恶地

thruster/'θrʌstə(r)/n. 助力器，（尤指航天器的）推进器

mph miles per hour 的缩写，意为每小时所行英里数；英里每小时

clutch/klʌtʃ/v. 握紧，抱紧；（因害怕或痛苦）突然抓住；n.（汽车等起换挡功能的）离合器踏板；[常用单数] 紧紧抓住

hover/'hɒvə(r)/v. 翱翔，盘旋；踌躇，彷徨（尤指在某人身边）；靠近（某事物）；处于不稳定状态

execute/'eksɪkjuːt/v.（尤指依法）处决，处死；实行，执行；成功地完成（技巧或动作）；制作，做成（艺术品）；[律] 执行（法令），使（法律文件）生效

skycrane/s'kaɪkr'eɪn/n. 空中吊车，空中起重机

maneuver/mə'nuːvə/n. 细致巧妙的移动，机动动作；策略，手段，花招；v.（使谨慎或熟练地）移动，运动；操纵，控制，使花招

snip/snɪp/v.（用剪刀快速）剪，剪断，剪开；n. 剪；剪东西的咔嚓声

traverse/trə'vɜːs/v. 横过，横越，穿过

retrieval/rɪ'triːvl/n. 取回；索回；数据检索

laser/'leɪzə(r)/n. 激光器

deploy/dɪ'plɔɪ/v. 部署，调度（军队或武器）；有效地利用；调动

rotorcraft/'rəʊtəkrɑːft/n. 旋翼机

elated/i'leɪtɪd/adj. 兴高采烈的，欢欣鼓舞的，喜气洋洋的

remark/rɪ'mɑːk/n. 谈论，言论，评述；v. 说起，谈论，评论

contingency/kən'tɪndʒənsi/n. 可能发生的事，偶发（或不测、意外）事件

tear sth. apart 撕毁；使分裂；使痛苦

spark/spɑːk/v. 引发，触发；冒火花，飞火星；n. 火花，火星；（指品质或感情）一星，丝毫，一丁点；生气，活力，才华；诱因，导火线

low-res 等同于 row-resolution，意为低分辨率

atop/ə'tɒp/*prep.* 在…顶上

Atlas V 宇宙神五号运载火箭

align/ə'laɪn/*v.* 排整齐，校准，（尤指）使成一条直线；使一致

orbit/'ɔːbɪt/*n.* （天体等运行的）轨道；（人、组织等的）影响范围，势力范围；*v.* 沿轨道运行；围绕…运动

UAE United Arab Emirates 的缩写，意为阿拉伯联合酋长国

probe/prəʊb/*n.* 探究；详尽调查；（不载人）航天探测器，宇宙探测航天器；探测仪，传感器，取样器；*v.* 盘问，追问，探究；用细长工具）探查，查看

uneventful/ˌʌnɪ'ventfl/*adj.* 平淡无奇的，平凡的，缺乏刺激的

insertion/ɪn'sɜːʃn/*n.* 插入，嵌入，插入物；（书、文章等中）添加的东西

trajectory/trə'dʒektəri/*n.* （射体在空中的）轨道，弹道，轨迹

bullseye/'bʊlzaɪ/*n.* 靶心，鹄的，命中靶心

boulder/'bəʊldə(r)/*n.* （受水或天气侵蚀而成的）巨石，漂砾

pit/pɪt/*n.* 深洞，深坑；矿井；*v.* 打洞

smorgasbord/'smɔːɡəsbɔːd/*n.* 自助餐

fleet/fliːt/*n.* 舰队；（一国的）全部军舰，海军；（同一机构或统一调度的）机群，车队；*adj.* 跑得快的，快速的

scatter/'skætə(r)/*v.* 撒，撒播；散开，四散，驱散；*n.* 散落，三三两两，零零星星

slate/sleɪt/*v.* （尤指在报纸上）批评，抨击；[常用被动] 预定，计划，安排；推举，选定

Notes

1. NASA：美国国家航天局 National Aeronautics and Space Administration，是美国联邦政府的独立机构，负责制定执行美国的民用太空计划及进行航空科学和空间科学研究。1958 年 7 月 29 日，美国总统艾森豪威尔签署《美国国家航空航天法案》创立 NASA，1958 年 10 月开始运作，取代前身美国国家航空咨询委员会（NACA）。自此，NASA 负责管理阿波罗登月计划、天空实验室和航天飞机等美国太空探索任务。

2. Perseverance：毅力号，是由美国国家航空航天局下属的喷气推进实验室制造，用于火星 2020 任务中的火星车。该探测器于美国东部时间 2020 年 7 月 30 日上午 7:50（世界协调时间 11:50）发射，于美国加利福尼亚时间 2021 年 2 月 18 日下午 3 时 55 分成功登陆火星，并降落在耶泽罗撞击坑。同年 3 月 5 日，毅力号在火星上完成首次行驶测试。毅力号的外观与好奇号大致上相同，携带 7 种科学仪器，23 个摄影镜头，2 个麦克风。任务计划探测耶泽罗撞击坑附近的火星表面。毅力号还携带了一台名为机智号的无人机，配合毅力号进行科学研究。2021 年 4 月 20 日，毅力号成功将火星大气的二氧化碳转化成氧，这是地球以外的首次造氧。2021 年 9 月 6 日，毅力号成功取得第一块火星岩石样本。

3. Jezero Crater：耶泽罗撞击坑，又译为耶泽洛撞击坑或杰泽罗撞击坑，是火星北半球的一座撞击坑，直径 47.52 千米，座落于伊希地平原与大瑟提斯高原的交界带北缘。

该撞击坑最晚约于 36 亿年前形成，内部富含黏土矿物，在形成初期极可能是一座长期存在的湖泊。撞击坑的名称"耶泽罗"源自波斯尼亚和黑塞哥维那中部的湖村，这个名称在许多斯拉夫语族语言中都是指"湖泊"。由于地质古老，地形丰富，加上可能保存早期生命讯息的三角洲，美国航太总署于 2018 年择定耶泽罗撞击坑为火星 2020 探测车任务的着陆地点。

4. Jet Propulsion Laboratory：喷气推进实验室（缩写为 JPL）位于美国加利福尼亚州帕萨迪那，是美国国家航空航天局的一个下属机构，行政上由加州理工学院管理，始建于 1936 年，主要负责为美国国家航空航天局开发和管理无人太空探测任务，同时也负责管理美国国家航空航天局的深空网络。

5. Ingenuity：机智号，也称"小机灵"（Ginny），是一台火星无人直升机，是第一架"在另一个星球上进行动力控制飞行"的飞行器。在火星 2020 任务中用来进行飞行技术验证，它可以提供目前轨道卫星或地面探测车和着陆器无法提供的独特视角。为探测器或人类提供高清晰度图像和侦察，并使探测车能够进入难以到达的地形。

6. Atlas V：宇宙神 5 号运载火箭，为洛克希德马丁公司所研制的不可重复使用的运载火箭，现由洛克希德马丁与波音公司研制，隶属联合发射同盟，航空喷气公司则负责宇宙神 5 型运载火箭固态助推器的研发及制造。时至 2015 年 10 月，宇宙神 5 型运载火箭已经发射 50 余次，其首航始于 2002 年 8 月，并保有相当完美的成功率。

7. United Launch Alliance：联合发射联盟（缩写为 ULA）为洛克希德·马丁太空系统与波音国防太空安全组成的合资公司，于 2006 年 12 月成立，整合了两家公司负责美国联邦政府发射服务的团队，美国联邦政府客户包括美国国防部、美国国家航空航天局及其他政府机构。

8. *The Verge*：美国的科技新闻及媒体网络，由 Vox Media 在纽约曼哈顿的办事处操作。网站发布新闻、长篇专题报道、产品评价、博客及娱乐节目。

9. European Space Agency：欧洲空间局（缩写为 ESA）是由欧洲数国政府组成的国际空间探测和开发组织，总部设在法国首都巴黎。ESA 目前共有 19 个成员国：奥地利、比利时、捷克、丹麦、芬兰、法国、德国、希腊、爱尔兰、意大利、卢森堡、荷兰、挪威、葡萄牙、西班牙、瑞典、瑞士、罗马尼亚以及英国；另外，加拿大是 ESA 的准成员国。法国是其主要贡献者。ESA 并非隶属欧盟的机构。欧盟辖下另有欧盟卫星中心（European Union Satellite Centre）。

Exercises

I. Getting the Message

Read the questions and complete the answers according to the text.

1. Why do engineers call the landing process "seven minutes of terror"?
_____

2. How did descent stage move itself far away from Perseverance?
_____

3. What did the NASA's top science official do with the printout of the mission's contingency plan in post-landing press conference?

_____

4. When would high-definition video of touching down be available?

_____

5. Why was The Jezero Crater the most challenging landing site NASA has faced?

_____

II. Languages Focus

A. *Match the following words in left with their explanations in right.*

1. perseverance   a. to move or make sb./sth. move suddenly forwards and/or downwards
2. plunge   b. to move or to make people or animals move very quickly in different directions
3. clutch   c. the quality of continuing to try to achieve a particular aim despite difficulties
4. hover   d. to do a piece of work, perform a duty, put a plan into action
5. execute   e. an event that may or may not happen
6. retrieval   f. a thorough and careful investigation of sth.
7. elated   g. to stay in the air in one place
8. contingency   h. very happy and excited because of sth. good that has happened or will happen
9. probe   i. to hold sb./sth. tightly
10. scatter   j. the process of getting sth. back, especially from a place where it should not be

B. *Fill in the blanks with the words or expressions given below. Change the form where necessary.*

| hover | elated | retrieval | probe | scatter |
| clutch | perseverance | execute | plunge | contingency |

1. We are going to _____ our campaign plan to the letter.
2. When the police arrived, the crowd _____ in all directions.
3. I was _____ by the prospect of the new job ahead.
4. This is a very good way to _____ softly.
5. He has never stopped trying and showed great _____.
6. A helicopter _____ overhead as one of the gang made a run for it.
7. Mr. Brown says Iran's _____ currency has made it harder for customers to pay.

8. I need to examine all possible _____.

9. Children _____ empty bowls form a queue.

10. The ship was buried, beyond _____, at the bottom of the sea.

III. Translation

1. NASA's Perseverance rover has successfully touched down on the surface of Mars after surviving a blazing seven-minute plunge through the Martian atmosphere.

_____

2. Enduring blazing heat, the rover was shielded by a protective shell and parachute to help slow itself down.

_____

3. NASA's top science official was elated and began his remarks on Perseverance's landing victory.

_____

4. Perseverance's journey through space was even more uneventful than expected.

_____

5. Its mix of different rock formations offers researchers a smorgasbord of potential samples to collect during its mission.

_____

IV. Discussion

The spaceflight company SpaceX established by the billionaire Elon Musk launched four private passengers into orbit in 2021 on the first mission to space with an all-civilian crew.

A reusable Falcon 9 rocket launched from Cape Canaveral, Florida, shortly after 8PM. EDT carrying Jared Isaacman, a 38-year-old tech entrepreneur, Sian Proctor, a 51-year-old geoscientist, Chris Sembroski, a 42-year-old aerospace data engineer, and Hayley Arceneaux, a 29-year-old physician assistant. The four-member crew will now orbit the planet for three days before returning to Earth's atmosphere and crashing into the Atlantic Ocean.

This successful launch marks a significant accomplishment for SpaceX and is beneficial to the developing space tourism sector. Jeff Bezos and Richard Branson, two rival billionaires, each soared to the edge of space two months ago in spacecraft created by their respective aerospace corporations. Both Bezos' Blue Origin and Branson's Virgin Galactic are intending to offer orbital joyrides for space passengers in the future, even though both of the flights during the summer were suborbital jaunts.

As governments and their space organizations no longer have exclusive access to the universe, the historic journey signals the next phase in human spaceflight development.

Work in pairs and discuss the following questions:

1. Do you think space tourism is possible for in the future?

2. What can people do when they travel through space?

3. Can you think of other questions related to space tourism?

The Scientific Exploration of Space

Since the war, and particularly during the last few years, a rapidly growing amount of effort has been devoted to the use of high-power rockets to carry instruments up to great heights above the earth; to launch artificial satellites and deep space probes. We have pointed out how much has been and can still be done from the earth's surface. Why then all this concentration on the use of rockets?

One of the main reasons is that our atmosphere, while beneficial for life in general, prevents us from seeing the universe in any but a very restricted range of light — almost entirely confined to visible light and to a relatively restricted range of radio waves, in fact. We must make observations from outside the atmosphere to study the ultra-violet light, X-rays, infrared rays and all those radio waves that cannot penetrate through our atmosphere. With instruments in artificial satellites circulating at heights of over 200 miles such observations can be made. What they will record, we do not know — if we did, it would not be worth going to all this trouble but there is scope here for astronomical studies for generations to come.

This is only one of the many major new possibilities for scientific research which are opened up by the development of rocket vehicles in the study of the earth's outer atmosphere, in meteorology, in the study of the space between the earth and the planets, and so on. There are four main categories of vehicles involved in this work, which has been called space research. First, there are vertical sounding rockets, which can go up to 1,000 miles or more, but are of most use below 200 miles. These rockets simply rise to the top of their trajectory and fall back to earth. Next, we have the artificial satellites revolving round the earth in elliptical paths, never penetrating closer than about 150 miles or so. A speed as high as 18,000 miles per hour must be given to a body to launch it as a satellite. If the satellite orbit is very elongated, so that it passes out to distances several times the earth's radius (4,000 miles), we have a deep space probe. The greater the launching speed, the greater the penetration into space before the return to earth. Eventually, when the speed reaches 25,000 miles per hour, the probe never returns but becomes a satellite of the sun, an artificial planet. Probes may be specially directed to pass near the moon, or hit the moon or become satellites of the moon. These are the lunar probes of which there have been a number of examples recently.

From the scientist's point of view, all these vehicles play a valuable part. The availability of artificial satellites does not make vertical sounding rockets obsolete and this is even more true of deep space and lunar probes in relation to artificial satellites. To the scientist the value of any particular launching is the success of the experiment concluded, not just the distance reached from the earth. Nor is he concerned with putting men in the vehicle, for the instruments can be made to operate automatically and to send back their readings to earth — even over distances of millions of miles — as coded radio signals.

Words & Expressions

confine/kən'faɪn/*v.* [常用被动] 限制，限定；[常用被动] 监禁，禁闭；使离不开（或受困于床、轮椅等）

ultra-violet/ˌʌltrə'vaɪəlɪt/*adj.* 紫外的

inferred/ˌɪnfrə'red/*adj.* 红外线的，使用红外线的

penetrate/'penɪtreɪt/*v.* 穿过；进入；渗透，打入（组织、团体等）；看透，透过…看见；洞察，发现，揭示；被领悟，被理解

scope/skəʊp/*n.*（做或实现某事的）机会，能力；（题目、组织、活动等的）范围；*v.* 仔细看，彻底检查

astronomical/ˌæstrə'nɒmɪkl/*adj.* 天文学的，天文的；（数量、价格等）极其巨大的

meteorology/ˌmiːtɪə'rɒlədʒi/*adj.* 气象学

revolve/rɪ'vɒlv/*v.* 旋转，转动；环绕

elliptical/ɪ'lɪptɪkl/*adj.* [语法] 省略的，隐晦的；椭圆的，椭圆形的

elongate/'iːlɒŋɡeɪt/*v.*（使）变长，伸长，拉长

radius/'reɪdɪəs/*n.* 半径（长度）；半径范围；周围；[解] 桡骨

obsolete/'ɒbsəliːt/*adj.* 淘汰的；废弃的；过时的

Notes

1. visible light：可见光，是电磁波谱中人眼可以感知的部分，可见光谱没有精确的范围；一般人的眼睛可以感知的电磁波的频率在 380～750THz，波长在 780～400nm。人眼可以看见的光的范围受大气层影响。大气层对于大部分的电磁辐射来讲都是不透明的，只有可见光波段和其他少数如无线电通讯波段等例外。

2. radio wave：无线电波，是指在自由空间（包括空气和真空）传播的射频频段的电磁波。无线电波的波长越短、频率越高，相同时间内传输的信息就越多。

3. Ultra-violet light：紫外线，是电磁波谱中频率为 750THz～30PHz，对应真空中波长为 400～10nm 辐射的总称，不能引起人们的视觉。它是频率比蓝紫光高的不可见光。

4. X-ray：X 射线，是一种频率极高，波长极短、能量很大的电磁波。X 射线的频率和能量仅次于伽马射线，频率范围 30PHz～300EHz，对应波长为 0.01～10nm，能量为 124eV～1.24MeV。X 射线具有穿透性，但人体组织间有密度和厚度的差异，当 X 射线透过人体不同组织时，被吸收的程度不同，经过显像处理后即可得到不同的影像。

5. infrared ray：红外线，又称红外辐射，介于可见光和微波之间，波长范围为 0.76～1000μm 的红外波段的电磁波。它是频率比红光低的不可见光。

6. deep space probe：深空探测器是指发射到地月系统之外的探测器；如果被派去探索其他行星，则被称为行星探测器。实验舱是一种小型无人实验室，通常在飞行后回收。

Exercises

I. Comprehension of the Text

Read the text and answer the following questions. Write the answers on the lines.

1. How can we see the universe according to the article?
   _____

2. Is the statement "the vertical sounding rockets only can be used below 200 miles high" true or false?
   _____

3. Is the statement "if launch a satellite, a speed as high as 18,000 miles per hour must be given" true or false?
   _____

4. Is the statement "our atmosphere prevents us from seeing the universe in any range of light" true or false?
   _____

5. What is the value of each launching to the scientist?
   _____

II. Main Details Comprehension

Directions: *In this section, you are going to read a passage with ten statements attached to it. Each statement contains information given in one of the paragraphs. Identify the paragraph from which the information is derived. You may choose a paragraph more than once. Each paragraph is marked with a letter.*

Some College Students are Angry that they have to Pay to Do their Homework

A) Digital learning systems now charge students for access codes needed to complete coursework, take quizzes, and turn in homework. As universities go digital, students are complaining of a new hit to their finances that's replacing-and sometimes joining-expensive textbooks: pricey online access codes that are required to complete coursework and submit assignments.

B) The codes — which typically range in price from $80 to $155 per course — give students online access to systems developed by education companies like McGraw Hill and Pearson. These companies, which long reaped big profits as textbook publishers, have boasted that their new online offerings, when pushed to students through universities they partner with, represent the future of the industry.

C) But critics say the digital access codes represent the same profit-seeking ethos (观念) of the textbook business, and are even harder for students to opt out of. While they could once buy second-hand textbooks, or share copies with friends, the digital systems are essentially impossible to avoid.

D) "When we talk about the access code we see it as the new face of the textbook monopoly (垄断), a new way to lock students around this system," said Ethan Senack, the higher education advocate for the U.S. Public Interest Research Group, to *BuzzFeed News*. "Rather than $250 (for a print textbook) you're paying $120," said Senack. "But because it's all digital it eliminates the used book market and eliminates any sharing and because homework and tests are through an access code, it eliminates any ability to opt out".

E) Sarina Harpet, a 19-year-old student at Virginia Tech, was faced with a tough dilemma when she first started college in 2015 — pay rent or pay to turn in her chemistry homework. She told BuzzFeed News that her freshman chemistry class required her to use Connect, a system provided by McGraw Hill where students can submit homework, take exams and track their grades. But the code to access the program cost $120 — a big sum for Harper, who had already put down $450 for textbooks, and had rent day approaching.

F) She decided to wait for her next work-study paycheck, which was typically $150—$200, to pay for the code. She knew that her chemistry grade may take a dive as a result. "It's a balancing act," she said. "Can I really afford these access codes now?" She didn't hand in her first two assignments for chemistry, which started her out in the class with a failing grade.

G) The access codes may be another financial headache for students, but for textbook businesses, they're the future. McGraw Hill, which controls 21% of the higher education market, reported in March that its digital content sales exceeded print sales for the first time in 2015. The company said that 45% of its $140 million revenue in 2015 "was derived from digital products".

H) A Pearson spokesperson told *BuzzFeed News* that "digital materials are less expensive and a good investment" that offer new features, like audio texts, personalized knowledge checks and expert videos. Its digital course materials save students up to 60% compared to traditional printed textbooks, the company added. McGraw Hill didn't respond to a request for comment, but its CEO David Levin told the *Financial Times* in August that "in higher education, the era of the printed textbook is now over".

I) The textbook industry insists the online systems represent a better deal for students. "These digital products aren't just mechanisms for students to submit homework, they offer all kinds of features," David Anderson, the executive director of higher education with the Association of American Publishers, told *BuzzFeed News*. "It helps students understand in a way that you can't do with print homework assignments".

J) David Hunt, an associate professor in sociology at Augusta University, which has rolled out digital textbooks across its math and psychology departments, told *BuzzFeed News* that he understands the utility of using systems that require access codes. But he doesn't require his students to buy access to a learning program that controls the class assignments. "I try to make things as inexpensive as possible," said Hunt, who uses free digital textbooks for his classes but designs his own curriculum. "The online systems may make my life a lot easier but I feel like I'm giving up control. The discussions are the things where my expertise can benefit the students most".

K) A 20-year-old junior at Georgia Southern University told *BuzzFeed News* that she normally spends $500－$600 on access codes for class. In one case, the professor didn't require students to buy a textbook, just an access code to turn in homework. This year she said she spent $900 on access codes to books and programs. "That's two months of rent," she said. "You can't sell any of it back. With a traditional textbook you can sell it for $30－$50 and that helps to pay for your new semester's books. With an access code, you're out of that money".

L) Benjamin Wolverton, a 19-year-old student at the University of South Carolina, told *BuzzFeed News* that "it's ridiculous that after paying tens of thousands in tuition we have to pay for all these access codes to do our homework." Many of the access codes he's purchased have been required simply to complete homework or quizzes. "Often it's only 10% of your grade in class." he said. "You're paying so much money for something that hardly affects your grade — but if you didn't have it, it would affect your grades enough. It would be bad to start out at a B or C." Wolverton said he spent $500 on access codes for digital books and programs this semester.

M) Harper, a poultry (家禽) science major, is taking chemistry again this year and had to buy anew access code to hand in her homework. She rented her economics and statistics textbooks for about $20 each. But her access codes for homework, which can't be rented or bought second-hand, were her most expensive purchases: $120 and $85.

N) She still remembers the sting of her first experience skipping an assignment due to the high prices. "We don't really have a missed assignment policy," she said. "If you miss it, you just miss it. I just got zeros on a couple of first assignments. I managed to pull everything back up. But as a scared freshman looking at their grades, it's not fun".

_____ 1. A student's yearly expenses on access codes may amount to their rent for two months.

_____ 2. The online access codes may be seen as a way to tie the students to the digital system.

_____ 3. If a student takes a course again, they may have to buy a new access code to submit their assignments.

_____ 4. McGraw Hill accounts for over one-fifth of the market share of college textbooks.

_____ 5. Many traditional textbook publishers are now offering online digital products, which they believe will be the future of the publishing business.

_____ 6. One student complained that they now had to pay for access codes in addition to the high tuition.

_____ 7. Digital materials can cost students less than half the price of traditional printed books according to a publisher.

_____ 8. One student decided not to buy her access code until she received the pay for her part-time job.

_____ 9. Online systems may deprive teachers of opportunities to make the best use of their expertise for their students.

_____ 10. Digital access codes are criticized because they are profit-driven just like the textbook business.

Ⅲ. Translation

Translate the five following sentences into English, using the words or expressions given in brackets.

1．手电筒勉强照见那幽暗处。（penetrate）

_____

2．随着技术的革新，许多传统技艺已被淘汰。（obsolete）

_____

3．他们答应了扩大该组织的活动范围。（scope）

_____

4．我在自己的村庄里过着非常封闭的生活。（confine）

_____

5．从孩提时代起，她的生活就一直以网球为中心。（revolve）

_____

Product Manual
信息类产品说明书的翻译原则

（一）客观

信息类产品说明书主要是客观地向消费者介绍产品的功能、特点、用法等，使用的语言需要严谨、规范、不夸大、不过分渲染，只对产品客观描述即可，引导读者按照一定的思维逻辑循序渐进，知道该做什么、怎么做，进而了解和正确使用该产品。这些内容带有描述说明的性质，客观而不带有感情色彩。例如：

(1) Siri lets you write and send a message, schedule a meeting, place a phone call, get directions, set a reminder, search the web, and much more — simply by talking naturally. Siri asks question if it needs clarification or more information. Siri also uses information from your contacts, music library, calendars, reminder, and so forth to understand what you're talking about.

Siri 能为您书写和发送信息、安排会议、拨打电话、获取路线、设定提醒事项、上网搜索等，只需您自然地说出来即可。如果 Siri 需要澄清或者更多信息，它会问问题。

Siri 也会使用来自通讯录、音乐库、提醒事项等的信息来理解您谈论的内容。

从中英文的对比可以看出,以上几句的翻译与原文结构基本相同,一些词语的排列及使用都做到了遵循原文,而且并没有对任何信息进行删除或者添加解释性翻译,字字句句都是原文的再现,这样的翻译方式可以将原文中的信息传达得清晰明了,有助于传播开发者的技术。

(2) Operate iPod in a place where the temperature is always between 0℃ and 35℃.

须在温度为 0~35℃的场所使用 iPod。

这是一个祈使句,原文希望用户能谨遵温度要求来使用该产品。因此,在翻译这个句子时应遵循客观原则,将这种语气表达出来。

(3) If a seventh device is connected, device A will no longer be memorized.

如果已连接第七台设备,音箱的内存将不再保存第一台设备的配对记录。

该例句中,原文中用的是"device A"(设备 A),在译文中,为了和前半句中的"a seventh"(第七台)保持一致,客观准确描述原文信息,将其翻译成"第一台"。

(二)简洁通顺又紧凑

产品说明书一方面向用户传达有关产品的信息,另一方面也具有广告的功能。为了让广大的消费者都能够阅读说明书的译文,获取有关产品的信息,说明书的翻译除要忠实地传达原文信息外,还要力求语言的简洁,从而使说明书的译文能被一般读者读懂,进而促使产品对读者产生吸引力,更好地提高产品的市场潜力。但是,要注意,英译汉时简洁并不意味着大白话,而应该注意措辞紧凑。例如:

(1) Should you encounter some problems during the installation or use of this computer, please refer to this trouble — shooting guide prior to calling the helpdesk. Look up the problem in the left column and then check the suggestions in the right column.

安装或使用本机如遇问题,请先阅读本疑难解决之说明,如不能解决问题,再致电客服部。请在左栏中查找问题,在右栏查看所建议的解决方法。

(2) If replacement pans are used in making repairs, these pans, may be remanufactured, or may contain remanufactured materials. If it is necessary to replace the entire product, it may be replaced with a remanufactured product.

若维修需用替换零部件,则这些零部件可以是翻新过的,或含有翻新过的材料。如有必要替换整个产品,则可能用翻新产品替换。

和原文相比,译文措辞比较严谨简洁,譬如第一句中的介词 in 省略不译,原因如上文所述;第二句中的代词 it、冠词 a 等都省略不译。因为,这一句中,第一个 it 是形式主语,汉语没有形式主语这种概念,第二个 it 指前文已提及的 entire product,汉语前面已经翻译了这一名词,所以后面不必重复,更不必使用"它"来代称,同时,汉语中没有表示一类的冠词,所以这些词语均省略不译,这样避免了啰唆与重复,使译文简洁易懂,且语义通顺紧凑。

(3) To obtain the best performance and enduring failure — free use, please read this instruction carefully.

请仔细阅读说明书,以便使本机发挥其最佳性能,经久耐用,不出故障。

原文中的"发挥"这一动词省略不译,"经久耐用,不出故障"译成 enduring failure —

free use，显得简单明了。

（三）专业又通俗

信息类产品说明书所介绍的产品大部分是专业性比较强的产品，那么产品说明书中难免会出现专业技术词汇。在翻译当中，术语的翻译一定要符合目的语的专业术语规范，但与此同时也要通俗易懂。否则，会让消费者感到疑惑。例如：

(1) Avoid using any combustible material near the appliance；comply with the operation instructions when cleaning anti — grease filters and when removing grease deposits for the appliance.

不得在抽油烟机附近使用任何易燃物；清洗除油烟过滤网罩和油垢时务必遵照操作说明。

这里的 combustible material、anti — grease filters、grease deposits 都属于专业术语，在译文中分别转换成"易燃物""除油烟过滤网罩"和"油垢"。

(2) The USB Driver allows the system to recognize the USB ports on the mainboard. You need to install this driver if you are running Windows 95.

USB 驱动程序可以使系统识别主板上的 USB 端口。如果您正在运行 Windows 95，则需要安装该驱动程序。

此句中的 USB Driver、USB ports、mainboard 都是计算机术语，分别译成了"USB 驱动程序""USB 端口"和"主板"。

(3) Equipped with a four-way reversion valve，a dual air flow system and fresh air damper, this air conditioner ensures comfortable temperatures in all season, supplies fresh air with a ventilator, filters dust and absorbs humidity. It creates an ideal environment for living and working. With it hermetically sealed compressor designed and manufactured in China, it is elegant, compact, efficient, reliable, low in voice, and easy to operate.

本型号空调器装有四通换向阀及高低两档风量和新风装置，因此可供冬暖夏凉之用，室内通风时能不断补充新鲜空气，过滤空气中的尘埃并吸收湿气，可提供一个较理想的生活与工作环境。由于该机采用自行设计制造的全封闭压缩机，整机结构紧凑，外形美观，效率高，噪音低，使用方便，性能稳定可靠。

原文中的"四通换向阀""高低两档风量""新风装置""全封闭压缩机"这些空调机常用术语分别译成了 four-way reversion valve、dual air flow system、flesh air damper、hermetically sealed compressor，保留了原文的技术性特点，符合技术说明书的特征。

(4) Use the Apple EarPods with Remote and Mic（iPhone 5, shown above）or the Apple EarPhones with Remote and Mic（iPhone 4S or earlier）to listen to music and video, and make phone calls.

使用 Apple EarPods with Remote and Mic 耳机或 Apple EarPhones with Remote and Mic 耳机（iPhone 4 或 iPhone 4S）来听音乐和视频以及打电话。

说明书的用户组要面向普通大众，除了专业，说明书的翻译也要通俗易懂。此处可以注意到原文括号中 earlier 在译文中译者将其固定改为 iPhone 4，此处的改译是为了消除歧义，不确定旧款到底是指 iPhone 3 还是 iPhone 4 等，而且避免读者进行不必要的推理，易于理解。

Unit 9　Space Technology

1. *Read the following paragraphs and then answer the questions.*

Configuring the Advanced Settings

4.1　Wireless

4.1.1 General

The General tab allows you to configure the basic wireless settings.

To configure the basic wireless settings:

(1) From the navigation panel, go to **Advanced Settings** > **Wireless** > **General** tab.

(2) Select 2.4GHz or 5GHz as the frequency band for your wireless network.

(3) Assign a unique name containing up to 32 characters for your SSID (Service Set Identifier) or network name to identify your wireless network. Wi-Fi devices can identify and connect to the wireless network via your assigned SSID. The SSIDs on the information banner are updated once new SSIDs are saved to the settings.

NOTE:　You can assign unique SSIDs for the 2.4 GHz and 5GHz frequency bands.

(4) In the **Hide SSID** field, select **Yes** to prevent wireless devices from detecting your SSID. When this function is enabled, you would need to enter the SSID manually on the wireless device to access the wireless network.

(5) Select any of these wireless mode options to determine the types of wireless devices that can connect to your wireless router:

- **Auto**: Select **Auto** to allow 802.11AC, 802.11n, 802.11g, and 802.11b devices to connect to the wireless router.

- **Legacy**: Select **Legacy** to allow 802.11b/g/n devices to connect to the wireless router. Hardware that supports 802.11n natively, however, will only run at a maximum speed of 54Mbps.

- **N only**: Select **N only** to maximize wireless N performance. This setting prevents 802.11g and 802.11b devices from connecting to the wireless router.

(6) Select the operating channel for your wireless router. Select **Auto** to allow the wireless router to automatically select the channel that has the least amount of interference.

(7) Select any of these channel bandwidth to accommodate higher transmission speeds:

- **40MHz:** Select this bandwidth to maximize the wireless throughput.

- **20MHz (default):** Select this bandwidth if you encounter some issues with your wireless connection.

(8) Select any of these authentication methods:

- **Open System**: This option provides no security.
- **Shared Key**: You must use WEP encryption and enter at least one shared key.

(1) What is SSID?

___

(2) Which Hz can you select as the frequency band for your wireless network?

___

(3) How to prevent wireless devices from detecting your SSID?

___

(4) If you encounter some issues with your wireless connection, which bandwidth should you select?

___

(5) How many authentication methods are mentioned in this user guide?

___

2. *Map reading and translation.*

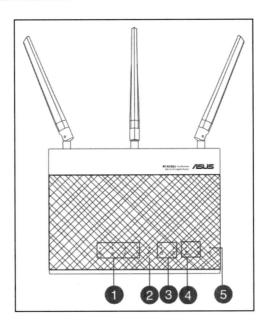

> ❶ **LAN 1~4 LED**
> **Off:** No power or no physical connection.
> **On:** Has physical connection to a local area.network (LAN).

❶ ___

> ❷ **WAN (Internet) LED**
> **Off:** No power or no physical connection.
> **On:** Has physical connection to a wide area.network (WAN).

❷ ___

Unit 9 Space Technology   137

> ❸ **USB 3.0/2.0 LED**
> **Off:** No power or no physical connection.
> **On:** Has physical connection to USB 3.0/2.0 devices.

❸ _____

> ❹ **2.4GHz LED/5GHz LED**
> **Off:** No 2.4GHz or 5GHz signal.
> **On:** Wireless system is ready.
> **Flashing:** Transmitting or receiving data via wireless connection.

❹ _____

> ❺ **Power LED**
> **Off:** No power.
> **On:** Device is ready.
> **Flashing slow:** Rescue mode
> **Flashing quick:** WPS is processing.

❺ _____

Workshop

Background

While astronomy — the study of celestial objects — has existed since the beginning of trustworthy written history, it was the development of large and relatively efficient rockets during the mid-twentieth century that allowed physical space exploration to become a reality.

There are some events leading to space exploration, including Galileo Galilei's first telescopic observation of the night sky, William Moore's first exposition of the rocket equation based on Newton's third law of motion, William Parsons' first proper observation of other galaxies, and Konstantin Tsiolkovsky's first proposal of space elevator.

The Soviet Union and the United States engaged in a "Space Race" that propelled the early period of space exploration. Many people consider the Soviet Union's Sputnik 1 launch in 1957, and the American Apollo 11's first Moon landing in 1969, to be the turning points for this early phase.

Focus switched from one-off missions to renewable hardware after the first 20 years of exploration, such as the Space Shuttle program, and from competitiveness to collaboration, such as with the International Space Station (ISS).

In the 2000s, China started a successful crewed spaceflight program, India launched Chandraayan 1, the European Union planned future crewed space flights, and Japan also did so. In the 21st century, China, Russia, and Japan have supported crewed trips to the Moon, while in the 20th and 21st centuries, the European Union has supported crewed missions to the Moon and Mars.

Task

1. Search more information about space exploration (e.g. history, future, or government budget)

2. Discuss the following questions based on what you have found:

(1) What are the benefits of space exploration for human beings?

(2) Is space exploration worthwhile considering its billions of expenditures?

Process

Step 1. The whole class is divided into several groups, with each group containing 3—4 students.

Step 2. Group members collect information by searching the Internet or interviewing your friends or classmates.

Step 3. Discuss the above two questions with group member.

Step 4. Each group delivers a presentation based on the interview and discussion.

Unit 10　Technology and Brain

Musk: Technology that Connects the Human Brain to Computers Is Not Far Off

At a Friday event, Elon Musk revealed more details about his mysterious neuroscience company Neuralink and its plans to connect computers to human brains. While the development of this futuristic-sounding tech is still in its early stages, the presentation was expected to demonstrate the second version of a small, robotic device that inserts tiny electrode threads through the skull and into the brain. Musk said ahead of the event he would "show neurons firing in real-time. The matrix in the matrix".

And he did just that. At the event, Musk showed off several pigs that had prototypes of the neural links implanted in their head, and machinery that was tracking those pigs' brain activity in real time. The billionaire also announced the Food and Drug Administration had awarded the company a breakthrough device authorization, which can help expedite research on a medical device.

Like building underground car tunnels and sending private rockets to Mars, this Musk-backed endeavor is incredibly ambitious, but Neuralink builds on years of research into brain-machine interfaces. A brain-machine interface is technology that allows for a device, like a computer, to interact and communicate with a brain. Neuralink, in particular, aims to build an incredibly powerful brain-machine interface, a device with the power to handle lots of data, that can be inserted in a relatively simple surgery. Its short-term goal is to build a device that can help people with specific health conditions.

The actual status of Neuralink's research has been somewhat murky, and Friday's big announcement happened as ex-employees complain of internal chaos at the company. Musk has already said the project allowed a monkey to control a computer device with its mind, and as the *New York Times* reported in 2019, Neuralink had demonstrated a system with 1,500 electrodes connected to a lab rat. Since then, Musk has hinted at the company's progress (at times on Twitter), though those involved have generally been close-lipped about the status of the research.

Musk opened Friday's event by emphasizing the wide variety of spinal and neurological conditions — including seizures, paralysis, brain damage, and depression — that Neuralink technology could help treat.

"These can all be solved with an implantable neural link," said Musk. "The neurons are like wiring, and you kind of need an electronic thing to solve an electronic problem".

But it's worth highlighting that Musk wants Neuralink to do far more than treat specific health conditions. He sees the technology as an opportunity to build a widely available brain-computer interface for consumers, which he thinks could help humans keep pace with increasingly powerful artificial intelligence.

So while modest, Neuralink's research already foreshadows how this technology could one day change life as we know it. At the same time, it's a reminder that the potential, eventual merging of humans with computers is destined to introduce a wide range of ethical and social questions that we should probably start thinking about now.

Founded in 2016, Neuralink is a neuroscience technology company focused on building systems with super-thin threads that carry electrodes. When implanted into a brain, these threads would form a high-capacity channel for a computer to communicate with the brain, a system supposed to be much more powerful than the existing brain-machine interfaces being researched.

One major barrier to inserting these incredibly tiny wires, which are thinner than a strand of human hair, is actually getting them past the skull and into the brain. That's why Neuralink is also developing an incredibly small robot that connects the electrode to humans through surgery that's about as intensive as a Lasik eye procedure. On Friday, Musk outlined how the company hopes to do the procedure without general anesthesia in a single-day hospital stay. That's the goal at least, and would represent a huge leap forward from previous brain-machine interfaces, which have required more invasive surgeries.

"We've been connecting forms of computers to brains for 20 or 30 years already," Nolan Williams, the director of Stanford's Brain Stimulation Lab, told Recode, referencing deep stimulation used for patients with Parkinson's as one example of connecting a brain and a computer.

"The brain itself uses certain frequencies and certain kinds of electrical thresholding to communicate with itself," Williams explained. "Your brain is a series of circuits that kind of intercommunicate and communicate between themselves".

Essentially, a brain-machine interface can use the electricity the brain already uses to function along with a series of electrodes to connect the brain with a machine. Neuralink cites previous examples in which humans have used electrodes to control cursors and robotic limbs with their minds as the basis for its system. But what's novel about Neuralink's plan is making the process of connecting a device with the brain minimal, while also massively increasing the number of electrodes engaged. The company wants to make brain-machine interfaces not only easier to install but also more powerful.

As the focus of Friday's event, Musk showed what the second generation of that robot will look like: a large white structure with five degrees of freedom.

"The robot is a super complicated, highly-precise machine which is able to both capture your brain and then with almost a sewing machine-like, micro-precise needle and thread, place the neural threads in the exact right location based on the surgeon decisions around what the safe locations are for the threads to be inserted," Afshin Mehin, a designer and founder of the firm Woke, which worked on the robot's outer device that holds the needle, told Recode.

The machine operates at a very small scale, and Neuralink hopes to expand its capabilities. For instance, the current robot has a 150 micrometer gripper, and an even tinier needle — less than 40 micrometers — which can "grasp the implant's threads then precisely insert each into the cortex while avoiding visible vasculature," according to Neuralink robotics director Ian O'Hara. He added in an emailed statement that, while the robot currently handles only the insertion of the threads, Neuralink is working to expand the robot's role in surgery to increase the number of patients it can help and make the procedure shorter.

Musk said that, in the past year, Neuralink simplified its plans for a wearable device that connects to the threads implanted in the user's brain. While the first generation of this device would have been installed behind a person's ear, the newest version is a small, coin-size device that would sit under the top of their skull.

"It's kind of like a Fitbit in your skull with tiny wires," explained Musk, who compared the device to a smart watch.

The research is still in early stages and, as it advances, will likely require focusing on how the technology can help people with specific, severe health conditions first, according to Stanford neurosurgery professor Maheen Adamson. While the medical applications of such technology could be wide-ranging, moving it from its current, nascent state will require the close oversight of the Food and Drug Administration, which would not comment specifically on Neuralink.

Words & Expressions

neuroscience/'njʊərəʊsaɪəns/*n.* 神经科学
futuristic/ˌfjuːtʃə'rɪstɪk/*adj.* 极其现代的；未来派的
electrode/ɪ'lektrəʊd/*n.* 电极
skull/skʌl/*n.* 颅骨，头（盖）骨；脑袋，脑子
matrix/'meɪtrɪks/*n.* ［数］矩阵；（人或社会成长发展的）社会环境，政治局势；线路网，道路网
show off 卖弄，炫耀
prototype/'prəʊtəˌtaɪp/*n.* 样机
implant/ɪm'plɑːnt/*v.* 灌输，注入（观念、看法等），（在思想上）生根；将（人造器官等）置入，（通常指通过手术）将…植入；*n.* （植入人体中的）移植物，植入物
expedite/'ekspədaɪt/*v.* 加快，加速
endeavor/ɪn'devə/*n.* （尤指新的或艰苦的）努力，尝试；*v.* 努力，尽力
murky/'mɜːki/*adj.* （液体）浑浊的，污浊的；（空气、光等）昏暗的，阴暗的，朦胧的；［贬义］隐晦的，含糊的，暧昧可疑的
spinal/'spaɪnl/*adj.* 脊的，脊柱的，脊髓的

seizure/ˈsiːʒə(r)/n. 起获，没收，充公，起获的赃物，没收的财产；夺取，占领，控制；疾病，尤指脑病的）侵袭，发作

paralysis/pəˈræləsɪs/n. 麻痹，瘫痪；（活动、工作等）能力的完全丧失，瘫痪

strand/strænd/n.（线、绳、金属线、毛发等的）股，缕；（观点、计划、故事等的）部分，方面；v. 使滞留；使搁浅

anesth. esia/ˌænəsˈθiːziə/n. 麻醉；感觉缺失，麻木

threshold/ˈθreʃhəʊld/n. 门槛，门口；阈，界，起始点；开端，起点，入门

circuit/ˈsɜːkɪt/n. 环行，环行路线；电路，线路；巡回，巡游

cursor/ˈkɜːsə(r)/n.（计算机荧光屏上的）光标，游标

limb/lɪm/n. 肢，臂，腿，翼，翅膀；有…肢（或翼、翅膀）的

sew/səʊ/v. 缝，做针线活；缝制，缝补，缝上

thread/θred/n.（棉、毛、丝等的）线；线索，脉络，思绪，思路，贯穿的主线；线状物，细细的一条；v. 穿（针），纫（针），穿过；（使）穿过，通过，穿行；穿成串，串在一起

cortex/ˈkɔːteks/n.［解］皮层，皮质，（尤指）大脑皮层

vasculature/ˈvæskjʊlətʃə(r)/n.［解］脉管系统

nascent/ˈnæsnt/adj. 新生的，萌芽的，未成熟的

oversight/ˈəʊvəsaɪt/n. 疏忽，忽略，失察；负责，照管

Notes

1. Elon Musk：埃隆·马斯克，曾取名马谊郎在台湾登记公司，企业家、商业大亨、美国工程院院士。他是 SpaceX 创始人、董事长、首席执行官、首席工程师，特斯拉投资人、首席执行官、产品设计师、前董事长，无聊公司创始人，Neuralink 和 OpenAI 联合创始人，同时也是 Twitter 的首席执行官、董事会唯一成员。2022 年，马斯克以 2190 亿美元财富成为世界首富。

2. Neuralink：Neuralink 是一个美国神经科技和脑机接口公司，由埃隆·马斯克和 8 名其他联合创办者创办，负责研发植入式脑机界面技术。公司的总部在美国加利福尼亚州旧金山。Neuralink 于 2016 年成立，并于 2017 年 3 月公之于众。2019 年 7 月 17 日，Neuralink 对外宣布该公司研发的一款脑机接口系统。2020 年 8 月 29 日，Neuralink 展示了一头被植入 Neuralink 设备的猪，Neuralink 设备成功读取猪大脑活动。

3. Stanford's Brain Stimulation Lab：斯坦福大学脑刺激实验室（BSL），利用新的脑刺激技术来探测和调节神经精神疾病/障碍的神经网络，以努力开发新的模型和新的治疗方法。该实验室专注于利用神经刺激来探索参与控制人类大脑冲突调节的神经元素。

4. Fitbit：Fitbit 是美国消费电子产品和健身公司，总部位于美国加利福尼亚州旧金山，主要产品包括活动追踪器、智能手表和无线可穿戴式智能产品等。该公司原名 Healthy Metrics Research，于 2007 年 10 月改为现名。Fitbit 的报告则显示其已出售超过 1 亿部设备，拥有 2800 万用户。

Exercises

I. Getting the Message

Read the questions and complete the answers according to the text.

1. What can help expedite research on a medical device?

_____

2. What diseases could Neuralink technology help treat?

_____

3. What can bring ethical and social questions in the future?

_____

4. Why is Neuralink is also developing an incredibly small robot?

_____

5. Where was the first generation of wearable device installed?

_____

II. Languages Focus

A. *Match the following words in left with their explanations in right.*

1. implant	a. the fact of making a mistake because you forget to do sth. or you do not notice sth.
2. expedite	b. to use a needle and thread to make stitches in cloth
3. endeavor	c. not clearly known and suspected of not being honest
4. murky	d. to put sth. into a part of the body for medical purposes, usually by means of an operation
5. seizure	e. the use of legal authority to take sth. from sb.; an amount of sth. that is taken in this way
6. paralysis	f. beginning to exist; not yet fully developed
7. threshold	g. to make a process happen more quickly
8. sew	h. a loss of control of, and sometimes feeling in, part or most of the body, caused by disease or an injury to the nerves
9. nascent	i. an attempt to do sth., especially sth. new or difficult
10. oversight	j. the point just before a new situation, period of life, etc.

B. *Fill in the blanks with the words or expressions given below. Change the form where necessary.*

oversight	seizure	sew	paralysis	endeavor
threshold	nascent	implant	murky	expedite

1. She made the dresses on the _____ machine.

2. Everyone in this _____ business is still struggling with basic issues.
3. The strike caused total _____ in the city.
4. Prejudices can easily become _____ in the mind.
5. She felt as though she was on the _____ of a new life.
6. Violators of the fishing regulations face _____ of the boat's catch.
7. They are _____ to protect trade union rights.
8. I didn't mean to leave her name off the list; it was an _____.
9. We have developed rapid order processing to _____ deliveries to customers.
10. The law here is a little bit _____.

III. Translation

Translate the following sentences into Chinese.

1. A brain-machine interface is technology that allows for a device, like a computer, to interact and communicate with a brain.

_____

2. Those involved have generally been close-lipped about the status of the research.

_____

3. It's worth highlighting that he wants the company to do far more than treat specific health conditions.

_____

4. The company wants to make brain-machine interfaces not only easier to install but also more powerful.

_____

5. While the first generation of this device would have been installed behind a person's ear, the newest version is a small, coin-size device that would sit under the top of their skull.

_____

IV. Discussion

Personal technology, such as smart speakers, smart watches, wearables, and VR headsets, is becoming more and more popular. We now rely more heavily on modern technologies for social interaction, entertainment, and educational experiences as a result of the COVID-19 epidemic. A growing number of us are using technology to enhance our reality as we spend more time at home. Our daily experiences are layered with biometric data, audio interactivity, and visual information via wearables like smart earphones, lenses, watches, rings, bracelets, and even textiles. With the emergence of the brain-computer interface (BCI), an even more personal connection is possible as wearable technology becomes more prevalent in our daily lives.

Both internal and exterior connections to the human brain are possible with BCIs. They are able to read brain activity, convert it into information, and then relay that information back to the brain. Technologists and businesspeople alike find the prospect of BCIs amplifying human intelligence to superhuman levels appealing, but it raises the issue of whether or not we, our organizations, and our technology systems are prepared for this transition.

Work in pairs and discuss the following questions:
1. How do BCIs benefit us?
2. What are issues or concerns caused by BCIs?
3. Are you willing to try BCI tech in the future?

Is It True that The Human Brain Is Only 10% Developed?

The enduring myth says that we only use 10% of our brains with 90% standing by for spare capacity. 75% of the public and 50% of science teachers have believed this myth. In the 1890's William James, the father of American Psychology, said that most of us do not meet our mental ability.

He meant this as a challenge to encourage us to develop ourselves mentally. This, together with science's inability to understand the role of our massive frontal lobes, resulted in most people misunderstanding James and believing that we do not use most of our brain. This could not be further from the truth.

Consider the percentage of total body energy the brain uses. Dogs and rats use 5% of total body energy to run their brains. Primates use 10% of body glucose and the human brain (2% of body mass) uses 20% of all available energy. Children use 50% of energy and infants use 60% to run their brain activity.

On a weight basis the human brains contain more neurons than any other species. We have 86 billion neurons, 40% more than an ape.

Half the energy we use in the brain is consumed pumping chemicals from one part of the brain to the other. This resets the chemicals which move in and out of the nerve coating to send nerve signals. Once a signal has passed through the nerve the chemicals need to be reset.

As we use so much energy just to keep the brain in a state of readiness, there is much less energy left for the nerves to "get things done". It would therefore be impossible to fire all the nerves of the brain at the same time; we need a way of saving energy.

By firing only the necessary parts of the brain at any one time, a process called "Sparse Coding", we can carry the most information using the least energy.

In the human brain, between 1% and 16% of brains cells should be active at any one time for the most efficient use of energy. One way of saving energy is to allow many functions to occur below the conscious level, using less energy but allowing us to perform many things at the same time.

Another way that we use less brain energy, just as we may use a road network to travel from Norwich to London, is in selecting the quickest way to travel depending on traffic and other conditions. Nerves also seek out the most efficient route of travel. So far from only using 10% of the brain, we really do use all of the brain at some point.

The brain, as well as all nerve tissue, will develop strong, reliable pathways when used often. This is why chiropractic care works so well.

Chiropractic adjustments have a powerful "resetting" effect on the nervous system, retuning the brain to accept nerve signals and clearly understand them. As good nerve signals often choose pathways that control other positive functions of the body such as increased immune system or improve healing rates — clients often report that they have better body functions, healing rates and sleep patterns as well as a reduction in symptoms such as pain.

The more we use a variety of nerve functions the more our body's display overall improved function. If a path is walked along regularly it becomes clear, so much so that two can walk abreast and eventually a bike or a small car can drive along it. This is the same with nerve signals.

Far from using only 10% of our brains we use 100% of our brains, only not at the same time.

Words & Expressions

stand by 做好准备；袖手旁观；继续支持（尤指处于困境者）；坚持（原有的决定、承诺或声明）

inability/ˌɪnə'bɪləti/n. 无能，无力，不能

lobe/ləʊb/n. （身体器官的）叶，（尤指）肺叶，脑叶

primate/'praɪmeɪt/n. 灵长类，灵长目动物；大主教，总主教

glucose/'ɡluːkəʊs/n. 葡萄糖，右旋糖

neuron/'njʊərɒn/n. [生] 神经元

pump/pʌmp/v. 用泵（或泵样器官等）输送；[液] 涌出，涌流，奔流；上下（或内外）快速摇动，急速摇晃；盘问，追问，一再探问；n. 抽水机，泵，打气筒

readiness/'redinəs/n. 准备就绪；愿意，乐意

sparse/spɑːs/adj. 稀少的，稀疏的，零落的

Sparse Coding 稀疏编码

tissue/'tɪʃuː/n. （人、动植物细胞的）组织；（尤指用作手帕的）纸巾，手巾纸

chiropractic/ˌkaɪərəʊ'præktɪk/n. 按摩（疗法），脊柱推拿（疗法）

retune/riː'tjuːn/v. 重新调谐，重新调整（频率、频道）

immune/ɪ'mjuːn/adj. 有免疫力的；不受影响的；受保护的，免除的，豁免的

symptom/'sɪmptəm/n. 症状；征候，征兆

abreast/ə'brest/adv. 并列，并排，并肩

Notes

1. William James：威廉·詹姆斯，美国心理学之父，美国本土第一位哲学家和心理学家，也是教育学家、实用主义的倡导者，美国机能主义心理学派创始人之一，也是美国最早的实验心理学家之一。1904 年当选为美国心理学会主席，1906 年当选为国家科学院院士。2006 年被美国的权威期刊《大西洋月刊》评为影响美国的 100 位人物之一（第 62 位）。

2. frontal lobe：额叶，大脑半球在中央沟以前、大脑外侧沟以上的部分，可分为背外侧面、内侧面和底面，与人的行为、学习和个性有关。

3. glucose：有机化合物葡萄糖，分子式 $C_6H_{12}O_6$。是自然界分布最广且最为重要的一种单糖，它是一种多羟基醛。纯净的葡萄糖为无色晶体，有甜味但甜味不如蔗糖，易溶于水，微溶于乙醇，不溶于乙醚。天然葡萄糖水溶液旋光向右，故属于"右旋糖"。葡萄糖在生物学领域具有重要地位，是活细胞的能量来源和新陈代谢中间产物，即生物的主要供能物质。植物可通过光合作用产生葡萄糖。在糖果制造业和医药领域有着广泛应用。

4. neuron：神经元即神经元细胞，是神经系统最基本的结构和功能单位。分为细胞体和突起两部分。细胞体由细胞核、细胞膜、细胞质组成，具有联络和整合输入信息并传出信息的作用；突起有树突和轴突两种。树突短而分枝多，轴突长而分枝少。末梢分布于某些组织器官内，形成各种神经末梢装置。感觉神经末梢形成各种感受器；运动神经末梢分布于骨骼肌肉，形成运动终极。

5. Sparce Coding：稀疏编码算法是一种无监督学习方法，它用来寻找一组"超完备"基向量来更高效地表示样本数据。稀疏编码算法的目的就是找到一组基向量，使得我们能将输入向量表示为这些基向量的线性组合。

Exercises

I. Comprehension of the Text

Read the text and answer the following questions. Write the answers on the lines.

1. Is the statement "babies use a higher percentage of energy to run brain activity than children" true or false?

_____

2. Is the statement "pumping chemicals from one area of the brain to another consumes half of the energy we utilize in the brain" true or false?

_____

3. Is the statement "firing all of the brain's neurons at once would be easy for people" true or false?

_____

4. What is the way for brain to save energy?

___

5. What is the result of using a variety of nerve functions more?

___

II. Main Details Comprehension

Directions: *In this section, you are going to read a passage with ten statements attached to it. Each statement contains information given in one of the paragraphs. Identify the paragraph from which the information is derived. You may choose a paragraph more than once. Each paragraph is marked with a letter.*

The Blessing and Curse of the People Who Never Forget

A handful of people can recall almost every day of their lives in enormous detail-and after years of research, neuroscientists are finally beginning to understand how they do it.

A) For most of us, memory is a mess of blurred and faded pictures of our lives. As much as we would like to cling on to our past, even the saddest moments can be washed away with time.

B) Ask Nima Veiseh what he was doing for any day in the past 15 years, however, and he will give you the details of the weather, what he was wearing, or even what side of the train he was sitting on his journey to work. "My memory is like a library of video tapes, walk-throughs of every day of my life from waking to sleeping," he explains.

C) Veiseh can even put a date on when those tapes started recording: 15 December 2000, when he met his first girlfriend at his best friend's 16th birthday party. He had always had a good memory, but the thrill of young love seems to have shifted a gear in his mind: from now on, he would start recording his whole life in detail. "I could tell you everything about every day after that".

D) Needless to say, people like Veiseh are of great interest to neuroscientists (神经科学专家) hoping to understand the way the brain records our lives. A couple of recent papers have finally opened a window on these people's extraordinary minds. And such research might even suggest ways for us all to relive our past with greater clarity.

E) "Highly superior autobiographical memory" (or HSAM for short), first came to light in the early 2000s, with a young woman named Jill Price. Emailing the neuroscientist and memory researcher Jim McGaugh one day, she claimed that she could recall every day of her life since the age of 12. Could he help explain her experiences?

F) McGaugh invited her to his lab, and began to test her: he would give her a date and ask her to tell him about the world events on that day. True to her word, she was correct almost every time.

G) It didn't take long for magazines and documentary film-makers to come to understand her "total recall", and thanks to the subsequent media interest, a few dozen other subjects (including Veiseh) have since come forward and contacted the team at the University of California, Irvine.

H) Interestingly, their memories are highly self-centred: although they can remember "autobiographical" life events in extraordinary detail, they seem to be no better than average at recalling impersonal information, such as random (任意选取的) lists of words. Nor are they necessarily better at remembering a round of drinks, say. And although their memories are vast, they are still likely to suffer from "false memories". Clearly, there is no such thing as a "perfect" memory — their extraordinary minds are still using the same flawed tools that the rest of us rely on. The question is, how?

I) Lawrence Patih is at the University of Southern Mississippi recently studied around 20 people with HSAM and found that they scored particularly high on two measures: fantasy proneness (倾向) and absorption. Fantasy proneness could be considered a tendency to imagine and daydream, whereas absorption is the tendency to allow your mind to become fully absorbed in an activity — to pay complete attention to the sensations (感受) and the experiences. "I'm extremely sensitive to sounds, smells and visual detail," explains Nicole Donohue, who has taken part in many of these studies. "I definitely feel things more strongly than the average person".

J) The absorption helps them to establish strong foundations for recollection, says Patihis, and the fantasy proneness means that they revisit those memories again and again in the coming weeks and months. Each time this initial memory trace is "replayed", it becomes even stronger. In some ways, you probably go through that process after a big event like your wedding day — but the difference is that thanks to their other psychological tendencies, the HSAM subjects are doing it day in, day out, for the whole of their lives.

K) Not everyone with a tendency to fantasies will develop HSAM, though, so Patihis suggests that something must have caused them to think so much about their past. "Maybe some experience in their childhood meant that they became obsessed (着迷) with calendars and what happened to them," says Patihis.

L) The people with HSAM I've interviewed would certainly agree that it can be a mixed blessing. On the plus side, it allows you to relive the most transformative and enriching experiences. Veiseh, for instance, travelled a lot in his youth. In his spare time, he visited the local art galleries, and the paintings are now lodged deep in his autobiographical memories.

M) "Imagine being able to remember every painting, on every wall, in every gallery space, between nearly 40 countries," he says. "That's a big education in art by itself." With this comprehensive knowledge of the history of art, he has since become a professional painter.

N) Donohue, now a history teacher, agrees that it helped during certain parts of her education: "I can definitely remember what I learned on certain days at school. I could imagine what the teacher was saying or what it looked like in the book."

O) Not everyone with HSAM has experienced these benefits, however. Viewing the past in high definition can make it very difficult to get over pain and regret. "It can be very hard to forget embarrassing moments," says Donohue. "You feel the same emotions — it is just as raw, just as fresh ... You can't turn off that stream of memories, no matter how hard you try." Veiseh agrees: "It is like having these open wounds — they are just a part of you," he says.

P) This means they often have to make a special effort to lay the past to rest. Bill, for instance, often gets painful "flashbacks", in which unwanted memories intrude into his consciousness, but overall he has chosen to see it as the best way of avoiding repeating the same mistakes. "Some people are absorbed in the past but not open to new memories, but that's not the case for me. I look forward to each day and experiencing something new".

_____ 1. People with HSAM have the same memory as ordinary people when it comes to impersonal information.

_____ 2. Fantasy proneness will not necessarily cause people to develop HSAM.

_____ 3. Veiseh began to remember the details of his everyday experiences after he met his first young love.

_____ 4. Many more people with HSAM started to contact researchers due to the mass media.

_____ 5. People with HSAM often have to make efforts to avoid focusing on the past.

_____ 6. Most people do not have clear memories of past events.

_____ 7. HSAM can be both a curse and a blessing.

_____ 8. A young woman sought explanation from a brain scientist when she noticed her unusual memory.

_____ 9. Some people with HSAM find it very hard to get rid of unpleasant memories.

_____ 10. A recent study of people with HSAM reveals that they are liable to fantasy and full absorption in an activity.

III. Translation

Translate the five following sentences into English, using the words or expressions given in brackets.

1. 有些家庭因无力支付医疗费用而得不到医治。（inability）

_____

2. 她的症状逐步恶化。（symptom）

_____

3. 他会不断了解最新消息。（abreast）

_____

4. 他误以为他的家人会支持他。（stand by）

_____

5. 他是个50来岁的矮胖男人，头发稀疏。（sparse）

_____

Product Manual
信息类产品说明书的翻译方法

（一）直译与意译

在信息类产品说明书的翻译过程中，直译是最常用的方法，也称对等译法。通常在目的语和源语中可以找到意义完全对等的单词或词组。采用直译法，可以保持原文的内容和形式，使得译文无论从内容上还是形式上都忠实于原文。例如：

(1) Insert the power cord into the power socket on the back of the loudspeaker.
将电源线插入音箱背面的电源插口。

(2) Connect the correct power cord to the wall socket.
将正确的电源线连接至墙上的电源插座。

(3) Push the SOURCE or WAKE button to choose your source or to switch between connected sources.
轻按 SOURCE/WAKE（音源/唤醒）按钮来选择音源，或在已连接的音源间切换。

以上例句多为产品的操作过程，在翻译这类讲解说明文时，按原文的顺序采用直译法，多使用简单句，使得译文简洁明了，通俗易懂，具有更强的可操作性。

意译是根据原文的大意来翻译，不作逐字逐句的翻译。内容忠实于原文，但不拘泥于原文的形式。可以通过转换表达形式，适当调整原文语序和成分的方法来使译文更符合语言的表达习惯。某些说明书中的术语在另一种语言中很难找到相对应的词汇来表达，或者字面的翻译不足以表达其专业含义时，可以采用意译的方式。例如：

(4) Embodying the raw, wayward spirit of rock n roll，the Kilburn portable active stereo speaker takes the unmistakable look and sound of Marshall, unplugs the chords, and takes the show on the road.

Kilburn 便携式立体声有源音箱外观质朴，具有 Marshall 音箱的完美音质，不需插电，随身携带，尽显率真本然的摇滚精神。

像这样的句子采取意译法，对原文的句子进行一些拆分，对语序进行适当的调整，在实现了忠实、通顺的基础上使译文兼具了意美和形美。如果按照原文直译，译文会显得不易理解，达不到准确、流畅的翻译效果。

(5) Select input as source by pushing the SOURCE/WAKE button until the input LED is lit(see page 015).
按下 SOURCE/WAKE（音源 / 唤醒）按钮，直至输入 LED 灯亮起，选择输入作为音源（请参阅第 207 页）。

由于这本便携式立体声有源音箱的产品说明书是一本多语言说明书，每种语言的说明文字按一定顺序排列，所以英文说明书中的第 15 页并非中文说明书的第 15 页，这里采用意译的方法译成中文说明书中对应的第 207 页，方便用户读者查找。

(6) When some part of the body is in con-tact with the receiving/transmitting system for the Bluetooth device or the Kilburn active loudspeaker.

当设备的某个部分与蓝牙设备或 Kilburn 有源音箱的接收/传送系统接触时。

Body 有物体的意思，但若直接翻译成"物体"显然也不够准确，根据上下文的意思，把 body 翻译成"设备"更能准确表达原文意思。

（二）增译和减译

增译就是在原文的基础上添加必要的单词、词组、分句或完整句，从而使译文在语法、语言形式上符合目标语的表达习惯。减译则与此相反，适当地删减原文的词句，以达到忠实于原文或获得通顺流畅的译文的目的。

(1) Electrical variations due to obstacles in the form of walls, corners, etc..

由于障碍物（如墙、角落等）而造成电气性能变化。

从这个例子中可以看到，若将"electrical variations"直译成"电的变化"，用户读者可能无法理解这句话的意思，所以此处增译"性能"一词，以帮助用户更好地理解。

(2) Click "Whiteboard Software".

单击"白板软件"按钮。

Whiteboard Software 后增译"按钮"一词。

(3) Panel Button ✕ : The thumbnail panel is closed when you click this button.

"面板关闭"按钮 ✕ :用户单击此按钮，缩率图面板即被关闭。

根据下文可知，此处如果仅翻译成"面板按钮"，冒号后的句子意义则没有起到对其的解释说明作用，此外意义也产生了偏差，所以此处"✕"，应顺应文意增译为"关闭"。

(4) This illustration intends to show the internal speaker layout.

此图旨在说明音箱的内部布局。

从译文可以看出此句话是配有图片的，用户读者可以很直观地看到音箱的网状盖板里面扬声器的布局，因此译文采用省译翻译法，原句中的 speaker 一词没有译出。

(5) Click "Next" Next＞ .

单击下一步按钮 下一步 。

可改译为：单击 下一步 。

Next 一词在计算机文本中译为"下一步"，若此处，将文字信息和图示信息全部翻译过来为"单击下一步 下一步 "，累赘反复，不符合软件说明书简洁大方的特点，故此处的文字信息忽略不译，用图示信息展现即可。

(6) They are Original size Original size , Small size Small size , Midimum size Middle size and Large size Large size .

他们分别是： 原始尺寸   小尺寸   中尺寸   大尺寸 。

此处选择用图片信息，而省略文字信息。一方面表示尺寸的语言描述和图示按钮信息所表达的意思一样。省略语言信息行文更加简洁。另一方面，图示信息更直观的方便用户按安装步骤操作。

1. *Read the following paragraphs and then answer the questions.*

Software Installation and Configuration

With the hardware installed, the final step is to install the GeForce Experience software to update your drivers and optimize your games.

1 Download and install GeForce Experience software.
- Go to http://www.geforce.com/geforce-experience and click **Download Now**.
- Accept the NVIDIA software license agreement by selecting **Agree and Continue**. GeForce Experience software begins to install.
- Select **Close** to finish the installation.

2 Optimize your installed games.
- Open GeForce Experience and click **Scan for Games** and click OK to scan your installed games.
- Click on **Optimize All** to optimize your game settings.

3 Get the latest drivers.
- Open GeForce Experience, log in, and select the **Drivers** tab.
- Select **Download Driver**. Your GPU driver begins to download.
- Select **Express Installation** when the download finishes. GeForce Experience begins to install the graphics driver.

Note: It may take several minutes for the installation to take place. Your screen may go blank for a few seconds one or more times during installation. This is normal.

- Click **CLOSE** when the driver install completes.

4 Congratulations! Your GeForce graphics card is now ready to use!

Note: If you have any questions about your NVIDIA product you can Chat live with NVIDIA Customer Care at www.nvidia.com/support or call 1-800-797-6530 (US) or 0800 404 7474 (UK).

(1) How many steps does it take to install the software?

(2) How to accept the NVIDIA software license agreement?

(3) How to optimize your game settings?

(4) Your screen may go blank for a few seconds one or more times during installation, is this normal?

(5) If you have any questions about your NVIDIA product, what can you do?

2. *Map reading and translation.*

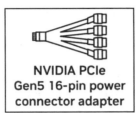

NVIDIA PCIe Gen5 16-pin power connector adapter

❶ _____

 Attention: Use only the included NVIDIA power connector adapter for your GeForce RTX 40 Series Founders Edition graphics card.

❷ _____

1. Connect the display(s) to the graphics card.
2. Reconnect your power cord to the PC.

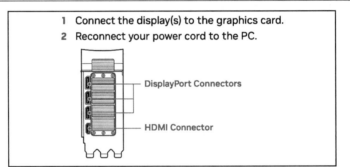

DisplayPort Connectors

HDMI Connector

❸ _____

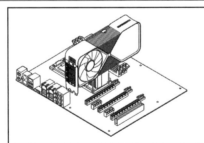

Install your GeForce RTX 4090 into the Primary PCI Express x16 slot (the Primary slot is the one closest to the CPU).

❹ _____

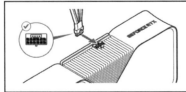

Connect at least three independent dedicated cables with 8-pin PCI Express plugs from the system power supply to the NVIDIA power connector adapter.

❺ _____

Workshop

Background

One hundred eleven years ago, E. M. Forster published a short story (*The Machine Stops*, 1909, *The Oxford and Cambridge Review*) about a futuristic scenario in which a mysterious machine controls everything, from food supply to information technologies. In a situation that evokes internet and digital media events of today, in this dystopia, all communication is remote and face-to-face meetings no longer happen. The machine controls the mindset, as it makes everybody dependent on it. In the short story, when the machine stops working, society collapses.

The story raises many questions, still relevant today, about the impact of digital media and related technology on our brains. This issue of *Dialogues in Clinical Neuroscience* explores in a multifaceted manner how, by what means, and with what possible effects digital media use affects brain function — for the good, the bad, and the ugly sides of human existence.

Overall, digital media use, from online gaming to smartphone/tablet or internet use, has revolutionized societies worldwide. In the UK alone, according to data collected by a regulatory agency for communication (Ofcom), 95% of people aged 16 to 24 years old own a smartphone and check it on average every 12 minutes. Estimates suggest that 20% of all adults are online more than 40 hours per week. There is no doubt that digital media, most of all the internet, are becoming important aspects of our modern life. Nearly 4.57 billion people worldwide have access to the internet, according to a report published on December 31, 2019. The speed of change is astonishing, with an exponential increase in the last decade. How and at what possible costs and/or benefits can our brain and mind adapt?

Task

1. Read the following part of article about the impact of the digital revolution on human brain and behavior:
   (1) Brain plasticity related to the use of digital media.
   (2) Influences on the developing brain.
   (3) Digital media on the aging brain.
2. Search more information related to above issues.
3. Discuss the impact of technology on brain development with your group members.

Process

Step 1. The whole class is divided into several groups, with each group containing 3—4 students.

Step 2. Group members collect information by reading the article and searching the Internet.

Step 3. Discuss the above question with group member.

Step 4. Each group delivers a presentation based on the information and discussion.

Unit 11   The World Is Changing Fast

What Is Digital Economy?

The digital economy is the economic activity that results from billions of everyday online connections among people, businesses, devices, data, and processes. The backbone of the digital economy is hyperconnectivity which means growing interconnectedness of people, organizations, and machines that results from the Internet, mobile technology and the internet of things (IoT).

The digital economy is taking shape and undermining conventional notions about how businesses are structured; how firms interact; and how consumers obtain services, information, and goods.

Professor Walter Brenner of the University of St. Gallen in Switzerland states: "The aggressive use of data is transforming business models, facilitating new products and services, creating new processes, generating greater utility, and ushering in a new culture of management".

Recently, *TechCrunch*, a digital economy news site, noted, "Uber, the world's largest taxi company, owns no vehicles. Facebook, the world's most popular media owner, creates no content. Alibaba, the most valuable retailer, has no inventory. And Airbnb, the world's largest accommodation provider, owns no real estate…Something interesting is happening".

What is it about these companies that allows them to re-imagine the traditional boundaries and value proposition of their industry? What can these young companies teach you about leading a digital transformation in your industry? How will you adapt to the emerging fluidity found in traditional roles?

There are some fundamental areas of digital transformation central to business success in the digital economy.

Future of Work

People regularly work from different offices, their home, or a local coffee shop – now even more so since the pandemic has pushed remote working to the fore. While where we work has changed, we all expect the same level of connectivity experienced in the physical office. The emergence of this flexible, global enterprise requires organizations to manage a dynamic ecosystem of talent and enable next-generation digital business processes that prove to be effective, even when distributed across various places and time zones.

The 2020 pandemic has certainly fast tracked this transition in some respects, at least in the short term, but has also highlighted the need for organizations to adopt a more open minded approach to longer term digital enablement of the workforce.

Customer Experience

In the digital economy, all customers — business-to-business as well as business-to-consumer alike — want to interact with businesses when and where they want and in a fashion that is most convenient for them. Additionally, customers desire engagement with brands through experiences that are seamless, omnichannel, direct, contextual, and personalized.

It has become crucial to give all customers a personalized and unique journey right from the minute they land on a business's website, all the way to making a purchase in your store and beyond.

The Internet of Things (IoT)

The Internet of Things (IoT) connects the digital and physical worlds by collecting, measuring, and analyzing data to predict and automate business processes.

As sensor prices continue to drop, we are on the cusp of an era where everything can be connected — people, businesses, devices, and processes — to each other. The melding of the physical and digital world brings every asset into a digital domain where software dominates.

IoT solutions enable businesses to analyze data generated by sensors on physical objects in a world of intelligent, connected devices. This data can transform businesses, revealing hidden patterns and insights that can help you make more informed decisions and take action more quickly.

When an organization can understand its physical and digital asset inventory at any given moment, it can operate with precision previously unimaginable, paving the way for the ultimate lean enterprise. This will not be a nice-to-have differentiator, but an imperative for any digital business within the next two years.

Digital Supply Networks

While the global middle class is expected to expand threefold by 2030, there is increasing pressure on essential business resources, which are growing at a slower rate of 1.5 times. The answer to this mismatch lies in how enterprises securely share data in real time to enable next-generation commerce applications to thrive.

The digitization of everything is creating new intelligent digital networks of networks that fundamentally change the way commerce is managed, optimized, shared, and deployed.

Words & Expressions

hyperconnectivity/ˈhaɪpəˌkɒnekˈtɪvɪti/n. 超高速连接，超级连接
interconnectedness/ˌɪntəkəˈnɛktnəs/n. 互联性
aggressive/əˈgresɪv/adj. 好斗的，挑衅的；积极进取的；非常严重的；强烈的
ushering/ˈʌʃərɪŋ/v. 开创，引导
pandemic/pænˈdemɪk/adj.（疾病）大规模流行的；n. 大流行病
ecosystem/ˈiːkəʊsɪstəm/n. 生态系统
omnichannel/ˈɒmnɪtʃænl/n. 多渠道
imperative/ɪmˈperətɪv/adj. 极重要的，必要的；命令的，强制的；n. 重要紧急的事，必要的事；祈使语气，祈使语气动词；命令
mismatch/ˌmɪsˈmætʃ/v. 使配错；使不适当地在一起；n. 错配，搭配不当；不匹配，不协调；实力悬殊（或不公平）的比赛
boundary/ˈbaʊndri/n. 分界线，边界；界限，范围；（板球）击球超过边界线得分
deploy/dɪˈplɔɪ/v. 部署，调度；利用
threefold/ˈθriːfəʊld/adj. 三倍的；三重的，有三部分的；adv. 三重地，三倍地
digitization/ˌdɪdʒɪtaɪˈzeɪʃn/n.[计] 数字化，数位化，数码化
optimize/ˈɒptɪmaɪz/v. 优化，充分利用（形势，机会，资源）；使（数据、软件等）优化；持乐观态度（＝optimise）
inventory/ˈɪnvəntri/n. 详细目录，清单；存货，库存；盘货，存货盘点；v. 开列清单
contextual/kənˈtekstʃuəl/adj. 上下文的，与语境相关的

Notes

1. the University of St. Gallen：圣加仑大学（Universität St.Gallen）（University of St. Gallen），圣加仑大学成立于 1898 年 5 月 25 日，是一所以经济、金融、法律和社会学为主的综合性大学。学校的管理学硕士项目（Master in Management）在 2014 年《金融时报》（*Financial Times*）的全球管理学硕士排名中位列 1 位。圣加仑大学商学院在 2015 年的欧洲商学院排名中位列第 4 位。

2. *TechCrunch*：是美国科技类博客，由互联网方面的律师 Michael Arrington 建立，主要报道新兴互联网公司、评论互联网新产品、发布重大突发新闻。*TechCrunch* 目前成为关注互联网和创业的重量级博客媒体，是美国互联网产业的风向标，里面的内容几乎成为风险投资和行业投资者的投资参考。

3. Alibaba：阿里巴巴集团控股有限公司（简称为阿里巴巴集团）2021 全财年收入 7172.89 亿元，是以曾担任英语教师的马云为首的 18 人于 1999 年在浙江省杭州市创立的公司。阿里巴巴集团经营多项业务，也从关联公司的业务和服务中取得经营商业生态系统上的支援。业务和关联公司的业务包括：淘宝网、天猫、聚划算、全球速卖通、阿里巴巴国际交易市场、1688、阿里妈妈、阿里云、蚂蚁金服、菜鸟网络等。

4. Airbnb：是 AirBed and Breakfast（Air-b-n-b）的缩写，中文名为爱彼迎。爱彼迎

是一家联系旅游人士和家有空房出租的房主的服务型网站,它可以为用户提供多样的住宿信息。2011 年,爱彼迎服务令人难以置信地增长了 800%。爱彼迎成立于 2008 年 8 月,总部设在美国加利福尼亚州旧金山。爱彼迎是一个旅行房屋租赁社区,用户可通过网络或手机应用程序发布、搜索度假房屋租赁信息并完成在线预定程序。据官网显示以及媒体报道,其社区平台在 191 个国家、65 000 个城市为旅行者们提供数以百万计的独特入住选择,不管是公寓、别墅、城堡还是树屋。爱彼迎被《时代周刊》称为"住房中的 EBay"。

5. The Internet of Things(IoT):这个专业词组最早由英国人 Kevin Ashton 在 1999 年提出。但物联网的概念则可追溯到 1995 年比尔·盖茨的《未来之路》(*The Road Ahead*)一书。物联网(Internet of Things)是指设备到互联网的连接。汽车、厨房电器,甚至心脏监视器都可以通过物联网连接。

I. Getting the Message

Read the questions and complete the answers according to the text.

1. What is digital economy?
_____

2. What's Walter Brenner idea?
_____

3. By what does (IoT) connect the digital and physical worlds?
_____

4. How will you adapt to the emerging fluidity found in traditional roles?
_____

5. How has the digital economy affected you?
_____

II. Languages Focus

A. *Match the following words in left with their explanations in right.*

1. aggressive	a. an epidemic that is geographically widespread; occurring throughout a region or even throughout the world
2. pandemic	b. having or showing determination and energetic pursuit of your ends
3. imperative	c. a mood that expresses an intention to influence the listener's behavior
4. mismatch	d. match badly; match two objects or people that do not go together
5. deploy	e. three times as great or many

6. threefold   f. place troops or weapons in battle formation
7. digitization   g. conversion of analog information into digital information
8. optimize   h. make optimal; get the most out of; use best
9. inventory   i. relating to or determined by or in context
10. contextual   j. a detailed list of all the items in stock

B. *Fill in the blanks with the words or expressions given below. Change the form where necessary.*

| ushering | aggressive | optimize | imperative | boundary |
| deploy | mismatch | contextual | inventory | threefold |

1. The key is to create a critical mass of leaders to _____ in change.
2. His style of argument in meetings is not so much _____ as pertinacious.
3. We allocate our resources effectively to _____ business potential.
4. The _____ mood is a kind of grammatical phenomenon.
5. Scientists continue to push back the _____ of knowledge.
6. It is a job in which a variety of professional skills will be _____.
7. Their marriage was a _____ they had little in common.
8. _____ clues can help one to find the meaning.
9. Is the shop _____ verified before the commencement of a sales promotion?
10. A _____ cord is not quickly broken.

III. Translation

Translate the following sentences into Chinese.

1. The digital economy is the economic activity that results from billions of everyday online connections among people, businesses, devices, data, and processes.

_____

2. The digital economy is taking shape and undermining conventional notions about how businesses are structured; how firms interact; and how consumers obtain services, information, and goods.

_____
_____

3. The aggressive use of data is transforming business models, facilitating new products and services, creating new processes, generating greater utility, and ushering in a new culture of management.

_____
_____

4. The world's largest taxi company, owns no vehicles. Facebook, the world's most popular media owner, creates no content. Alibaba, the most valuable retailer, has no inventory.

And Airbnb, the world's largest accommodation provider, owns no real estate...Something interesting is happening.

5. The Internet of Things (IoT) connects the digital and physical worlds by collecting, measuring, and analyzing data to predict and automate business processes.

Ⅳ. Discussion

ChatGPT is a language model developed by Open AI that can understand and communicate with human language. It has been trained on large amounts of text data and can generate different text types and code.

Simply put, ChatGPT is a computer program that can speak and understand like a human. It has learned many words and sentences from books and articles, so it knows how to combine words into sentences. It can complete given text prompts, answer questions, and even create new text. It can be fine-tuned for specific purposes, such as answering questions, translating languages, and summarizing text.

Now please the next questions:

1. How will ChatGPT benefit students?
2. How will ChatGPT negatively affect students?
3. What are the benefits of ChatGPT for teachers?
4. What are the negative effects of ChatGPT on teachers?
5. What are the practical applications of ChatGPT in education?

The Future of Information and Education

For centuries, education has consisted primarily of students sitting before an instructor in a classroom setting, learning via lecture and rote memorization from textbooks. It wasn't a perfect system, but it served its purpose as a generally effective way to educate the masses.

In recent years, however, educational technology has seen an incredible evolution, dramatically upgrading the way teachers teach and students learn. First-generation advances are already in use in classrooms around the world, and the future promises even more. Here are some emerging technological trends.

Virtual Reality

Imagine you're a sixth-grader assigned to write a class report about African elephants.

Virtual reality technology, initially designed for video games, would make such an assignment easier — and a lot more fun — by placing you in the middle of an incredibly realistic elephant herd. Without leaving your classroom, you would see up close what African elephants look like, what they eat, how they interact, and more.

Virtual reality provides a revolutionary educational opportunity in that it can take students anywhere they would like to go around the world, to galaxies beyond, and even through time itself. This kind of immersive experience facilitates learning through interaction — a dramatic step forward from traditional book learning. Best of all, it's appropriate for teaching everything from history to science to literature.

Holographic Technology

Like virtual reality, holographic technology is able to give students a more immersive educational experience by creating three-dimensional images of people, places, and objects. Through holograms, which use light beams to work their magic, students might be able to view medieval London, study Triceratops, or watch Abraham Lincoln deliver the Gettysburg Address, all in the comfort of the classroom.

The almost limitless capabilities of holographic technology can make learning more fun and exciting and can increase the amount of information students are able to absorb and retain on a given topic. In this way, holographic technology makes an effective complement to virtual reality, in terms of instructional content and stimulating student interest.

Cloud Computing

Cloud computing has proved to be a real groundbreaker by providing easy accessibility to information and courseware stored on remote cloud servers anytime and anyplace. All you need is an Internet-connected device, and the world's collective knowledge is literally at your fingertips.

The benefits of app-enabled cloud computing to education are tremendous. One of the most important is freedom. Users can collaborate with instructors and fellow students at any time, no matter where the user might be. Cloud computing also makes available a virtual library of class materials, including textbooks and curricula, for downloading and use at any time. Data storage issues become a thing of the past.

Adaptive Learning

Not everyone learns at the same pace or as effectively through traditional educational methods. As a result, many students are left behind on the education continuum, which can have negative lifelong consequences. Adaptive learning aids students by incorporating unique technologies to adapt educational materials to a student's individual needs.

What makes adaptive learning effective is the use of learning analytics based on data gathered from students. It uses these analytics to determine how an individual learns best, then adapts the learning materials accordingly over the course of the class. If it finds that a person learns better by watching videos rather than reading a textbook, for example, it will incorporate more videos into the curriculum.

3D Printing

Many people learn better when they have something tangible to work with, a physical object they can hold in their hands and get their head round. Low-cost 3D printers now make that possible.

3D printers are able to manufacture almost anything a student can imagine, whether it's for a second grader who has designed her own wildly imaginative race car or for a veterinary student in need of artificial dog bones on which to practice surgery. 3D printers have proved so effective at on-the-spot manufacturing that they have been used at the International Space Station.

In addition to meeting students where their imaginations crest, 3D printers help make learning a more interactive experience by encouraging students to conceive something, then manufacture it. In so doing, learning goes from conceptual to concrete in a matter of minutes.

Collaborative Learning Technology

Thanks to the ubiquitousness of cell phones, tablets, and other digital devices, it's never been easier to connect with the world around us. Personal devices can be used to facilitate a connected form of learning that encourages students to discuss topics with peers in and outside the classroom, share their knowledge, and educate each other.

Words & Expressions

galaxies/'gæləksi/*n.* 星系；银河，银河系（the Galaxy）；群英，人才荟萃

evolution/iːvə'luːʃ(ə)n/*n.* 进化（论）；演变，发展；（气体的）释放，（热量的）散发；队形变换，位置变换

interact/ˌɪntər'ækt/*v.* 相互交流，互动；相互作用，相互影响

immersive/ɪ'mɜːsɪv/*adj.* （计算机系统或图像）沉浸式虚拟现实的

holographic/hɒlə'græfɪk/*adj.* 全息的；全部手写的

holograms/'hɒləgræm/*n.* [激光] 全息图；全息照相；综合衍射图（hologram 的复数）

Triceratops/traɪ'serətɒps/*n.* 三角恐龙

curricula/kə'rɪkjʊlə/*n.* 课程（curriculum 的复数形式）

continuum/kən'tɪnjuəm/*n.* 连续统；连续统一体；闭联集

tangible/'tændʒəb(ə)l/*adj.* 明确的，真实的；可触摸的，可感知的；*n.* 可触知的东西

veterinary/'vetərəneri/*adj.* 兽医的；*n.* 兽医

crest/krest/*n.* （山）顶，（浪）峰；（家族、城镇、机构等作为标记的）饰章，徽章；鸟冠，羽冠；（昔日士兵帽子上的）羽饰；*v.* 到达山顶（或浪峰）；到达洪峰，达到顶点；（波浪）形成峰；饰有（或系有）冠状饰物（be crested with）

conceptual/kən'septʃuəl/*adj.* 概念的，观念的

Collaborative/kəˈlæbərətɪv/*adj.* 合作的，协作的
ubiquitous/juːˈbɪkwɪtəs/*adj.* 普遍存在的，无所不在的

Notes

1. Abraham Lincoln：亚伯拉罕·林肯（Abraham Lincoln，1809—1865 年），美国政治家、战略家、第 16 任总统。林肯是首位共和党籍总统，在任期间主导废除了美国黑人奴隶制。

2. the Gettysburg Address：葛底斯堡演说发表于美国南北战争期间，是美国前总统林肯最著名的演说，也是美国历史上被人引用最多的演说。1863 年 11 月 19 日，林肯在宾夕法尼亚州的葛底斯堡的葛底斯堡国家公墓揭幕式上发表此次演说，哀悼在葛底斯堡之役中阵亡的将士。

3. cloud computing：云计算，指将各种服务存储在互联网上供用户临时使用的计算机应用模型。

4. 3D printers：3D 打印机，简称为 3DP，是一位名为恩里科·迪尼（Enrico Dini）的发明家设计的一种神奇的打印机，不仅可以"打印"一幢完整的建筑，甚至可以在航天飞船中给宇航员打印任何所需的物品的形状。但是 3D 打印出的是物体的模型，并不能打印出物体的功能。

Exercises

I. Comprehension of the Text

Read the text and answer the following questions. Write the answers on the lines.

1. What opportunities does virtual reality offer for education?
_____

2. In what ways does holographic technology help students?
_____

3. What are the benefits of app-enabled cloud computing to education?
_____

4. What makes adaptive learning effective?
_____

5. What can 3D printer make for a student?
_____

II. Main Details Comprehension

Directions: *In this section, you are going to read a passage with ten statements attached to it. Each statement contains information given in one of the paragraphs. Identify the paragraph from which the information is derived. You may choose a paragraph more than* *once. Each paragraph is marked with a letter.*

Do In-Class Exams Make Students Study Harder?

Research suggests they may study more broadly for the unexpected rather than search for answers.

A) I have always been a poor test-taker. So it may seem rather strange that I have returned to college to finish the degree I left undone some four decades ago. I am making my way through Columbia University, surrounded by students who quickly supply the verbal answer while I am still processing the question.

B) Since there is no way for me to avoid exams, I am currently questioning what kind are the most taxing and ultimately beneficial. I have already sweated through numerous in-class midterms and finals, and now I have a professor who issues take-home ones. I was excited when I learned this, figuring I had a full week to do the research, read the texts, and write it all up. In fact, I was still rewriting my midterm the morning it was due. To say I had lost the thread is putting it mildly.

C) As I was suffering through my week of anxiety, overthinking the material and guessing my grasp of it, I did some of my own polling among students and professors. David Eisenbach, who teaches a popular class on U.S. presidents at Columbia, prefers the in-class variety. He believes students ultimately learn more and encourages them to form study groups. "That way they socialize over history outside the class, which wouldn't happen without the pressure of an in-class exam," he explained, "Furthermore, in-class exams force students to learn how to perform under pressure, and essential work skill".

D) He also says there is less chance of cheating with the in-class variety. In 2012, 125 students at Harvard were caught up in a scandal when it was discovered they had cheated on a take-home exam for a class entitled "Introduction To Congress". Some colleges have what they call an "honor code", though if you are smart enough to get into these schools, you are either smart enough to get around any codes or hopefully, too ethical to consider doing so. As I sat blocked and clueless for two solid days, I momentarily wondered if I couldn't just call an expert on the subject matter which I was tackling, or someone who took the class previously, to get me going.

E) Following the Harvard scandal, Mary Miller, the former dean of students at Yale, made an impassioned appeal to her school's professors to refrain from take-hone exams. "Students risk health and well being, as well as performance in other end-of-term work, when faculty offers take-home exams without clear, time-limited boundaries," she told me. "Research now shows that regular quizzes, short essays, and other assignments over the course of a term better enhance learning and retention".

F) Most college professors agree the kind of exam they choose largely depends on the subject. A quantitative-based one, for example, is unlikely to be sent home, where one could ask their older brothers and sisters to help. Vocational-type classes, such as computer science or journalism, on the other hand, are often more research-oriented and lend themselves to take-home testing. Chris Koch, who teaches "History of Broadcast Journalism" at Montgomery Community College in Rockville, Maryland, points out that reporting is about investigation rather than the memorization of minute details. "In my field, it's not what you know — it's what you know how to find out," says Koch. "There is way too much information, and more coming all the time, for anyone to remember. I want my students to search out the answers to questions by using all the resources available to them".

G) Students' test-form preferences vary, too, often depending on the subject and course difficulty. "I prefer take-home essays because it is then really about the writing, so you have time to edit and do more research," says Elizabeth Dresser, a junior at Barnard. Then there is the stress factor. Francesca Haass, a senior at Middlebury, says, "I find the in-class ones are more stressful in the short term, but there is immediate relief as you swallow information like mad, and then you get to forget it all. Take-homes require thoughtful engagement which can lead to longer term stress as there is never a moment when the time is up." Meanwhile, Olivia Rubin, a sophomore at Emory, says she hardly even considers take-homes true exams. "If you understand the material and have the ability to articulate (说出) your thoughts, they should be a breeze".

H) How students ultimately handle stress may depend on their personal test-taking abilities. There are people who always wait until the last minute, and make it much harder than it needs to be. And then there those who, not knowing what questions are coming at them, and having no resources to refer to, can freeze. And then there are we rare folks who fit both those descriptions.

I) Yes, my advanced age must factor into the equation (等式), in part because of my inability to access the information as quickly. As another returning student at Columbia, Kate Marber, told me, "We are learning not only all this information, but essentially how to learn again. Our fellow students have just come out of high school. A lot has changed since we were last in school".

J) If nothing else, the situation has given my college son and me something to share, When I asked his opinion on this matter, he responded, "I like in-class exams because the time is already reserved, as opposed to using my free time at home to work on a test," he responded. It seems to me that a compromise would be receiving the exam questions a day or two in advance, and then doing the actual test in class the ticking clock overhead.

K) Better yet, how about what one Hunter College professor reportedly did recently for her final exam: She encouraged the class not to stress or even study, promising that, "It is going to be a piece of cake." When the students came in, sharpened pencils in hand, there was not a bluebook in sight. Rather, they saw a large chocolate cake and they each were given a slice.

_____1. Elderly students find it hard to keep up with the rapid changes in education.

_____2. Some believe take-home exams may affect students' performance in other courses.

_____3. Certain professors believe in-class exams are ultimately more helpful to students.

_____4. In-class exams are believed to discourage cheating in exams.

_____5. The author was happy to learn she could do some exams at home.

_____6. Students who put off their work until the last moment often find the exams more difficult than they actually are.

_____7. Different students may prefer different types of exams.

_____8. Most professors agree whether to give an in-class or a take-home exam depends on type of course being taught.

_____9. The author dropped out of college some forty years ago.

_____10. Some students think take-home exams will eat up their free time.

Ⅲ. Translation

Translate the five following sentences into English, using the words or expressions given in brackets.

1．由于我无法避免考试，我目前在思考哪种考试是最具挑战性和最终有益的。（taxing）

_____

2．研究表明，他们可能更倾向于广泛学习以应对意外情况，而不是寻找答案。（unexpected）

_____

3．当我坐在那里两天却毫无进展时，我瞬间想知道我是否可以直接找一个熟悉这个问题的专家，或者找一个之前上过这门课的人来帮助我。（blocked and clueless）

_____

4．大多数大学教授都认为他们选择的考试类型在很大程度上取决于学科。例如，以数量为基础的考试不太可能被带回家，因为这样人们就可以请他们的兄弟姐妹帮忙。另外还有更注重研究能力的职业类课程，如计算机科学或新闻学也同样。（research-oriented）

_____

5．学生最终如何处理压力可能取决于他们个人的考试能力。总有些人等拖延到最后一刻，给事情增加不必要的困难。（ultimately）

_____

Part C

Product Manual
产品说明书的翻译策略 1——名词化和定语后置

在英语说明书翻译中，名词化和定语后置是两种常见的语法结构调整策略，它们通常用于强调特定的概念或使语句更加简练。在翻译说明书时需要调整语言使其更符合中文的表达方式，更易于读者理解。

（一）名词化 (Nominalization)

在翻译名词化时，理解原文的具体上下文和意图是关键，以确保翻译能够有效地传达产品说明书的信息，因此在翻译时可以采用以下策略：

（1）保留名词形式。如果原文中的名词化术语在中文中也有相应的专业术语，并且保留原文能够更好地传达意思，可以考虑直接保留名词形式。例如：

Data integration
数据集成

（2）翻译为名词短语。将名词化的术语翻译为中文名词短语，使之更符合中文的表达方式。例如：

User engagement
用户参与

（3）使用动词或动名词形式。将名词化的术语翻译为中文中的动词或动名词形式，使之更符合中文语境。例如：

Performance optimization
性能优化

（4）根据上下文选择合适表达。在翻译时要考虑整个说明书的语境，选择最符合情境的翻译方式，确保翻译的结果既准确又自然。例如：

Efficiency enhancement
提升效能

（二）定语后置（Attributive Postposition）

在英文说明书中，定语后置的结构常见，尤其是在描述产品特性、功能或规格时。在翻译时，一般要将原文中的形容词短语放在名词后面，以保持中文语序；另外，要注意保持句子结构的清晰，确保读者能够准确理解。

（1）with 结构的翻译。

A system with advanced features
具有先进特性的系统

（2）定语从句的翻译。

The software, which is user-friendly, …
用户友好的软件…

（3）介词短语后置的翻译。

A device for data storage
数据存储的设备

这些策略的灵活运用有助于保持翻译文本的自然度和流畅度，同时使得中文读者更容易理解。在使用这些策略时，翻译者需要根据上下文和句子的整体结构来决定最合适的表达方式。

1. *Read the following paragraphs and then answer the questions.*

User's manual of GoPro HERO9 Black

Setting the Screen Orientation

You can easily switch between landscape and portrait shots by rotating your camera. HERO9 Black can even capture photos and videos right-side up when it's mounted upside down.

The orientation is locked in when you press the Shutter button ⃝. If your camera tilts during recording, like on a roller coaster, your footage will tilt with it. You'll capture every twist and turn.

LOCKING THE ORIENTATION
HERO9 Black lets you lock the screen in landscape or portrait orientation. This is especially useful when you're using body and handheld mounts. That's when accidentally shooting in the wrong orientation is mostly likely to happen.

Swipe down on the rear screen to access the Dashboard.
1. Turn your camera to the orientation you want.
2. Tap 🧭 on the Dashboard.

The screen is now locked and will match the orientation of your camera.

Heads Up: Locking the screen in this way will only work when the Orientation is set to All (default) in Preferences.

SETTING LANDSCAPE LOCK
You can also set your GoPro to record only in landscape orientation.

Swipe down on the rear screen to access the Dashboard.
1. Swipe left and tap Preferences > Displays > Orientation.
2. Switch from Auto (default) to Landscape.

Your GoPro will record right-side up whether your camera is right-side up or upside down. You can also lock the orientation on the Dashboard.

(1) What feature of the HERO9 Black allows users to easily switch between landscape and portrait shots?

(2) How does the camera handle capturing photos and videos when mounted upside down?

(3) What happens to the footage if the camera tilts during recording?

(4) What is the purpose of locking the screen orientation in HERO9 Black?

(5) How is the Dashboard accessed on the HERO9 Black?

2. *Map reading and translation.*

With your camera off and battery removed, insert the SD card into the card slot with the label facing the battery compartment.

You can eject the card by pressing it into the slot with your fingernail.

❶

Connect your camera to a USB charger or computer using the included USB-C cable.

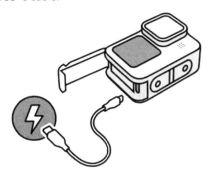

It takes about 3 hours for the battery to fully charge. The camera status light will turn off when it's done. To learn more, see *Battery Information (page 113)*.

❷

Unplug the cable and shut the door when charging is complete. Be sure the door latch is closed and locked before using your camera.

❸

DURATION CAPTURE
Use duration capture to set how long your GoPro records before it stops. It's available in Video, TimeWarp, Time Lapse, and Night Lapse modes in increments from 15 seconds to 3 hours.

❹

WHITE BALANCE
White Balance lets you adjust the color temperature of videos and photos to optimize for cool or warm lighting conditions. Scroll between the options to see a live preview of each setting, and then tap the one you want.

Options for this setting are Auto (default), 2300K, 2800K, 3200K, 4000K, 4500K, 5000K, 5500K, 6000K, 6500K, and Native. Lower values will give you warmer tones.

You can also choose Auto to let your GoPro set the White Balance or the Native setting to create a minimally color-corrected file that allows for more precise adjustments in post-production.

❺

Workshop

Background

Today, with the development of the technology and the diversity of the mass media, advertising has influenced us pervasively in our daily life. However, whatever the promotive strategies advertising takes, language is the main carrier of message all along, as *The Language of Advertising*, by Vestergaard & Schroder, says, "Advertising takes many forms, but in most of them language is of crucial importance." Advertising language is a style of immediate impact and rapid persuasion. The point of an advertisement is to persuade you of the merits of a particular product or service, in order that you will take out some of your money. What are the unique features that separate advertising language from any other kind of language? How can you design an effective and impressive advertising message?

Task

You are going to collect and analyze various advertisements from different media. Then, summarize the features of advertising language. Finally, you may try to design an advertising message for one product in our daily life.

Process

Step 1. Form groups of 5－6 students. Complete the task in groups.

Step 2. Collect as many advertisements as possible from different newspapers, magazines, radio, TV, and the Internet.

Step 3. Analyze various advertisements and summarize the features of advertising language.

Step 4. Select one product around us and try to design an effective and impressive advertising message for it of your own.

Step 5. Report your findings about advertising language and your own advertising message in written form and make an oral presentation in class as well.

Unit 12　ChatGPT

ChatGPT Is a Tipping Point for AI

  Less than two weeks ago, OpenAI released ChatGPT, a powerful new chatbot that can communicate in plain English using an updated version of its AI system. While versions of GPT have been around for a while, this model has crossed a threshold: It's genuinely useful for a wide range of tasks, from creating software to generating business ideas to writing a wedding toast. While previous generations of the system could technically do these things, the quality of the outputs was much lower than that produced by an average human. The new model is much better, often startlingly so.

  At first glance, ChatGPT might seem like a clever toy. On a technical level, it doesn't work differently than previous AI systems, it's just better at what it does. Since its release, Twitter has been flooded with examples of people using it to strange and absurd ends: writing weight-loss plans and children's books, and offering advice on how to remove a peanut butter sandwich from a VCR in the style of the *King James Bible*.

  There are other reasons to be skeptical besides the unusual use cases. Most pointedly, despite years of hype, AI notoriously only sort of works in most applications outside of data analysis. It's pretty good at steering cars, but sometimes it rams into another vehicle. Mostly, it provides good answers to queries, but sometimes it seems to make up the results entirely.

  But a deeper exploration reveals much more potential. And the more you look, the more you see what has changed with this model — and why it seems like a tipping point.

  ChatGPT, now open to everyone, has made an important transition. Until now, AI has primarily been aimed at problems where failure is expensive, not at tasks where occasional failure is cheap and acceptable — or even ones in which experts can easily separate failed cases from successful ones. A car that occasionally gets into accidents is intolerable. But an AI artist that draws some great pictures, but also some bad ones, is perfectly acceptable. Applying AI to the creative and expressive tasks (writing marketing copy) rather than dangerous and repetitive ones (driving a forklift) opens a new world of applications.

  What are those applications, and why do they matter so much?

  First, not only can this AI produce paragraphs of solidly written English (or French, or Mandarin, or whatever language you choose) with a high degree of sophistication, it can also create blocks of computer code on command. To give you an idea of what this looks like, I introduced my undergraduate entrepreneurship students to the new AI system, and before I was done talking, one of my students had used it to create the code for a startup prototype using code libraries they had never seen before. They completed a four-hour project in less than an hour.

This is a major change. Massive increases in speed have been seen in a randomized trial of AI code tools. One good programmer can now legitimately do what not so long ago was the work of many, and people who have never programmed will soon be able to create workable code as well.

Second, it has an incredible capacity to perform different kinds of writing with more significant implications than might be initially apparent. The use of AI in writing can greatly increase the productivity of businesses in a variety of industries. By utilizing AI's ability to quickly and accurately generate written content, businesses can save time and resources, allowing them to focus on other important tasks. This is particularly beneficial for industries such as marketing and advertising, consulting, and finance, where high-quality written materials are essential for communicating with clients and stakeholders. Additionally, AI can also be useful for industries such as journalism and publishing, where it can help generate articles and other written content with speed and accuracy. Overall, the use of AI in writing will greatly benefit businesses by allowing them to produce more written materials in less time.

An AI wrote the previous paragraph. It also actively revised it in response to my criticism to improve the material. In tests of whether it could make other parts of my job as a professor easier, it took seconds to write a reasonable course syllabus, class assignments, grading criteria, even lecture notes that could be potentially useful with some editing.

A final reason why this will be transformative: The limits of the current language model are completely unknown. Using the public mode, people have used ChatGPT to do basic consulting reports, write lectures, produce code that generates novel art, generate ideas, and much more. Using specialized data, it's possible to build each customer their own customized AI that predicts what they need, responds to them personally, and remembers all their interactions. This isn't science fiction. It is entirely doable with the technology just released.

So, after reading this article, I hope you immediately start experimenting with AI (for free, here) and start high-level discussions about the implications: for your company, your industry, and the rest of the world. Integrating AI into our work — and our lives — will bring sweeping changes. Right now, we're just scratching the surface of what those might be.

Words & Expressions

in plain English 用平白的语言（或文字）
threshold/'θreʃhəʊld/ n. 门槛，门口；阈，界，起始点；开端，起点
toast/təʊst/ n. 干杯，祝酒，敬酒；烤面包片，吐司；v. 为⋯举杯敬酒；烤（尤指面包）

startling/'stɑːtlɪŋ/*adj.* 惊人的，让人震惊的；（颜色）极鲜亮的
at first glance 乍一看（指对某事物进行初步观察或评估时的第一印象）
skeptical/'skeptɪkl/*adj.* 怀疑的
pointedly/'pɔɪntɪdli/*adv.* 明确地；尖锐地，直言不讳地
hype/haɪp/*n.*（电视、广播等中言过其实的）促销广告，促销讨论；*v.* 夸张地宣传（某事物）
notorious/nəʊ'tɔːriəs/*adj.* 声名狼藉的，臭名昭著的
ram/ræm/*v.* 和⋯相撞，撞击；塞进，挤进
forklift/'fɔːklɪft/*n.* 叉车，铲车
entrepreneurship/ˌɒntrəprə'nɜːʃɪp/*n.* 企业家（身份、行为）；企业家精神
prototype/'prəʊtətaɪp/*n.* 原型，雏形，最初形态
legitimate/lɪ'dʒɪtɪmət/*adj.* 正当合理的，合情合理的；合法的，法律认可的，法定的
implication/ˌɪmplɪ'keɪʃn/*n.* 可能的影响（或作用、结果）；含意，暗指；（被）牵连，牵涉
stakeholder/'steɪkhəʊldə(r)/*n.*（某组织、工程、体系等的）参与人，参与方；有权益关系者
syllabus/'sɪləbəs/*n.* 教学大纲
doable/'duːəbl/*adj.* 可做，可行
sweeping/'swiːpɪŋ/*adj.* 影响广泛的，大范围的，根本性的；（过分）笼统的，一概而论的

Notes

1. OpenAI：OpenAI 是美国一个人工智能研究实验室，由非营利组织 OpenAI Inc. 和其营利组织子公司 OpenAI LP 所组成。OpenAI 进行 AI 研究的目的是促进和发展友好的人工智能，使人类整体受益。OpenAI 系统运行在微软基于 Azure 的超级计算平台上。该组织于 2015 年由萨姆·阿尔特曼、里德·霍夫曼、杰西卡·利文斯顿、埃隆·马斯克、伊尔亚·苏茨克维、沃伊切赫·扎伦巴、彼得·泰尔等人在旧金山成立。

2. ChatGPT：全称聊天生成预训练转换器（Chat Generative Pre-trained Transformer），是 OpenAI 开发的人工智能聊天机器人程序，于 2022 年 11 月推出。ChatGPT 目前仍以文字方式交互，而除了可以用人类自然对话方式来交互，还可以用于较为复杂的语言工作，包括自动生成文本、自动问答、自动摘要等多种任务。如在自动文本生成方面，ChatGPT 可以根据输入的文本自动生成类似的文本（剧本、歌曲、企划等）；在自动问答方面，ChatGPT 可以根据输入的问题自动生成答案。还有编写和调试计算机程序的能力。在推广期间，所有人可以免费注册，并在登录后免费使用 ChatGPT 与 AI 机器人对话。

Exercises

I. Getting the Message

Read the questions and complete the answers according to the text.

1. How is the new version of GPT different from the old ones?
   _____

2. What are some drawbacks of AI mentioned in the article?
   _____

3. Which problems has AI primarily aimed at?
   _____

4. What tasks does AI help the author accomplish?
   _____

5. What are advantages of using specialized data in the use of ChatGPT?
   _____

II. Languages Focus

A. *Match the following words in left with their explanations in right.*

1. notorious	a.	a possible effect or result of an action or a decision
2. sweeping	b.	the floor or ground at the bottom of a doorway, considered as the entrance to a building or room
3. implication	c.	the first design of sth. from which other forms are copied or developed
4. startling	d.	for which there is a fair and acceptable reason
5. legitimate	e.	having an important effect on a large part of sth.
6. entrepreneurship	f.	well known for being bad
7. stakeholder	g.	the state of being an entrepreneur, or the activities associated with being an entrepreneur
8. prototype	h.	extremely unusual and surprising
9. skeptical	i.	having doubts that a claim or statement is true or that sth. Will happen
10. threshold	j.	a person or company that is involved in a particular organization, project, system, etc., especially because they have invested money in it

B. *Fill in the blanks with the words or expressions given below. Change the form where necessary.*

startling	skeptical	threshold	legitimate	sweeping
ram	notorious	prototype	stakeholder	implication

during training. The less familiar it is then the higher the text's perplexity is, meaning "it's more likely to be human-written", Mr. Tian said.

It then measures burstiness by scanning the text to see how variable it is. For example, does the text have a mix of short versus long sentences? Or does the writing appear to be more levelled and uniform?

"If you plot precisely over time, a human-written article will vary a lot," Mr. Tian said. "It would go up and down, it would have sudden spikes".

He is still working on improving GPTZero, but he has released a beta version for public use. In a tweet, he demonstrated how the app can successfully sniff out the difference between an essay published in *the New Yorker* magazine versus a letter written by ChatGPT.

He said he has also since tested it out by feeding the app BBC articles written by journalists, versus articles written by ChatGPT using the same headline as a prompt. (Mr. Tian formerly worked with the BBC's investigations unit). He said the app successfully guessed the difference between the texts with a less than 2% false positive rate.

Since its launch, Mr. Tian's app has been used by thousands of people. He said he has since been contacted by teachers and university admissions officers from around the world who are interested in how it works.

While GPTZero was created to combat academic plagiarism, Mr. Tian said he sees apps like his being used to address other issues that will come with the rising popularity of artificial intelligence such as online disinformation campaigns.

He is, however, not opposed to artificial intelligence — in fact, he said he was very excited about its emergence, and has found it useful in helping him to write computer code and solve other problems. But he said it was important to develop safeguards for any new technology as it gives its use a sense of credibility.

But he said that, above all, the popularity of his app speaks to "a human urge to know the truth".

Words & Expressions

packed/pækt/*adj.* 异常拥挤的，挤满人的；有大量…的，…极多的

thesis/'θiːsɪs/*n.* 论文；毕业论文，学位论文

display/dɪ'spleɪ/*v.* 陈列，展出；显露，表现（特性或情感等）；*n.* 陈列，展览；展示；表演；（特性、情感或能力的）表现，表露

sinister/'sɪnɪstə(r)/*adj.* 邪恶的，险恶的，不祥的，有凶兆的

malware/'mælwɛə/*n.* 恶意软件

perplexity/pə'pleksəti/*n.* 困惑，迷惘；难以理解的事物，疑团

scan/skæn/*v.* 粗略地读，浏览，翻阅；细看，察看，审视，端详；*n.* 扫描检查

versus/'vɜːsəs/*prep.* （表示两队或双方对阵）对，诉，对抗；（比较两种不同想法、选择等）与…相对，与…相比

level /ˈlevl/ v. 使平坦，使平整；摧毁，夷平（建筑物或树林）；使相等，使平等，使相似

spike /spaɪk/ n. 尖状物，尖头，尖刺；猛增，急升；穗，穗状花序；v. 用尖物刺入（或扎破）；拒绝发表，阻止…传播，阻挠；迅速升值，急剧增值

demonstrate /ˈdemənstreɪt/ v. 证明，论证，说明；表现，显露

sniff /snɪf/ v.（吸着气）嗅，闻；抽鼻子（尤指哭泣、患感冒等时出声地用鼻子吸气）；抱怨；不以为然地说；n. 感觉，察觉；吸气（声），抽鼻子（声）；嗅，闻；微小的可能性

prompt /prɒmpt/ n. 提词，提示；提示符；v. 促使，导致，激起；鼓励，题型，提醒（某人说话）；adj. 迅速的，及时的；adv. 准时地

combat /ˈkɒmbæt/ v. 防止，减轻；战斗，与…搏斗；n. 搏斗，打仗，战斗

plagiarism /ˈpleɪdʒərɪzəm/ n. 抄袭，剽窃；剽窃作品

disinformation /ˌdɪsˌɪnfəˈmeɪʃn/ n.（尤指政府机构故意发布的）虚假信息，假消息

Notes

1. Princeton University：普林斯顿大学，简称普林斯顿，位于美国新泽西州的普林斯顿市，是世界著名的私立研究型大学，也是常春藤盟校成员，与哈佛大学、耶鲁大学齐名。普林斯顿大学成立于1746年，前身是"新泽西学院（College of New Jersey）"，是九所在美国革命前成立的殖民地学院之一，同时也是美国第四古老的高等教育机构。学校在1747年移至纽瓦克，最终在1756年搬到了现在的普林斯顿市，并于1896年正式更名为"普林斯顿大学"。在流行文化中，普林斯顿大学往往令人联想到阿尔伯特·爱因斯坦、艾伦·图灵、约翰·纳什等著名学者。

2. Toronto：多伦多，简称多市，又名图麟都，是加拿大安大略省首府，加拿大最大城市。多伦多坐落在安大略湖西北岸的南安大略地区。多伦多市是大多伦多地区的心脏地区，也是安大略省南部人口稠密区（称作金马蹄地区）的一部分。作为加拿大的经济中心，多伦多是一个世界级城市，也是世界上最大的金融中心之一。

3. GPTZero：GPTZero是一个网站，其主要功能是预测文档是否由大型语言模型编写，提供句子、段落和文档级别的预测。GPTZero作为一个分类模型，主要作用是识别英语文章中哪些由人工写作、哪些由人工智能生成。

Exercises

I. Comprehension of the Text

Read the text and answer the following questions. Write the answers on the lines.

1. What happened when students were asked to distinguish what had been written by a human and what had been generated by AI?

2. When and where did Edward Tian develop GPTZero?

3. What does GPTZero evaluate when it analyses an article?

4. According to Edward Tian, what is the feature of an article written by a human being?

5. What was Edward Tian's initial purpose of creating GPTZero?

II. Main Details Comprehension

Directions: *In this section, you are going to read a passage with ten statements attached to it. Each statement contains information given in one of the paragraphs. Identify the paragraph from which the information is derived. You may choose a paragraph more than once. Each paragraph is marked with a letter.*

How Work Will Change When Most of us Live to 100

A) Today in the United States there are 72,000 centenarians (百岁老人). Worldwide, probably 450,000. If current trends continue, then by 2050 there will be more than a million in the US alone. According to the work of Professor James Vaupel and his co-researchers, 50% of babies born in the US in 2007 have a life expectancy of 104 or more. Broadly the same holds for the UK, Germany, France, Italy and Canada, and for Japan 50% of 2007 babies can expect to live to 107.

B) Understandably, there are concerns about what this means for public finances given the associated health and pension challenges. These challenges are real, and society urgently needs to address them. But it is also important to look at the wider picture of what happens when so many people live for 100 years. It is a mistake to simply equate longevity (长寿) with issues of old age. Longer lives have implications for all of life, not just the end of it.

C) Our view is that if many people are living for longer, and are healthier for longer, then this will result in an inevitable redesign of work and life. When people live longer, they are not only older for longer, but also younger for longer. There is some truth in the saying that "70 is the new 60" or "40 the new 30." If you age more slowly over a longer time period, then you are in some sense younger for longer.

D) But the changes go further than that. Take, for instance, the age at which people make commitments such as buying a house, getting married, having children, or starting a career; These are all fundamental commitments that are now occurring later in life. In 1962, 50% of Americans were married by age 21. By 2014, that milestone (里程碑) had shifted to age 29.

E) While there are numerous factors behind these shifts, one factor is surely a growing realization for the young that they are going to live longer. Options are more valuable the longer they can be held. So if you believe you will live longer, then options become more valuable, and early commitment becomes less attractive. The result is that the commitments that previously characterized the beginning of adulthood are now being delayed, and new patterns of behavior and a new stage of life are emerging for those in their twenties.

F) Longevity also pushes back the age of retirement, and not only for financial reasons. Yes, unless people are prepared to save a lot more, our calculations suggest that if you are now in your mid-40s, then you are likely to work until your early 70s; and if you are in your early 20s, there is a real chance you will need to work until your late 70s or possibly even into your 80s. But even if people are able to economically support a retirement at 65, over thirty years of potential inactivity is harmful to cognitive (认知的) and emotional vitality. Many people may simply not want to do it.

G) And yet that does not mean that simply extending our careers is appealing. Just lengthening that second stage of full-time work may secure the financial assets needed for a 100-year life, but such persistent work will inevitably exhaust precious intangible assets such as productive skills, vitality, happiness, and friendship.

H) The same is true for education. It is impossible that a single shot of education, administered in childhood and early adulthood, will be able to support a sustained, 60-year career. If you factor in the projected rates of technological change, either your skills will become unnecessary, or your industry outdated. That means that everyone will, at some point in their life, have to make a number of major reinvestments in their skills.

I) It seems likely, then' that the traditional three-stage life will evolve into multiple stages containing two, three, or even more different careers. Each of these stages could potentially be different. In one the focus could be on building financial success and personal achievement, in another on creating a better work/life balance, still another on exploring and understanding options more fully, or becoming an independent producer, yet another on making a social contribution. These stages will span sectors, take people to different cities, and provide a foundation for building a wide variety of skills.

J) Transitions between stages could be marked with sabbaticals (休假) as people find time to rest and recharge their health, re-invest in their relationships, or improve their skills. At times, these breaks and transitions will be self-determined, at others they will be forced as existing roles, firms, or industries cease to exist.

K) A multi-stage life will have profound changes not just in how you manage your career, but also in your approach to life. An increasingly important skill will be your ability to deal with change and even welcome it. A three-stage life has few transitions, while a multi-stage life has many. That is why being self-aware, investing in broader networks of friends, and being open to new ideas will become even more crucial skills.

L) These multi-stage lives will create extraordinary variety across groups of people simply because there are so many ways of sequencing the stages. More stages mean more possible sequences.

M) With this variety will come the end of the close association of age and stage. In a three-stage life, people leave university at the same time and the same age, they tend to start their careers and family at the same age, they proceed through middle management all roughly the same time, and then move into retirement within a few years of each other. In a multi-stage life, you could be an undergraduate at 20, 40, or 60; a manager at 30, 50, or 70; and become an independent producer at any age.

N) Current life structures, career paths, educational choices, and social norms are out of tune with the emerging reality of longer lifespans. The three-stage life of full-time education, followed by continuous work, and then complete retirement may have worked for our parents or even grandparents, but it is not relevant today. We believe that to focus on longevity as primarily an issue of aging is to miss its full implications. Longevity is not necessarily about being older for longer. It is about living longer, being older later, and being younger longer.

_____ 1. An extended lifespan in the future will allow people to have more careers than now.

_____ 2. Just extending one's career may have both positive and negative effects.

_____ 3. Nowadays, many Americans have on average delayed their marriage by some eight years.

_____ 4. Because of their longer lifespan, young people today no longer follow the pattern of life of their parents or grandparents.

_____ 5. Many more people will be expected to live over 100 by the mid-21st century.

_____ 6. A longer life will cause radical changes in people's approach to life.

_____ 7. Fast technological change makes it necessary for one to constantly upgrade their skills.

_____ 8. Many people may not want to retire early because it would do harm to their mental and emotional well-being.

_____ 9. The close link between age and stage may cease to exist in a multi-stage life.

_____ 10. People living a longer and healthier life will have to rearrange their work and life.

III. Translation

Translate the five following sentences into English, using the words or expressions given in brackets.

1. 这项研究也证明了肥胖和死亡率之间的直接关系。(demonstrate)

_____

2. 输入了无效信息将显示错误代码。(display)

_____

3. 猛烈的暴风雨夷平了甘蔗种植园，也摧毁了家园。(level)

_____

4. 由于火势蔓延，人们须要立即采取行动。(prompt)

_____

5．政府正在采取措施，打击滥用毒品。（combat）

Product Manual
产品说明书的翻译策略 2——简单句

在说明书翻译中，使用简单句结构是一种常见的翻译策略，特别是当目标语言的语法结构与源语言有差异时。简单句结构清晰，用词简单明了，适用于描述事实、指导操作、传递信息等场景。在翻译时，简单句可以更清晰地传达信息，减少歧义，并使翻译更易于理解。以下是一些关于简单句在说明书翻译中的具体应用：

（一）避免复杂结构

尽量避免过于复杂的语法结构，以确保读者能够迅速理解句子的主旨。例如：

In the event that the user encounters any issues, it is recommended that they contact our customer support department.
如果用户遇到任何问题，建议他们联系我们的客户支持部门。

（二）清晰表达动作和结果

将动作和结果直接表达在简单句中，避免过多的修饰性词语。例如：
Press the button to start the operation, and you will see the indicator light turn green.
按下按钮启动操作，您会看到指示灯变为绿色。

（三）直接陈述事实

使用简单句来直接陈述事实，强调清晰而直接的表达方式。例如：
The product is designed for use in extreme weather conditions.
该产品设计用于在极端天气条件下使用。

（四）避免长句子

将长句子分割为简单句，以避免读者在理解时感到困惑。例如：
To operate the equipment, first, make sure it is properly connected to the power source, and then, press the power button located on the control panel.
操作设备时，首先确保它已正确连接到电源，然后按控制面板上的电源按钮。

（五）强调步骤和顺序

在描述步骤或顺序时，使用简单句来明确表达每个步骤。例如：
Step 1: Connect the device to your computer using the provided USB cable. Step 2: Turn on the device by pressing the power button.

Unit 12　ChatGPT 　185

步骤 1：使用提供的 USB 电缆将设备连接到计算机。步骤 2：按下电源按钮开启设备。

在说明书的翻译中，应遵循保持语言简练、通顺，准确传达原文意思的重要原则，简单句的翻译策略有助于确保说明书的目标语言版本清晰、简洁，并能够有效地传达产品使用和操作的信息。

1. *Read the following paragraphs and then answer the questions.*

User's manual of Vivitek Projector

Introduction

The User's Manual describes the installation, setup and operation of the DU8090Z projector and provides assistance to the installation personnel and the end-user to fully develop the performance of the projector. VIVITEK has made every effort to ensure that the information in the Manual is correct at the time of printing. The contents may be frequently updated due to the continuously product improvement and customer feedback.
You can find the latest version of the Manual and the manual of other Vivitek products on www.vivitekcorp.com.

Installing the projector
The high quality display effect can be guaranteed only when the projector is correctly installed. Generally, the light source facing the screen should be reduced or eliminated as much as possible. The contrast of the image will be obviously reduced if the light directly shines on the screen, such as the beam from windows or the searchlight cast on the image. The image may become faded and not bright.

Precautions for Installation

Caution:
- Projector installation must be done by a qualified professional. Contact your dealer for more information. It is not recommended you install the projector yourself.
- With ceiling installation, use approved mounting hardware & M4 screws; maximum depth of screw: 14 mm. Contact your dealer for information about mounting the projector on a ceiling.
- Only use the projector on a solid, level surface, serious injury and damage can occur if the projector is dropped.

Caution:
- Ensure that the hot air from the exhaust vent is not sucked into the projector.
- Ensure the air intake and exhaust vents are unobstructed and keep the required distance from any object. Below is required minimum distance between the vent and any object.
- All added enclosures should pass a certified thermal evaluation to ensure that the projector does not recycle exhaust air, as this may cause the projector to shut down even if the enclosure temperature is with the acceptable operation temperature range.

(1) What are the reasons mentioned for the potential frequent updates of the Manual?

(2) Where can users find the latest version of the Manual for the DU8090Z projector and other Vivitek products?

(3) What is recommended to do if the customer wants to install the projector?

(4) What is the maximum depth of the screws recommended for ceiling installation?

(5) According to the caution provided, where is it recommended to use the projector to avoid serious injury and damage?

2. *Map reading and translation.*

CAUTION To turn off main power, ensure to unplug from power outlet.

❶ _____

CAUTION To prevent electric shock, do not open the cabinet. There are high-voltage components inside. Refer service to qualified service personnel.

❷ _____

CAUTION The symbol warns the user about electric shock caused by voltage not insulated. Therefore, it is dangerous to make any kind of contact with any parts of inside units.

❸ _____

CAUTION To prevent the projector from electrical discharge or electric shock, do not expose the projector to rain or moist environment. Do not use the plug with an extension cord or an outlet unless all the prongs can be fully inserted.

❹ _____

This symbol alerts the user that important information which should be read carefully to avoid problems concerning the operation and maintenance.

❺ _____

Workshop

Background

An academic paper entitled *Chatting and Cheating: Ensuring Academic Integrity in the Era of ChatGPT* was published recently in an education journal, describing how artificial intelligence (AI) tools "raise a number of challenges and concerns, particularly in relation to academic honesty and plagiarism".

What readers — and indeed the peer reviewers who cleared it for publication — did not know was that the paper itself had been written by the controversial AI chatbot ChatGPT.

"We wanted to show that ChatGPT is writing at a very high level," said Prof Debby Cotton, director of academic practice at Plymouth Marjon University, who pretended to be the paper's lead author. "This is an arms race," she said. "The technology is improving very fast and it's going to be difficult for universities to outrun it".

Cotton, along with two colleagues from Plymouth University who also claimed to be co-authors, tipped off editors of the journal *Innovations in Education and Teaching International*. But the four academics who peer-reviewed it assumed it was written by these three scholars.

For years, universities have been trying to banish the plague of essay mills selling pre-written essays and other academic work to any students trying to cheat the system. But now academics suspect even the essay mills are using ChatGPT, and institutions admit they are racing to catch up with — and catch out — anyone passing off the popular chatbot's work as their own.

The Observer has spoken to a number of universities that say they are planning to expel students who are caught using the software.

Task

1. Write an essay on the use of AI in writing a paper.
2. Use the ChatGPT to generate the same paper.
3. Compare the two essays and discuss the following questions:
(1) What are the differences between two essays?
(2) What are the possible disadvantages of using AI to "write" an academic paper?
(3) How to detect plagiarism with the assistance of AI and how to prevent it?

Process

Step 1. The whole class is divided into several groups, with each group containing 3—4 students.

Step 2. Group members complete the first and second.

Step 3. Each group discusses three questions in Task 3.

Step 4. Each group delivers a presentation based on what they found.

Unit 13 Eco-network

US Launches Eco-network

Ready or not, the era of big data is coming to ecology. After years of discussion and debate, the United States is moving forward with an environmental monitoring network that promises to help transform a traditionally small-scale, local science into a continental-scale group enterprise.

The National Ecological Observatory Network (NEON) will consist of 20 "core" observatories representing distinct eco-regions throughout the United States. These will be bolstered by temporary stations that can be relocated wherever data need to be collected. The sites will house equipment and host visiting researchers, while gathering a range of environmental data over at least three decades.

The result will be a vast database that scientists can mine to tackle broad questions such as how global warming, pollution and land-use change are affecting ecosystems across the country. "NEON is really about trying to understand the biology of the entire continent rather than the biology of a specific place," says David Schimel, the project's chief science officer, based in Boulder, Colorado.

Conceived more than a decade ago, NEON has already spent just over US$80 million planning the network and developing instruments, and has a staff of about 140, including some 60 scientists and engineers. But the project, which is run by an independent body — NEON, Inc. — didn't clear its final hurdle until 28 July, when the National Science Foundation (NSF) awarded it $434 million over the next decade, with $12.5 million to be spent in the current fiscal year.

The money could jump-start site preparation and construction as early as this year. Schimel says that NEON expects to begin work near its home base in Colorado and in the northeast and to expand from there. The first data, from sensors placed on towers, submerged in streams and buried in soils, should come next year — a trickle that project members hope will become a torrent by 2016, when the project will be fully operational.

"It's a huge step forward," says Sandy Andelman, an ecologist who heads a network of tropical ecology sites through Conservation International in Arlington, Virginia. But, she cautions, NEON will create a massive new data set that few environmental scientists know how to use today. "Being able to manage and process and make sense of those data is going to be a huge challenge," Andelman says.

Once the entire network is up and running, some 15,000 sensors will work in concert with scientists on the ground to supply roughly 500 distinct categories of data ranging from basic weather readings to concentrations of ozone in the air and nitrogen in the soils, leaves and streams. Scientists will collect tens of thousands of samples, including soil, water, plants and small mammals. At the same time, aerial surveys will analyze broader land-use trends as well as details such as leaf chemistry and carbon stocks, and satellite data will expand coverage over the entire continent.

NEON's draft scientific plan, released on 4 August, identifies climate, land use and invasive species as drivers of ecosystem change that can be studied through their impact on bio-diversity, biogeochemical and hydrological cycles and the spread of infectious diseases. By gathering data over large territories and long periods of time, NEON will aim to give scientists the statistical power they need to tease out subtle trends in a shifting ecological balance. For this reason, rather than focusing on regional investigations, the research stations are mainly designed to gather data in a uniform manner that can be used in larger network studies.

"The big intellectual hurdle was the transition from a series of largely regional sites to an integrated system," says James Collins, an ecologist at Arizona State University in Tempe, who as head of the biological sciences directorate at the NSF during 2005－2009 helped to mould the proposal into its current form.

Over the years the project has battled against scepticism. Early on, Steven Wofsy, an atmospheric chemist at Harvard University in Cambridge, Massachusetts, and a pioneer of carbon studies at the Harvard Forest ecological research centre, feared that NEON would generate more data than value. Today he gives NEON credit for putting high-profile critics — including himself — on its scientific advisory board to address any problems head on.

Wofsy remains sceptical of big science projects that promise to open up a new field with lots of data that scientists haven't necessarily said they want. But he commends NEON for developing a plan to tackle scientific questions that will play out over decades.

"If these guys are successful, they will have the goods on some really big ecological questions," Wofsy says. "Scientists who are interested in addressing those problems will have to make the effort to learn how to use those data".

Words & Expressions

ecology/iˈkɒlədʒi/n. 生态；生态学
continental/ˌkɒntɪˈnentl/adj. 大洲的；大陆的
bolster/ˈbəʊlstə(r)/v. 改善，加强
conceive/kənˈsiːv/v. 想出（主意、计划等）；想象，构想，设想；怀孕，怀（胎）
hurdle/ˈhɜːdl/n. 难关，障碍；（供人或马在赛跑中跨越的）栏架，跨栏；v.（奔跑中）跳越（某物）

fiscal/'fɪskl/*adj.* 财政的；国库的，国家岁入的
jump-start/'dʒʌmp stɑːt/*v.* 全力以赴启动，加大力度以加快启动
submerge/səb'mɜːdʒ/*v.* （使）潜入水中，没入水中，浸没，淹没；湮没，湮灭，掩盖（思想、感情等）
stream/striːm/*n.* （液/气）流；（人/车）流；一连串，接二连三，源源不断（的事情）；*v.* 流，流动，流出；鱼贯而行，一个接一个地移动；飘动，飘扬
trickle/'trɪkl/*n.* 细流，涓流；稀稀疏疏缓慢来往的东西；*v.* （使）滴，淌，小股流淌；（使）慢慢走，缓慢移动
torrent/'tɒrənt/*n.* 急流，激流，湍流，洪流；迸发，连发，狂潮
ozone/'əʊzəʊn/*n.* 臭氧
nitrogen/'naɪtrədʒən/*n.* 氮；氮气
mammal/'mæml/*n.* 哺乳动物
aerial/'eəriəl/*adj.* 空中的，空气中的，地表以上的；从飞机上的
invasive/ɪn'veɪsɪv/*adj.* 侵入的，侵袭的；切入的，开刀的
hydrological/ˌhaɪdrə'lɒdʒɪkəl/*adj.* 水文的
infectious/ɪn'fekʃəs/*adj.* 传染性的，感染的（尤指通过呼吸）
territory/'terətri/*n.* 领土，版图，领地；（个人、群体、动物等占据的）领域，管区，地盘；（某人负责的）地区
tease out 提炼（信息）
subtle/'sʌtəl/*adj.* 不易察觉的，微妙的；机智的，狡猾的；敏锐的，头脑灵活的
scepticism/'skeptɪsɪzəm/*n.* 怀疑态度；怀疑主义

Notes

1. National Ecological Observatory Network：美国国家生态观测站网络（NEON），是由美国国家科学基金会资助的巴特尔纪念研究所运营的大型设施项目。NEON 自 2019 年开始全面运行，收集并提供生物圈对土地利用和气候变化的生态响应以及与地圈、水圈和大气反馈的长期标准化数据。NEON 是一个大陆规模的研究平台，用于了解生态系统如何以及为什么发生变化。

2. Boulder：博尔德，又译圆石市，是美国科罗拉多州的一个城市，位于州府丹佛西北，是圆石郡郡治。面积 65.7 平方千米，2020 年人口 108 250 人，是科罗拉多州第十一大城市。

3. National Science Foundation：国家科学基金会（缩写为 NSF），是美国政府独立机构，由美国国会于 1950 年创立。该机构支持除医学领域外的科学和工程学基础研究和教育，负责医学的同类机构为国家卫生研究院。美国国家自然科学基金会资助的项目占美国联邦政府资助的美国大学基础研究的 20%。在某些领域，如数学、计算机科学、经济学和社会科学，NSF 是主要的联邦赞助者。

4. Conservation International：保护国际（缩写为 CI），是一个非政府组织，总部设在美国华盛顿特区。其创建于 1987 年，目前有超过 900 位雇员，在超过 40 个国家进行保护工作，其中 90%的雇员是这些国家的公民，以非洲、亚洲、大洋洲与南美洲中部

雨林的发展中国家为主。CI 在全球生物多样性保护的需求最迫切的地区工作，包括生物多样性热点地区、重要的海洋生态系统区，以及生物多样性丰富的荒野地区。保护国际并以和各地非政府组织与原住民形成伙伴关系而著称。

5. Arlington：阿灵顿县是美国弗吉尼亚州东北部的一个县，位于波托马克河西岸，哥伦比亚特区对岸。原来是特区的一部分，但美国国会在 1846 年 7 月 9 日退回给弗吉尼亚州。面积 26 平方英里（67.7 平方千米），是美国地理面积最小的自治县。2020 年，该县的人口估计为 238 643 人。按人口计算，阿灵顿是弗吉尼亚州第六大县。

6. Arizona State University：亚利桑那州立大学（缩写为 ASU），是美国亚利桑那州的一所公立研究型大学。该校由分散在凤凰城大都会区各地的 5 个校区与在哈瓦苏湖城的一个校区所组成，共拥有 22 个学院，是美国学生最多的大学之一。亚利桑那州立大学在 2019 年 QS 世界大学排名中排第 212 位。

Exercises

I. Getting the Message

Read the questions and complete the answers according to the text.

1. What is the function of the environmental monitoring network launched by the United States?
   _____
2. What can the data collected from the monitoring be used for?
   _____
3. Where were the sensors which collocated first data placed?
   _____
4. What are the challenges when using the environmental monitoring network?
   _____
5. What was the scientist's concern over the environmental monitoring network?
   _____

II. Languages Focus

A. *Match the following words in left with their explanations in right.*

1. stream   a. a continuous flow of liquid or gas/people or vehicles
2. territory   b. spreading very quickly and difficult to stop
3. invasive   c. an infectious disease can be passed easily from one person to another, especially through the air they breathe
4. conceive   d. not very noticeable or obvious
5. infectious   e. an area that one person, group, animal, etc. considers as their own and defends against others who try to

enter it

6. torrent   f. to improve sth. or make it stronger

7. submerge   g. a problem or difficulty that must be solved or dealt with before you can achieve sth.

8. hurdle   h. to form an idea, a plan, etc. in your mind; to imagine sth.

9. bolster   i. a large amount of water moving very quickly

10. subtle   j. to go under the surface of water or liquid; to put sth. or make sth. go under the surface of water or liquid

B. *Fill in the blanks with the words or expressions given below. Change the form where necessary.*

submerge	hurdle	torrent	subtle	bolster
infectious	territory	stream	invasive	conceive

1. Hopes of an early cut in interest rates _____ confidence.
2. Two-thirds of candidates fail at this first _____ and are sent home.
3. Those suffering from _____ diseases were separated from the other patients.
4. The plot of the film is ingeniously _____.
5. Although I believe taxes will go up, I also believe it will be done _____.
6. After the winter rains, the stream becomes a raging _____.
7. Carter's fourth album definitely moves into uncharted _____.
8. Her _____ car was discovered in the river by police divers.
9. They found _____ cancer during a routine examination.
10. Refugees have been _____ into neighbouring country for months.

III. Translation

Translate the following sentences into Chinese.

1. These will be bolstered by temporary stations that can be relocated wherever data need to be collected.

_____

2. The money could jump-start site preparation and construction as early as this year.

_____

3. But, she cautions, NEON will create a massive new data set that few environmental scientists know how to use today.

_____

4. Over the years the project has battled against scepticism.

_____

5. Scientists who are interested in addressing those problems will have to make the effort to learn how to use those data.

IV. Discussion

Developments of technology are causing ecological problems, including ecological damage, environmental problem, resource scarcity, etc. Some people think the solution is that everyone accepts a simpler life, while others believe that technology can solve these problems.

Work in pairs to discuss both views and give your own opinion.

Experts Are Warning AI Could Lead to Human Extinction

Think about that for a second. Really think about it. The erasure of the human race from planet Earth.

That is what top industry leaders are frantically sounding the alarm about. These technologists and academics keep smashing the red panic button, doing everything they can to warn about the potential dangers artificial intelligence poses to the very existence of civilization.

On Tuesday, hundreds of top AI scientists, researchers, and others — including OpenAI chief executive Sam Altman and Google DeepMind chief executive Demis Hassabis — again voiced deep concern for the future of humanity, signing a one-sentence open letter to the public that aimed to put the risks the rapidly advancing technology carries with it in unmistakable terms.

"Mitigating the risk of extinction from AI should be a global priority alongside other societal-scale risks such as pandemics and nuclear war," said the letter, signed by many of the industry's most respected figures.

It doesn't get more straightforward and urgent than that. These industry leaders are quite literally warning that the impending AI revolution should be taken as seriously as the threat of nuclear war. They are pleading for policymakers to erect some guardrails and establish baseline regulations to defang the primitive technology before it is too late.

Dan Hendrycks, the executive director of the Center for AI Safety, called the situation "reminiscent of atomic scientists issuing warnings about the very technologies they've created. As Robert Oppenheimer noted, 'We knew the world would not be the same'".

"There are many 'important and urgent risks from AI', not just the risk of extinction; for example, systemic bias, misinformation, malicious use, cyberattacks, and weaponization," Hendrycks continued. "These are all important risks that need to be addressed".

And yet, it seems that the dire message these experts are desperately trying to send the public isn't cutting through the noise of everyday life. AI experts might be sounding the alarm, but the level of trepidation — and in some cases sheer terror — they harbor about the technology is not being echoed with similar urgency by the news media to the masses.

Instead, broadly speaking, news organizations treated Tuesday's letter — like all of the other warnings we have seen in recent months — as just another headline, mixed in with a garden variety of stories. Some major news organizations didn't even feature an article about the chilling warning on their website's homepages.

To some extent, it feels eerily reminiscent of the early days of the pandemic, before the widespread panic and the shutdowns and the overloaded emergency rooms. Newsrooms kept an eye on the rising threat that the virus posed, publishing stories about it slowly spreading across the world. But by the time the serious nature of the virus was fully recognized and fused into the very essence in which it was covered, it had already effectively upended the world.

History risks repeating itself with AI, with even higher stakes. Yes, news organizations are covering the developing technology. But there has been a considerable lack of urgency surrounding the issue given the open possibility of planetary peril.

Perhaps that is because it can be difficult to come to terms with the notion that a Hollywood-style science fiction apocalypse can become reality, that advancing computer technology might reach escape velocity and decimate humans from existence. It is, however, precisely what the world's most leading experts are warning could happen.

It is much easier to avoid uncomfortable realities, pushing them from the forefront into the background and hoping that issues simply resolve themselves with time. But often they don't — and it seems unlikely that the growing concerns pertaining to AI will resolve themselves. In fact, it's far more likely that with the breakneck pace in which the technology is developing, the concerns will actually become more apparent with time.

As Cynthia Rudin, a computer science professor and AI researcher at Duke University, told CNN on Tuesday: "Do we really need more evidence that AI's negative impact could be as big as nuclear war?"

Words & Expressions

erasure/ɪˈreɪʒə(r)/*n.* 擦掉，抹掉；消除，消灭；删除

frantic/ˈfræntɪk/*adj.* 紧张忙乱的，手忙脚乱的；（由于恐惧或担心）无法控制感情的，发狂似的

smash/smæʃ/*v.* （哗啦一声）打碎，打破，破碎；（使）猛烈撞击，猛烈碰撞；捣毁；打败；粉碎；使结束；*n.* 破碎，打碎，破碎（或打碎）的哗啦声；撞车

mitigate/ˈmɪtɪɡeɪt/*v.* 减轻；缓和

pandemic/pænˈdemɪk/*n.* （全国或全球性）流行病；大流行病

straightforward/ˌstreɪt'fɔːwəd/*adj.* 简单的，易懂的，不复杂的；坦诚的，坦率的，率直的

impend/ɪm'pɛnd/*v.* （胁迫之事）即将发生，正在逼近

plead/pliːd/*v.* 恳求；表示服罪/不服罪；解释，推说，找借口；为…辩护；声援；支持

erect/ɪ'rekt/*v.* 建立，建造；竖立，搭起；创立，设立；*adj.* 垂直的，竖直的；直立的

guardrail/'ɡɑːdˌreɪl/*n.* 护栏

baseline/'beɪslaɪn/*n.* 基础；起点；（网/棒球场的）底/垒线

defang/diː'fæŋ/*v.* 使无害，使无效

reminiscent/ˌremɪ'nɪsnt/*adj.* 使回忆起（人或事）的；回忆过去的，怀旧的，缅怀往事的

atomic/ə'tɒmɪk/*adj.* 原子的，与原子有关的

malicious/mə'lɪʃəs/*adj.* 怀有恶意的，恶毒的

dire/'daɪə(r)/*adj.* 极其严重的，危急的；极糟的，极差的

trepidation/ˌtrepɪ'deɪʃn/*n.* 惊恐，恐惧，不安

eerily/'ɪərəli/*adv.* 可怕地，奇异地

fuse/fjuːz/*v.* （使）融合，熔接，结合；*n.* 保险丝，熔断器；导火线，导火索

essence/'esns/*n.* 本质，实质，精髓；香精，精油

upend/ʌp'end/*v.* 翻倒，倒放；使颠倒

peril/'perəl/*n.* 严重危险；祸害，险情

velocity/və'lɒsəti/*n.* （沿某一方向的）速度；高速，快速

decimate/'desɪmeɪt/*v.* 大量毁灭，大批杀死（某地区的动物、植物或人）；严重破坏，大大削弱

forefront/'fɔːfrʌnt/*n.* （运动、活动的）前沿；（思考、关注的）重心

pertain/pə'teɪn/*v.* 存在，适用

breakneck/'breɪknek/*adj.* 飞速惊险的

Notes

1. Google DeepMind：前称 DeepMind 科技（DeepMind Technologies Limited），是一家英国的人工智能公司。公司创建于 2010 年，在 2014 年被谷歌收购。DeepMind 于 2014 年开始开发人工智能围棋软件 AlphaGo。

2. The Center for AI Safety：人工智能安全中心（CAIS），是一家总部位于美国旧金山的研究和实地建设非营利组织。CAIS 以通过开展安全研究、建立人工智能安全研究人员领域和倡导安全标准，降低与人工智能相关的社会规模风险为使命，从事人工智能安全地开发和使用。

3. Duke University：杜克大学，是一所位于美国北卡罗来纳州达勒姆的一所私立男女合校研究型大学。杜克大学为美国最顶尖的学府之一，有"南方哈佛"之称，其 2021 年录取率为 4.3%。虽然目前的学校创建于 1924 年，但杜克大学的历史实际上可以回溯到 1859 年时在今日现址创立的三一学院或更早的布朗学校（Brown's Schoolhouse，于 1838 年创立于同州的兰道夫县）。截至 2019 年 10 月，杜克大学的

历届校友、教授及研究人员中，共有 15 位诺贝尔奖得主、3 位图灵奖得主。

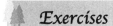

I. Comprehension of the Text

Read the text and answer the following questions. Write the answers on the lines.

1. What is the main aim of executives signing the open letter to the public?
   _____

2. What are essential risks existing in AI?
   _____

3. Is the statement "the news media and the masses hold the same concern over AI as experts do" true or false?
   _____

4. Is the statement "the general public suffered panic at the early stage of the pandemic" true or false?
   _____

5. Is the statement "the problems raised by AI might be as serve as those brought by nuclear weapons" true or false?
   _____

II. Main Details Comprehension

Directions: *In this section, you are going to read a passage with ten statements attached to it. Each statement contains information given in one of the paragraphs. Identify the paragraph from which the information is derived. You may choose a paragraph more than once. Each paragraph is marked with a letter.*

Do Parents Invade Children's Privacy When They Post Photos Online?

A) When Katlyn Burbidge's son was 6 years old, he was performing some ridiculous song and dance typical of a first-grader. But after she snapped a photo and started using her phone, he asked her a serious question: "Are you going to post that online?" She laughed and answered, "Yes, I think I will." What he said next stopped her. "Can you not?"

B) That's when it dawned on her: She had been posting photos of him online without asking his permission. "We're big advocates of bodily autonomy and not forcing him to hug or kiss people unless he wants to, but it never occurred to me that I should ask his permission to post photos of him online," says Burbidge, a mom of two in Wakefield, Massachusetts. "Now when I post a photo of him online, I show him the photo and get his okay".

C) When her 8-month-old is 3 or 4 years old, she plans to start asking him in an age-appropriate way, "Do you want other people to see this?" That's precisely the approach that two researchers advocated before a room of pediatricians (儿科医生) last week at the American Academy of Pediatrics meeting, when they discussed the 21st century challenge of "sharenting", a new term for parents' online sharing about their children. "As advocates of children's rights, we believe that children should have a voice about what information is shared about them if possible", says Stacey Steinberg, a legal skills professor at the University of Florida Levin College of Law in Gainesville.

D) Whether it's ensuring that your child isn't bullied over something you post, that their identity isn't digitally "kidnapped", or that their photos don't end up on a half dozen child pornography (色情) sites, as one Australian mom discovered, parents and pediatricians are increasingly aware of the importance of protecting children's digital presence. Steinberg and Bahareh Keith, an assistant professor of pediatrics at the University of Florida College of Medicine, say most children will likely never experience problems related to what their parents share, but a tension still exists between parents' rights to share their experiences and their children's rights to privacy.

E) "We're in no way trying to silence parents, voices," Steinberg says. "At the same time, we recognize that children might have an interest in entering adulthood free to create their own digital footprint." They cited a study presented earlier this year of 249 pairs of parents and their children in which twice as many children as parents wanted rules on what parents could share. "The parents said, 'We don't need rules-we're fine', and the children said, 'Our parents need rules', Keith says. "The children wanted autonomy about this issue and were worried about their parents sharing information about them".

F) Although the American Academy of Pediatrics offers guidelines recommending that parents model appropriate social media use for their children, it does not explicitly discuss oversharing by parents. "I think this is a very legitimate concern, and I appreciate their drawing our attention to it", David Hill, a father of five, says. He sees a role for pediatricians to talk with parents about this, but believes the messaging must extend far beyond pediatricians, offices. "I look forward to seeing researchers expand our understanding of the issue so we can translate it into effective education and policy," he says.

G) There's been little research on the topic, Steinberg wrote in a law article about this issue. While states could pass laws related to sharing information about children online, Steinberg feels parents themselves are generally best suited to make these decisions for their families. "While we didn't want to create any unnecessary panic, we did find some concerns that were troublesome, and we thought that parents or at least physicians should be aware of those potential risks," Steinberg says. They include photos repurposed for inappropriate or illegal means, identity theft, embarrassment, bullying by peers or digital kidnapping.

H) But that's the negative side, with risks that must be balanced against the benefits of sharing. Steinberg pointed out that parental sharing on social media helps build communities, connect spread-out families, provide support and raise awareness around important social issues for which parents might be their children's only voice.

I) A C. S. Mott survey found among the 56 percent of mothers and 34 percent of fathers who discussed parenting on social media, 72 percent of them said sharing made them feel less alone, and nearly as many said sharing helped them worry less and gave them advice from other parents. The most common topics they discussed included kids' sleep, nutrition, discipline, behavior problems and day care and preschool.

J) "There's this peer-to-peer nature of health care these days with a profound opportunity for parents to learn helpful tips, safety and prevention efforts, pro-vaccine messages and all kinds of other messages from other parents in their social communities", says Wendy Sue Swanson, a pediatrician and executive director of digital health at Seattle Children's Hospital, where she blogs about her own parenting journey to help other parents. "They're getting nurtured by people they've already selected that they trust." she says.

K) "How do we weigh the risks, how do we think about the benefits, and how do we alleviate the risks?" she says. "Those are the questions we need to ask ourselves, and everyone can have a different answer".

L) Some parents find the best route for them is not to share at all. Bridget O'Hanlon and her husband, who live in Cleveland, decided before their daughter was born that they would not post her photos online. When a few family members did post pictures, O'Hanlon and her husband made their wishes clear. "It's been hard not to share pictures of her because people always want to know how babies and toddlers (学走路的孩子) are doing and to see pictures, but we made the decision to have social media while she did not," O'Hanlon said. Similarly, Alison Jamison of New York decided with her husband that their child had a right to their own online identity. They did use an invitation-only photo sharing platform so that friends and family, including those far away, could see the photos, but they stood firm, simply refusing to put their child's photos on other social media platforms.

M) "For most families, it's a journey. Sometimes it goes wrong, but most of the time it doesn't," says Swanson, who recommends starting to ask children permission to post narratives or photos around ages 6 to 8. "We'll learn more and more what our tolerance is. We can ask our kids to help us learn as a society what's okay and what's not".

N) Indeed, that learning process goes both ways. Bria Dunham, a mother in Somerville, Massachusetts, was so excited to watch a moment of brotherly bonding while her first-grader and baby took a bath together that she snapped a few photos. But when she considered posting them online, she took the perspective of her son: How would he feel if his classmates, parents saw photos of him chest-up in the bathtub? "It made me think about how I'm teaching him to have ownership of his own body and how what is shared today endures into the future," Dunham says. "So I kept the pictures to myself and accepted this as one more step in supporting his increasing autonomy".

_____ 1. Steinberg argued parental sharing online can be beneficial.

_____ 2. According to an expert, when children reach school age, they can help their parents learn what can and cannot be done.

_____ 3. One mother refrained from posting her son's photos online when she considered the matter from her son's perspective.

_____ 4. According to a study, more children than parents think there should be rules on parents' sharing.

_____ 5. Katlyn Burbidge had never realized she had to ask her son's approval to put his photos online.

_____ 6. A mother decided not to post her son's photo online when he asked her not to.

_____ 7. A woman pediatrician tries to help other parents by sharing her own parenting experience.

_____ 8. There are people who decide simply not to share their children's photos online.

_____ 9. Parents and physicians should realize sharing information online about children may involve risks.

_____ 10. Parents who share their parenting experiences may find themselves intruding into their children's privacy.

III. Translation

Translate the five following sentences into English, using the words or expressions given in brackets.

1．她一再纠缠医生，恳求他做点什么。（plead）

2．咨询的本质是倾听并把那些被咨询者的观点考虑进来。（essence）

3．廉价进口严重削弱了英国的自行车工业。（decimate）

4．用法说明还算简单易懂。（straightforward）

5．植树造林减轻了土壤侵蚀。（mitigate）

Part C

Product Manual
产品说明书的翻译策略 3——条件句

在说明书翻译中，条件句的翻译是至关重要的，因为它们通常涉及产品使用的特定条件或情境。

（一）条件句翻译的适用结构

在翻译条件句时，关键是理解条件和结果之间的关系，并使用与中文语境相符的表达方式。确保翻译的语气和语法结构符合原文，以保持准确的信息传达。以下句式常见于说明书的条件句翻译：

（1）使用"如果…那么…"结构。例如：
If the device is not connected, an error message will be displayed.
如果设备未连接，将显示错误消息。
（2）使用"在…的情况下"结构。例如：
In case of low battery, please recharge the device.
在电量低的情况下，请给设备充电。
（3）使用"只有当…才"结构。例如：
The function is available only when the software is updated.
只有当软件更新时，该功能才可用。
（4）使用"除非…否则"结构。例如：
The door cannot be opened unless the safety switch is turned off.
除非关闭安全开关，否则门无法打开。
（5）使用"在…期间"结构。例如：
During setup, ensure that all connections are secure.
在设置过程中，请确保所有连接都牢固。

（二）条件句翻译的注意事项

（1）时态一致性。确保条件从句和主句的时态在翻译中保持一致。

（2）逻辑清晰度。保持逻辑清晰度，以确保读者能够准确理解条件与结果之间的关系。

（3）考虑上下文。在翻译条件句时，要考虑整体文章，确保条件的表达方式符合产品的使用场景和实际情境。

（4）保持简洁明了。尽量保持翻译的简洁明了，以便用户容易理解，不要使条件句过于复杂。

（5）测试可行性。在翻译完成后，可以进行一些可行性测试，确保条件句的表达不会引起歧义或混淆。

这些建议有助于确保条件句的翻译在语法、逻辑和文化层面上都是准确的，以提供清晰而有效的产品使用指导。

1. *Read the following paragraphs and then answer the questions.*

Seagate Mobile HDD User's Guide

5.0　About (SED) Self-Encrypting Drives

Self-encrypting drives (SEDs) offer encryption and security services for the protection of stored data, commonly known as "protection of data at rest." These drives are compliant with the Trusted Computing Group (TCG) Opal Storage Specifications as detailed in the following:

Trusted Computing Group (TCG) Documents (apply to Self-Encrypting Drive models only)
　　　　　TCG Storage Architecture Core Specification, Version 2.0
　　　　　TCG Storage Security Subsystem Class Opal Specification, Version 2.0
　　　　　(see www.trustedcomputinggroup.org)

In case of conflict between this document and any referenced document, this document takes precedence.

The Trusted Computing Group (TCG) is an organization sponsored and operated by companies in the computer, storage and digital communications industry. Seagate's SED models comply with the standards published by the TCG.

Unit 13 Eco-network

To use the security features in the drive, the host must be capable of constructing and issuing the following two SATA commands:
- Trusted Send
- Trusted Receive

These commands are used to convey the TCG protocol to and from the drive in their command payloads.

5.1 Data Encryption

Encrypting drives use one inline encryption engine for each drive employing AES-256 data encryption in Cipher Block Chaining (CBC) mode to encrypt all data prior to being written on the media and to decrypt all data as it is read from the media. The encryption engine is always in operation and cannot be disabled.

The 32-byte Data Encryption Key (DEK) is a random number which is generated by the drive, never leaves the drive, and is inaccessible to the host system. The DEK is itself encrypted when it is stored on the media and when it is in volatile temporary storage (DRAM) external to the encryption engine. A unique data encryption key is used for each of the drive's possible 16 data bands (see Section 5.5, Data Bands).

5.2 Controlled Access

The drive has two security providers (SPs) called the "Admin SP" and the "Locking SP." These act as gatekeepers to the drive security services. Security-related commands will not be accepted unless they also supply the correct credentials to prove the requester is authorized to perform the command.

5.2.1 Admin SP

The Admin SP allows the drive's owner to enable or disable firmware download operations (see Section 5.4, Drive Locking). Access to the Admin SP is available using the SID (Secure ID) password or the MSID (Manufacturers Secure ID) password.

5.2.2 Locking SP

The Locking SP controls read/write access to the media and the cryptographic erase feature. Access to the Locking SP is available using the Admin or User passwords.

5.2.3 Default password

When the drive is shipped from the factory, all passwords are set to the value of MSID. This 32-byte random value can only be read by the host electronically over the interface. After receipt of the drive, it is the responsibility of the owner to use the default MSID password as the authority to change all other passwords to unique owner-specified values.

5.2.4 ATA Enhanced Security

The drive can utilize the system's BIOS through the ATA Security API for cases that do not require password management and additional security policies.

Furthermore, the drive's ATA Security Erase Unit command shall support both Normal and Enhanced Erase modes with the following modifications/additions:

Normal Erase: Normal erase feature shall be performed by changing the Data Encryption Key (DEK) of the drive, followed by an overwrite operation that repeatedly writes a single sector containing random data to the entire drive. This write operation bypasses the media encryption. On reading back the overwritten sectors, the host will receive a decrypted version, using the new DEK of the random data sector (the returned data will not match what was written).

Enhanced Erase: Enhanced erase shall be performed by changing the Data Encryption Key of the drive.

(1) What are the two SATA commands that the host must be capable of constructing and issuing to use the security features in the drive?

(2) What encryption algorithm and mode are employed for data encryption in these drives?

(3) What are the two security providers (SPs) in the drive, and what functions do they perform?

(4) What is the default password set when the drive is shipped from the factory?

(5) How can the drive utilize the system's BIOS through the ATA Security API?

2. *Map reading and translation.*

Idle and standby timers
Each time the drive performs an active function (read, write or seek), the standby timer is reinitialized and begins counting down from its specified delay times to zero. If the standby timer reaches zero before any drive activity is required, the drive makes a transition to standby mode. In both Idle and standby mode, the drive accepts all commands and returns to active mode when disk access is necessary.

❶ _____

Radio and television interference. This equipment generates and uses radio frequency energy and if not installed and used in strict accordance with the manufacturer's instructions, may cause interference to radio and television reception.

❷ _____

The drive has a 32-byte hardware RNG that it is uses to derive encryption keys or, if requested to do so, to provide random numbers to the host for system use, including using these numbers as Authentication Keys (passwords) for the drive's Admin and Locking SPs.

❸ _____

In case of conflict between this document and any referenced document, this document takes precedence.

❹ _____

Unless otherwise noted, all specifications are measured under ambient conditions, at 25°C, and nominal power. For convenience, the phrases *the drive* and *this drive* are used throughout this manual to indicate the following drive models:

The specification summaries listed in the following tables are for quick reference. For details on specification measurement or definition, refer to the appropriate section of this manual.

❺ _____

Workshop

Background

Artificial intelligence (AI) is often presented in binary terms in both popular culture and political analysis. Either it represents the key to a futuristic utopia defined by the integration of human intelligence and technological prowess, or it is the first step toward a dystopian rise of machines. This same binary thinking is practiced by academics, entrepreneurs, and even activists in relation to the application of AI in combating climate change. The technology industry's singular focus on AI's role in creating a new technological utopia obscures the ways that AI can exacerbate environmental degradation, often in ways that directly harm marginalized populations. In order to utilize AI in fighting climate change in a way that both embraces its technological promise and acknowledges its heavy energy use, the technology companies leading the AI charge need to explore solutions to the environmental impacts of AI.

AI and the broader internet and communications industry have increasingly come under fire for using exorbitant amounts of energy. Take data processing, for example. The supercomputers used to run cutting-edge AI programs are powered by the public electricity grid and supported by back up diesel-powered generators. Training a single AI system can emit over 250,000 pounds of carbon dioxide. In fact, the use of AI technology across all sectors produces carbon dioxide emissions at a level comparable to the aviation industry. These additional emissions disproportionately impact historically marginalized communities who often live in heavily polluted areas and are more directly affected by the health hazards of pollution.

Recently, AI scientists and engineers have responded to these critiques and are considering new sources for powering data farms. However, even new, ostensibly more sustainable energy sources such as rechargeable batteries can exacerbate climate change and harm communities. Most rechargeable batteries are built using lithium, a rare earth metal whose extraction can have negative effects for marginalized communities. Lithium extraction, which is fueled by an increasing demand for cleaner energy sources, demands enormous water usage, to the tune of 500,000 gallons of water for every ton of lithium extracted. In Chile, the second largest producer of lithium in the world, indigenous communities like the Copiapó people in the North often clash with mining companies over land and water rights. These mining activities are so water intensive, the Institute for Energy Research reports that in Salar de Atacama they consumed 65 percent of the region's water. This water loss damages and permanently depletes wetlands and water sources, which has caused native species of flora and fauna to become endangered and affected local populations. Portraying lithium as "clean" energy simply because it is less environmentally disastrous than diesel or coal is a false dichotomy, which discourages stakeholders from pursuing newer, greener energy sources.

Task

1. Search more information about impacts of high technology/AI on ecology.

2. Discuss the following questions based on what you have found:

(1) Do the positive effects of high technology/AI on ecology outweigh the negative effects?

(2) How to alleviate ecological problems raised by using high technology/AI?

Process

Step 1. The whole class is divided into several groups, with each group containing 3—4 students.

Step 2. Group members collect information by searching the Internet or interviewing your friends or classmates.

Step 3. Discuss the above two questions with group member.

Step 4. Each group delivers a presentation based on the information and discussion.

Unit 14 Technology and Entertainment

Why Hollywood Really Fears Generative AI

Unions representing actors and writers are negotiating with major studios to stop AI from running riot in the industry. Their concerns are very real.

The future of Hollywood looks a lot like Deepfake Ryan Reynolds selling you a Tesla. In a video, since removed but widely shared on Twitter, the actor is bespectacled in thick black frames, his mouth mouthing independently from his face, hawking electric vehicles: "How much do you think it would cost to own a car that's so awesome?"

On the verisimilitude scale, the video, which originally circulated last month, registered as blatantly unreal. Then its creator, financial advice YouTuber Kevin Paffrath, revealed he had made it as a ploy to attract the gaze of Elon Musk. (Which it did: the Tesla CEO replied to Paffrath's tweet with a "nice.") Elsewhere on Twitter, people beseeched Reynolds to sue. Instead, his production company responded with a similarly janky video in which a gray-looking Musk endorsed gin made by Aviation, a company Reynolds co-owns. That video has also since been deleted.

"Finance guy sucks up to Musk on Twitter" is far from earth-shattering news, but the exchange is indicative of a much bigger problem: AI is making it possible for anyone to deepfake famous faces into whatever video they like. And actors, in turn, are becoming increasingly aware of the potential of AI to encroach on their work. With the Writers Guild of America already on strike, in part because of a similar threat, upcoming negotiations between the actors' union and studios will likely reference images like Fake Bruce Willis and Fake Ryan Reynolds as the latest steps toward a future dominated by AI.

The hype around the technology means it will be a focus of the talks, especially given that contracts are negotiated just once every three years, explains Duncan Crabtree-Ireland, executive director and chief negotiator for the Screen Actors Guild — American Federation of Television and Radio Artists (SAG-AFTRA). "Considering how far [AI has] advanced in the last 18 months, it's hard even to imagine where it'll be in three years," he says.

In a message asking its members to authorize a strike, the guild noted that it was seeking a contract that would protect members from losing income due to "unregulated use of generative AI." The deadline is Monday, June 5; on June 7, SAG-AFTRA begins negotiations with the Alliance of Motion Picture and Television Producers (AMPTP), which represents the studios. If actors go on strike, it would be the first time since 2000.

SAG has been concerned about machine learning tools since the days of pixelated sports video games. Back then, the guild worried about how easy it was for game studios to insert pro athletes into *Madden* games. Now, Hollywood studios are de-aging Harrison Ford and recreating the voices of the dead.

Given this, it's not hard to imagine a future in which a wide-eyed actor signs up for one season of a vampire TV show, and then two seasons later, their AI replacement busts out of a coffin. Meanwhile, they receive no additional compensation, even if the AI-generated character was based on their likeness and performance.

"The nature of the impact on performers is unique, especially with generative AI tools that can be used to recreate a performer image, likeness, or voice persona, or to do things that they didn't originally contemplate ever doing," says Crabtree-Ireland. "That's a concern".

Actors, like all Americans, are protected against commercial appropriation of their identity by the right of publicity — also known as name, image, and likeness rights. SAG wants to buttress these protections and stomp out exploitative terms like the vampire example by adding "informed consent" into future contracts: Certain kinds of AI use must be disclosed and compensated, the union argues.

But writers cannot lean on publicity rights in the same way. If they own the rights, they can seek recourse or compensation if their work is scraped by large language models, or LLMs, but only if the resulting work is deemed a reproduction or derivative of their script. "If the AI has learned from hundreds of scripts or more, this is not very likely," says Daniel Gervais, a professor of intellectual property and AI law at Vanderbilt University.

And it's this scraping, applied to performers, that concerns talent representatives. Entertainment lawyer Leigh Brecheen says she's most worried about her clients' valuable characteristics being extracted in a way that isn't easily identifiable. Imagine a producer conjuring a digital performance with the piercing intensity of Denzel Washington while entirely skirting his wages. "Most negotiated on-camera performer deals will contain restrictions against the use of name, likeness, performance in any work other than the one for which they are being hired," Brecheen says. "I don't want the studio to be able to use the performance to train AI either." This is why, as Crabtree-Ireland explains, it is crucial to reframe AI works as an amalgam of countless humans.

But will people care if what they're watching was made by an AI trained on human scripts and performances? When the day comes that ChatGPT and other LLMs can produce filmable scenes based on simple prompts, unprotected writers' rooms for police procedurals or sitcoms would likely shrink. Voice actors, particularly those not already famous for on-camera performances, are also in real danger. "Voice cloning is essentially now a solved problem," says Hany Farid, a professor at the University of California, Berkeley who specializes in analyzing deepfakes.

Short term, most AI-generated actors may come off like Fake Ryan Reynolds: ghoulishly unlikeable. It seems more likely that people will accept audiobooks made by AI or a digitally rendered Darth Vader voice than a movie resting on the ripped shoulders of an AI-sculpted

GigaChad-esque action hero.

Long term, though, if AI replicants escape the uncanny valley, audiences of the future may not care whether the actor in front of them is human. "It's complicated," says Matthew Sag, a professor of law and artificial intelligence at Emory University. "The job of writing can be encroached on in a marginal or progressive way. Performers are likely to be replaced in an all-or-nothing way".

As the actors' union and Hollywood studios head into talks next week, the key concern will be economic fairness: The union states that it has become increasingly difficult for guild members to "maintain a middle-class lifestyle." There is a modern disconnect between a film or TV show's success and residual compensation, unions argue, as well as longer gaps between increasingly shorter seasons, which means less time spent working.

In this context, AI could be Hollywood's next gambit to produce more content with fewer humans. Like the AI-generated Reynolds, the whole thing would be banal if it wasn't so critical. As such, union strikes remain a possibility. "They've got a 2023 business model for streaming with a 1970 business model for paying performers and writers and other creatives in the industry," says Crabtree-Ireland. "That is not OK".

Words & Expressions

generative/'dʒenərətɪv/*adj*. 有生产力的，有生殖力的；（语言学）生成的
negotiate /nɪ'gəʊʃieɪt/*v*.（尤指在商业或政治上）谈判，磋商，洽谈；商定，达成协议
bespectacled/bɪ'spektəkld/*adj*. 戴眼镜的
frame/freɪm/*n*. 框架，边框；构架，支架；体格，骨架；眼镜框
hawk/hɔːk/*n*. 鹰，隼；鹰派分子，主战分子；*v*. 叫卖，兜售；咳痰
awesome /'ɔːsəm/*adj*. 让人惊叹的，令人敬畏的；非常棒的，极佳的
verisimilitude/ˌverɪsɪ'mɪlɪtjuːd/*n*. 逼真，貌似真实；逼真的事物
circulate/'sɜːkjəleɪt/*v*.（液体或气体）环流，循环；传播，流传；传阅，传送
register/'redʒɪstə(r)/*n*. 登记表，注册簿；*v*. 登记，注册
blatantly/'bleɪtəntli/*adv*. 公然地；喧闹地；看穿了地
ploy/plɔɪ/*n*. 策略；活动；工作
gaze/geɪz/*v*. 凝视，注视；*n*. 凝视，注视
tweet /twiːt/*n*.（小鸟的）啁啾声，啾啾声；在推特网上发的贴子；*v*. 啾啾地叫；在推特网上发微博；在推特网上（与人）发信息
beseech/bɪ'siːtʃ/*vt*. 恳求，哀求；乞求，急切地要求得到
sue/suː/*v*. 起诉，指向法院提起诉讼
jank/dʒæŋk/*adj*. 质量极差的；不可靠的；多余的；无意义的；愚蠢的
endorse/ɪn'dɔːs/*v*.（公开）赞同，认可；（在广告中对某种产品）宣传，吹捧
suck/sʌk/*v*. 吸，吮，啜
earth-shattering/'ɜːθ ˌʃætərɪŋ/*adj*. 惊天动地的；极其重大的

indicative/ɪn'dɪkətɪv/adj. 指示的，表明的，象征的；陈述（语气）的
deepfake/di:pfeɪk/ v. 深度伪造；n. 深度伪造
encroach/ɪn'krəʊtʃ/v. 逐步侵占（侵犯），蚕食；侵占（土地）
upcoming/'ʌpkʌmɪŋ/adj. 即将来临的
hype/haɪp/n. 大肆的宣传广告，炒作；（为做广告而进行的）欺骗；v.（通过传媒）大肆宣传；使（人）兴奋，使（人）活跃
authorize/'ɔ:θəraɪz/v. 批准，许可；授权
guild/gɪld/n. 协会；（中世纪的）行会，同业公会；（生态）共位群，功能群
pro/prəʊ/n.〈非正式〉专业人士，职业选手；好处，赞成的论点；赞成者，支持者
vampire/'væmpaɪə (r)/n.（故事中的）吸血鬼；（喻）无情掠夺者，吸血鬼
bust out 挣脱，逃脱：从限制或束缚中挣脱出来，通常指从监狱或困境中逃脱
coffin/'kɒfɪn/n. 棺材；vt. 把（尸体）装入棺材；收殓
compensation/ˌkɒmpen'seɪʃ(ə)n/n. 赔偿金，补偿金；弥补，抵消；报酬，薪水
likeness/'laɪknəs/n. 相似，相像；样子，肖像，照片，画像；相似物
persona/pə'səʊnə/n. 表面形象，伪装；（作家创作或演员饰演的）人物，角色
contemplate/'kɒntəmpleɪt/v. 沉思，深思熟虑；盘算，打算；凝视，注视；考虑接受（发生某事的可能性）
buttress/'bʌtrəs/n. 扶壁；山边扶壁状凸出部分；支持力量；v. 支持；用扶壁支撑（建筑物等）
stomp/stɒmp/v.（尤指生气时）跺脚，重踩；跳顿足舞
exploitative/ɪk'splɔɪtətɪv/adj. 剥削的；利用的；开发资源的
consent/kən'sent/n. 许可，允许；同意，赞同；v. 赞同，准许，同意
lean on 依靠：指在需要支持或帮助时，依赖某人或某物
scrap/skræp/n.（纸、布等的）碎片，小块；v.（因不切实际而）放弃，抛弃（计划、体系）；把（旧机器、旧汽车等当）作废料处理，报废；〈非正式〉打架，吵架；激烈竞争
derivative/dɪ'rɪvətɪv/n. 派生物，衍生物；派生词；（金融）衍生工具（产品）；微商
extract/'ekstrækt/n. 选段，引文；v. 提取，提炼；取出，拔出；摘录
conjure/'kʌndʒə (r)/v. 变魔术，使…变戏法般地出现（或消失）；想象出，设想出
pierce/pɪəs/v.（锋利尖锐物体）刺入，刺穿；（在身体某部位）扎眼，穿孔（以佩戴珠宝）；（声或光）穿过，透入；冲过，突破；让某人心如刀割，深深地打动
on-camera 出镜头出现在电视上镜内表演电视上
amalgam/ə'mælgəm/n.［材］汞合金，［化工］汞齐；混合物
filmable/'fɪlməb(ə)l/adj. 可拍成电影的
prompt/prɒmpt/v. 促使，导致；鼓励，提示（说话者）；adj. 迅速的，立刻的
procedural/prə'si:dʒərəl/adj. 程序上的
sitcom/'sɪtkɒm/n. 情景喜剧
come off 脱落，从某个位置或表面分离出来；成功：实现预期的结果或效果
ghoulish/'gu:lɪʃ/adj. 食尸鬼似的；令人毛骨悚然的
unlikeable/ˌʌn'laɪkəbl/adj. 不可爱的；不讨喜的

audiobook/'ɔ:diəubuk/*n*. 有声读物（把文字录制成语音的"有声书"）
rip/rɪp/*v*. （使）撕裂，（使）划破；迅速扯开，猛力去除；抢掠，剥夺
uncanny/ʌn'kæni/*adj*. 神秘的；离奇的；可怕的
all-or-nothing/ˌɔ:l ɔ:'nʌθɪŋ/*adj*. 孤注一掷的，要么全有要么全无的
residual/rɪ'zɪdjuəl/*adj*. 残留的；（数量）剩余的；（物质状态在成因消失后）剩余的
gambit/'gæmbɪt/*n*. 话题；开始；以取得优势的开局棋法；开场白
banal/bə'nɑ:l/*adj*. 平淡无奇的，平庸的，陈腐的
critical/'krɪtɪk(ə)l/*adj*. 批判的，爱挑剔的；极其重要的
streaming/'stri:mɪŋ/*n*. 串流，流式传播；流媒体

Notes

1. SAG：美国演员工会（Screen Actors Guild）的缩写。该工会设有美国演员工会奖（Screen Actors Guild Awards，SAG Awards），于1995年创办。美国演员工会奖设有电影、电视两大类奖以及终身成就奖，每届共颁发16个奖项，由随机抽取产生的美国演员工会奖提名委员会投票产生提名名单，后由随机抽取的美国演员工会活跃会员进行最终的投票产生奖项得主。美国演员工会奖一般于每年1月底至3月初在美国洛杉矶圣殿剧院（Shrine Auditorium）举办，每年举办一届。美国演员工会奖是美国业界推崇的奖项之一，好莱坞年度重要奖项之一，与金球奖、英国电影学院奖、评论家选择奖合称为奥斯卡金像奖四大风向标。

2. Pixel：像素，是组成计算机数位影像（位图）的最小单位。像素图像（pixel iconography），顾名思义就是以像素为单位，一个点一个点去绘制出图像，也有人称之为点画法或像素艺术（Pixel Art）。最早出现在20世纪中后期计算机应用程序的图像（Icon），以及早期的8位元电子游戏，21世纪以来，被广泛应用在因特网、GUI（Graphic User Interface）以及行动游戏中等。基本上只要具备铅笔工具的影像处理软件都可以画，如PhotoShop或PhotoImpact等。

3. Generative AI：生成式AI，即通过各种机器学习（ML）方法从数据中学习工件的组件（要素），进而生成全新的、完全原创的、真实的工件（一个产品或物品或任务），这些工件与训练数据保持相似，而不是复制。简单理解，生成式AI就是利用现有文本、音频文件或图像创建新内容的技术。使用生成AI，计算机检测与输入相关的基本模式并生成类似内容。

4. LLM：大型语言模型，也叫大语言模型、大模型（Large Language Model，LLM；Large Language Models，LLMs），是指包含数千亿（或更多）参数的语言模型，这些参数是在大量文本数据上训练的，如模型GPT-3、PaLM.Galactica和LLaMA。具体来说，LLM建立在Transformer架构之上，其中多头注意力层堆叠在一个非常深的神经网络中。现有的LLM主要采用与小语言模型类似的模型架构（即Transformer）和预训练目标（即语言建模）。

Unit 14 Technology and Entertainment   209

Exercises

I. Getting the Message

There are 5 questions in this section. Read the questions and complete the answers according to the text.

1. What are Unions representing actors and writers negotiating?
_____

2. Why did YouTuber Kevin Paffrath make a video widely shared on Twitter?
_____

3. Why was Writers Guild of America on strike?
_____

4. What are the impacts of Generative AI on performers?
_____

5. What is the future of AI in the long term?
_____

II. Languages Focus

A. *Match the following words in left with their explanations in right.*

1. generative   a. to look steadily at sb./sth. for a long time
2. negotiate   b. to give official permission for sth., or for sb. to do sth.
3. awesome   c. having the ability of producing or orginating
4. circulate   d. very impressive or very difficult and perhaps rather
                         frightening
5. gaze   e. things that make a bad situation better
6. sue   f. to do clever tricks such as making things seem to
                         appear or disappear as if by magic
7. authorize   g. expressing disapproval of sb./sth. and saying what you
                         think is bad about them
8. compensation   h. to try to reach an agreement by formal discussion
9. conjure   i. to send goods or information to all the people in a
                         group
10. critical   j. to formally ask for sth., especially in court

B. *Fill in the blanks with the words or expressions given below. Change the form where necessary.*

| negotiate | awesome | gaze | tweet | bust out |
| lean on | film | sitcom | uncanny | critical |

1. I find it _____ that they seem to have an atmosphere just like a planet.

2. The former form takes *The Pianist* as an example to make a delicate watch Polanski's skill to change the literature structure into _____ one.

3. "Maybe you _____ your left arm too much," the doctor concluded, suggesting I see a bone doctor.

4. I have a blog in several leading portals in China, and also _____.

5. The rent is a matter for _____ between the landlord and the tenant.

6. I am getting bored of this party, let's _____ of here.

7. This mutual _____ is a major part of the attachment between mother and child.

8. Nearly a decade ago it was predicted that viewers of "Friends", a popular _____, would soon be able to purchase a sweater like Jennifer Aniston's with a few taps on their remote control.

9. The economy is just one of several _____ problems the country is grappling with.

10. Even though you have an _____ product, if no one knows about it, it doesn't do anyone any good.

Ⅲ. Translation

Translate the following sentences into Chinese.

1. The hype around the technology means it will be a focus of the talks, especially given that contracts are negotiated just once every three years, explains Duncan Crabtree-Ireland.

_____

2. Back then, the guild worried about how easy it was for game studios to insert pro athletes into Madden games.

_____

3. Actors, like all Americans, are protected against commercial appropriation of their identity by the right of publicity — also known as name, image, and likeness rights.

_____

4. "Most negotiated on-camera performer deals will contain restrictions against the use of name, likeness, performance in any work other than the one for which they are being hired," Brecheen says.

_____
_____

5. Voice actors, particularly those not already famous for on-camera performances, are also in real danger.

_____

IV. Discussion

Artificial intelligence is a kind of modern emerging science and technology that expands human thinking, and it has formed an independent branch in the process of the development of computer science. Through the proper application of artificial intelligence technology in movies, the development of modern movies can be promoted to a certain extent. However, artificial intelligence also hinders the development of modern films to a certain extent. It is difficult to truly reflect the professional quality of actors by relying on artificial intelligence, and it is also a certain challenge to reveal the true feelings of films.

Work in pairs and discuss about your opinions on the role of AI in the the film industry, and then write down your opinions.

Applications of AI in the Media & Entertainment Industry

The media and entertainment industry has been one of the earliest adopters of artificial intelligence (AI). AI has transformed the way content is created, delivered, and consumed.

The growing ubiquity of content creation tools like high-resolution cameras, content creation software, and smartphones is allowing pretty much anyone to create, publish, and distribute written, audio, and video content.

This trend is further accelerated by the proliferation of the internet, which has led to the replacement of traditional media channels like cable and radio with on-demand streaming platforms like Netflix and YouTube. As a result, consumers have potentially limitless options to choose from, in terms of media consumption.

Thus, media companies are facing the need to raise the quantity as well as the quality of content they create to attract as many consumers as they can to drive higher value. To help them achieve this objective, media companies are adopting advanced technologies like AI.

The use of Artificial Intelligence in the media and entertainment industry is helping media companies to improve their services and enhance the customer experience. Here are a few use cases of AI in media and AI in entertainment that are transforming the industry:

Metadata Tagging:

With countless pieces of content being created every minute, classifying these items and making them easy to search for viewers becomes a herculean task for media company employees. That's because this process requires watching videos and identifying objects, scenes, or locations in the video to classify and add tags.

To perform this task on a large scale, media creators and distributors like CBS interactive are using AI-based video intelligence tools to analyze the contents of videos frame by frame and identify objects to add appropriate tags.

This technology is being used by content creators or media publishing, hosting, and broadcasting platforms like NFL Media to organize their media assets in a highly structured and precise manner. As a result, regardless of its volume, all the content owned by media companies becomes easily discoverable.

Content Personalization:

Leading Music and video streaming platforms like Spotify and Netflix are successful because they offer content to people belonging to all demographics, having different tastes and preferences. Such companies are using AI and machine learning algorithms to study individual user behavior and demographics to recommend what they may be most interested in watching or listening to next keeping them constantly engaged. As a result, these AI-based platforms are providing customers with content that caters to their specific likings, thus offering them a highly personalized experience.

Reporting Automation:

In addition to automating day-to-day or minute-by-minute operations, AI is also helping media companies to make strategic decisions. For instance, leading media and broadcasting companies are using machine learning and natural language generation to create channel performance reports from raw analytics data shared by BARC.

The weekly data that is usually received from the Broadcast Audience Research Council of India (BARC) is generally in the form of voluminous Excel sheets. Analyzing these sheets on a weekly basis to derive and implement meaningful learnings proves to be quite daunting for the analytics team.

Predictive Analytics:

Another application of AI in the media and entertainment industry is predictive analytics. AI-powered predictive analytics is used to forecast box office revenues, TV ratings, and other performance metrics.

Predictive analytics helps media and entertainment companies make informed decisions about content production, advertising, and distribution. For example, Nielsen's AI-powered predictive analytics model can forecast TV ratings for upcoming shows. The model analyzes historical data and social media trends to predict the success of a show before it airs.

Similarly, AI-powered predictive analytics can forecast box office revenues for upcoming movies, helping studios make decisions about distribution and marketing.

AI-powered virtual assistants and chatbots are also improving customer engagement and collecting data about user preferences and behavior.

Virtual assistants such as Apple's Siri and Amazon's Alexa use natural language processing to interact with users and perform tasks. Chatbots are AI-powered programs that can engage in conversations with users.

Media and entertainment companies are using virtual assistants and chatbots to provide personalized recommendations, answer customer inquiries, and provide customer support. For example, the NBA uses Facebook Messenger chatbots to interact with fans, providing them with real-time updates, scores, and highlights.

AI has transformed the media and entertainment industry, from personalization of content to predictive analytics and virtual assistants. AI-powered algorithms are being used to create personalized content recommendations, forecast performance metrics, and interact with customers. However, there are ethical considerations that need to be addressed, such as job displacement, bias, and privacy.

Subtitle Generation:

International media publishing companies need to make their content fit for consumption by audiences belonging to multiple regions. To do so, they need to provide accurate multilingual subtitles for their video content. Manually writing subtitles for multiple shows and movies in dozens of languages may take hundreds or even thousands of hours for human translators. Youtube's artificial intelligence allows publishers to add automatic transcription to their videos.

Besides, it may also be difficult to find the right human resources to translate content for certain languages. Additionally, human translation can also be prone to errors. To overcome these challenges, media companies are leveraging AI-based technologies like natural language processing and natural language generation. For example, YouTube's AI allows its publishers to automatically generate closed captions for videos uploaded on the platform, making their content easily accessible.

As competition and the need for efficiency continue to rise in the industry, the role of AI in entertainment is only expected to grow in the coming years. By exploring and experimenting with the above and other AI use cases, media and entertainment companies are maximizing their business performance by enhancing the user experience and entertainment value delivered by them with greater efficiency.

Words & Expressions

ubiquity/juː'bɪkwəti/*n.* 普遍存在；到处存在
accelerate/ək'seləreɪt/*v.* （使）加快，促进；（车辆或驾驶者）加速
proliferation/prə,lɪfə'reɪʃn/*n.* （数量的）激增，剧增；（细胞、有机体的）繁殖，增生
tag/tæg/*n.* 标签；称呼，诨名；（电子）追踪器
herculean/,hɜːkjuˈliːən/*adj.* 力大无比的；困难的；赫拉克勒斯的
regardless of 不管，不顾
personalize/'pɜːsənəlaɪz/*vt.* 使个性化；把…拟人化
algorithms/'ælgərɪðəmz/*n.* 算法；算法式（algorithm 的复数）
demographics/,demə'græfɪks/*n.* 人口统计资料
cater to 迎合，满足
automation/,ɔːtə'meɪʃ(ə)n/*n.* 自动化
raw/rɔː/*adj.* 生的，未煮过的；天然的，未经加工的；（信息）未经处理的，原始的

revenue/'revənju:/n.（企业、组织的）收入，收益；（政府的）税收；税务局
metrics/'metrɪks/n. 度量；作诗法；韵律学
air/eə(r)/ v. 使公开，宣扬；（使）通风；（使）晾干
multilingual/ˌmʌlti'lɪŋgwəl/adj. 使用多种语言的；n. 使用多种语言的人
subtitle/'sʌbtaɪtl/n.（电影或电视上的）字幕（subtitles）；副标题，小标题；v. 为（电影，节目）提供字幕；为（作品，文章）提供副标题
manually/'mænjuəli/adv. 手动地；用手
be prone to 易于
leverage/'li:vərɪdʒ/n. 影响力，手段；杠杆力，杠杆作用；杠杆比率；v. 举债经营；充分利用（资源、观点等）
caption/'kæpʃ(ə)n/n.（图片的）说明文字；（电影或电视的）字幕；（法律文件的）开端部分；v. 给…加文字说明
daunting/'dɔ:ntɪŋ/adj. 使人畏惧的，使人气馁的

Notes

1. Netflix：美国奈飞公司，简称网飞，是一家会员订阅制的流媒体播放平台，总部位于美国加利福尼亚州洛斯盖图。成立于 1997 年，曾经是一家在线 DVD 及蓝光租赁提供商，用户可以通过免费快递信封租赁及归还网飞库存的大量影片实体光盘。网飞已经连续 5 次被评为顾客最满意的网站。可以通过计算机、电视机及平板电脑、手机收看电影、电视节目，可通过 Wii，Xbox360，PS3 等设备连接电视机。网飞大奖赛从 2006 年 10 月开始，网飞公开了大约 1 亿个 1～5 的匿名影片评级，数据集仅包含了影片名称、评价星级和评级日期，没有任何文本评价的内容。比赛要求参赛者预测网飞的客户分别喜欢什么影片，要把预测的效率提高 10%以上。

2. Metadata：元数据，又称中介数据、中继数据，为描述数据的数据（data about data），主要是描述数据属性（property）的信息，用来支持如指示存储位置、历史数据、资源查找、文件记录等功能。元数据算是一种电子式目录，为了达到编制目录的目的，必须在描述并收藏数据的内容或特色，进而达成协助数据检索的目的。都柏林核心集（Dublin Core Metadata Initiative，DCMI）是元数据的一种应用，它在 1995 年由国际图书馆电脑中心（OCLC）和美国国家超级计算应用中心（NCSA）联合赞助的研讨会上制定，旨在创建一套描述网络上电子文件特征的标准。

Exercises

I. Comprehension of the Text

Read the text and answer the following questions. Write the answers on the lines.

1. How many use cases of AI in media and entertainment industry are mentioned in the text?

2. According to the text, what has become a herculean task for media company employees?

_____

3. How do some Leading Music and Video streaming platforms achieve Content Personalization?

_____

4. What can virtual assistants and chatbots do for media and entertainment companies?

_____

5. What are AI-powered algorithms being used to?

_____

II. Main Details Comprehension

Directions: *In this section, you are going to read a passage with ten statements attached to it. Each statement contains information given in one of the paragraphs. Identify the paragraph from which the information is derived. You may choose a paragraph more than once. Each paragraph is marked with a letter.*

Science of Setbacks: How Failure Can Improve Career Prospects

A) How do early career setbacks affect our long-term success? Failures can help us learn and overcome our fears. But disasters can still wound us. They can screw us up and set us back. Wouldn't it be nice if there was genuine, scientifically documented truth to the expression "What doesn't kill you makes you stronger?".

B) One way social scientists have probed the effects of career setbacks is to look at scientists of very similar qualifications. These scientists, for reasons that are mostly arbitrary, either just missed getting a research grant or just barely made it. In social sciences, this is known as examining "near misses" and "narrow wins" in areas where merit is subjective. That allows researchers to measure only the effects of being chosen or not. Studies in this area have found conflicting results. In the competitive game of biomedical science, research has been done on scientists who narrowly lost or won grant money. It suggests that narrow winners become even bigger winners down the line. In other words, the rich get richer.

C) A 2018 study published in *the Proceedings of the National Academy of Sciences*, for example, followed researchers in the Netherlands. Researchers concluded that those who just barely qualified for a grant were able to get twice as much money within the next eight years as those who just missed out. And the narrow winners were 50 percent more likely to be given a professorship.

D) Others in the US have found similar effects with National Institutes of Health early-career fellowships launching narrow winners far ahead of close losers. The phenomenon is often referred to as the Matthew effect, inspired by *the Bible's* wisdom that to those who have, more will be given: There's a good explanation for the phenomenon in the book *The Formula: The Universal Laws of Success* by Albert Laszlo Barabasi. According to Barabasi, it's easier and less risky for those in positions of power to choose to hand awards and funding to those who've already been so recognized.

E) This is bad news for the losers. Small early career setbacks seem to have a disproportionate effect down the line. What didn't kill them made them weaker. But other studies using the same technique have shown there's sometimes no penalty to a near miss. Students who just miss getting into top high schools or universities do just as well later in life as those who just manage to get accepted. In this case, what didn't kill them simply didn't matter. So is there any evidence that setbacks might actually improve our career prospects? There is now.

F) In a study published in *Nature Communications*, Northwestern University sociologist Dashun Wang tracked more than 1, 100 scientists who were on the border between getting a grant and missing out between 1990 and 2005. He followed various measures of performance over the next decade. These included how many papers they authored and how influential those papers were, as measured by the number of subsequent citations. As expected, there was a much higher rate of attrition (减员) among scientists who didn't get grants. But among those who stayed on, the close losers performed even better than the narrow winners. To make sure this wasn't by chance, Wang conducted additional tests using different performance measures. He examined how many times people were first authors on influential studies, and the like.

G) One straightforward reason close losers might outperform narrow winners is that the two groups have comparable ability. In Wang's study, he selected the most determined, passionate scientists from the loser group and culled (剔除) what he deemed the weakest members of the winner group. Yet the persevering losers still came out on top. He thinks that being a close loser might give people a psychological boost, or the proverbial kick in the pants.

H) Utrecht University sociologist Arnout van de Rijt was the lead author on the 2018 paper showing the rich get richer. He said the new finding is apparently reasonable and worth some attention. His own work showed that although the narrow winners did get much more money in the near future, the actual performance of the close losers was just as good".

I) He said the people who should be paying regard to the Wang paper are the funding agents who distribute government grant money. After all, by continuing to pile riches on the narrow winners, the taxpayers are not getting the maximum bang for their buck if the close losers are performing just as well or even better. There's a huge amount of time and effort that goes into the process of selecting who gets grants, he said, and the latest research shows that the scientific establishment is not very good at distributing money. "Maybe we should spend less money trying to figure out who is better than who," he said, suggesting that some more equal dividing up of money might be more productive and more efficient. Van de Rijt said he's not convinced that losing out gives people a psychological boost; It may yet be a selection effect. Even though Wang tried to account for this by culling the weakest winners, it's impossible to know which of the winners would have quit had they found themselves on the losing side.

J) For his part, Wang said that in his own experience, losing did light a motivating fire. He recalled a recent paper he submitted to a journal, which accepted it only to request extensive editing, and then reversed course and rejected it. He submitted the unedited version to a more respected journal and got accepted.

K) In sports and many areas of life, we think of failures as evidence of something we could have done better. We regard these disappointments as a fate we could have avoided with more careful preparation, different training, a better strategy, or more focus. And there it makes sense that failures show us the road to success. These papers deal with a kind of failure people have little control over-rejection. Others determine who wins and who loses. But at the very least, the research is starting to show that early setbacks don't have to be fatal. They might even make us better at our jobs'. Getting paid like a winner, though? That's a different matter.

_____1. Being a close loser could greatly motivate one to persevere in their research.

_____2. Grant awarders tend to favor researchers already recognized in their respective fields.

_____3. Suffering early setbacks might help people improve their job performance.

_____4. Research by social scientists on the effects of career setbacks has produced contradictory findings.

_____5. It is not to the best interest of taxpayers to keep giving money to narrow winners.

_____6. Scientists who persisted in research without receiving a grant made greater achievements than those who got one with luck, as suggested in one study.

_____7. A research paper rejected by one journal may get accepted by another.

_____8. According to one recent study, narrow winners of research grants had better chances to be promoted to professors.

_____9. One researcher suggests it might be more fruitful to distribute grants on a relatively equal basis.

_____10. Minor setbacks in their early career may have a strong negative effect on the career of close losers.

Ⅲ. Translation

Translate the five following sentences into English, using the words or expressions given in brackets.

1. 这个饭店的老板又增加了很多快餐品种来迎合年轻消费者的口味。（cater to）

_____

2. 假如一整天你的鼠标都处于同一个地方，那么你易患重复性压迫损伤。（be prone to）

_____

3. 志愿者的目的是帮助灾难受害者，不论他们的种族或国籍。（regardless of）

_____

4．强大的编辑功能可以一幕一幕地编辑。（frame by frame）

5．你也可以参加直播或点播的运动课程。（on-demand）

Product Manual
产品说明书的翻译策略 4——祈使句

祈使句在说明书中用于给用户指导、命令或建议，通常以动词开头。在翻译祈使句时，需要注意语气的转换以及表达方式的灵活运用，也要保持语言的见解、明了，以保留原文的明确性和紧迫感。

（一）祈使句翻译常用话术

（1）使用"请"或"请您"来翻译请求或建议。例如：
Press the button to start the device.
请按下按钮启动设备。
（2）使用"请勿"或"切勿"来翻译禁止性的指令。例如：
Do not immerse the device in water.
请勿将设备浸入水中。
（3）使用"确保"或"务必"来翻译强调性的指令。例如：
Ensure that all connections are secure.
确保所有连接都牢固。
（4）使用"在…之前"来表达时间顺序。例如：
Insert the battery before powering on the device.
在开启设备之前插入电池。
（5）使用"避免"来翻译提醒或建议避免某些情况。例如：
Avoid exposing the device to direct sunlight.
避免将设备暴露在直射阳光下。

（二）祈使句翻译注意事项

（1）加强明确性。为了保持指示的明确性，可以使用更具体的动作描述或明确的词汇。
（2）保持简练。祈使句通常要求简洁明了，避免冗长的表达，使指示更容易理解。
（3）保持整体一致性。保持翻译的一致性，确保祈使句在整个文档中使用相似的表达方式，以避免混淆。
（4）考虑文化因素。了解目标语言用户的文化背景，选择在该文化中常见的表达方式。

Unit 14　Technology and Entertainment 219

（5）测试可行性。在翻译完成后，进行一些可行性测试，以确保翻译的祈使句能够准确地引导用户进行操作。

通过综合运用这些策略，可以确保祈使句在翻译中既保留原文的指示性和紧迫感，又能够适应目标语言和文化环境，为用户提供明确的操作指导。

1. *Read the following paragraphs and then answer the questions.*

Litheli Battery Power User's Guide

NOTE: The Battery Pack comes partly charged.
Charge the Battery Pack prior to first use, ideally at least 60 minutes.
Always pull out the Power Plug of the Charger
from the mains before removing or connecting the Battery Pack to the charger.
Never charge the Battery Pack when the ambient temperature is below 10 °C or above 40 °C.
Rest the Charger for at least 15 minutes between successive charging sessions.
If no Battery Pack is inserted into the Charger and the
charger is connected to mains, the Charging Status LED flashes green.

1. Align the Battery Pack to the rails of the Charger and slide it in. Ensure it clicks noticeably in place.

2. Connect the Power Plug of the Charger with the mains. The Charging Status LED lights up red. The continuously lit green Charging Status LED indicates that the charging process is complete.

3. Disconnect the Power Plug of the Charger from the mains and remove the Battery Pack from the charger.

4. Attach the Battery Pack back to the product (see "Installing and Removing Battery Pack").

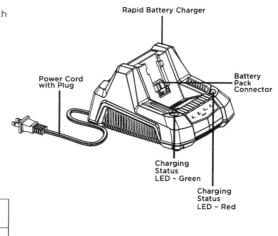

Charging status LEDs

Green LED flashes without battery pack	Charger ready
Green LED lights up with battery pack	Battery pack fully charged
Red LED lights up with battery pack	Battery pack charging
Red and green LEDs flashing	Battery pack defect
Red and green LEDs continuously lit	Battery pack too cold or warm

(1) What is the suggested minimum charging time before the first use?

(2) What are the temperature limits for charging the Battery Pack, and why is it important to adhere to them?

(3) What is the recommended rest period for the Charger between successive charging sessions?

(4) What does a continuously lit green Charging Status LED indicate during the charging process?

(5) Under what circumstances do the red and green LEDs continuously flash, and what does it indicate?

2. *Map reading and translation.*

> ⚠ **WARNING**
>
> Read this material before using this product. Failure to do so can result in serious injury. SAVE THIS MANUAL.

❶ _____

> When unpacking, make sure that the product is intact and undamaged. If any parts are missing or broken, please contact us: WWW.LITHELI.COM.

❷ _____

> **Dress Properly**—Do not wear loose clothing or jewelry. They can be caught in moving parts. Use of rubber gloves and substantial footwear is recommended when working outdoors. Wear protective hair covering to contain long hair.

❸ _____

> **Do Not Force Appliance** - It will do the job better and with less likelihood of injury at the rate for which it was designed.

❹ _____

> **TO PREVENT SERIOUS INJURY FROM ACCIDENTAL OPERATION:** Make sure that the Power Switch/Trigger is in the off-position and remove Battery Pack before setting up the appliance.

❺ _____

Workshop

Background

The media and entertainment industry is becoming increasingly digital, data-driven, and complex. They are facing the need to raise the quantity as well as the quality of content they create to attract as many consumers as they can to drive higher value. To help them achieve this objective, media companies are adopting advanced technologies like AI. In automating repetitive tasks, AI plays a significant role in enhancing efficiency and contributing to profitable growth.

Task

1. Interview some classmates and your families on this topic.
2. Search more information online.

Process

Step 1. Complete the task in groups. Form small groups with 5—6 students respectively.
Step 2. Interview your parents and search information online.
Step 3. Have a discussion with your classmates on the innovative ways of creating and sharing content with AI.
Step 4. Make an oral presentation in class.

Unit 15 Technology and Home Security

AI: the Future of Home Security

In the U.S alone, it's estimated that three out of four homes will be broken into within the next twenty years. Sadly, police clear only 13% of reported burglaries due to lack of physical evidence or witnesses. But all this could change thanks to artificial intelligence.

As home security systems and IoT technologies combine, we're seeing a new class of smarter intruder alarms emerging. This includes mechanisms that boast improved accuracy in intrusion detection while reducing the incidence of false alarms.

IHS Markit research suggests that this is just the beginning for AI enhanced intruder systems and that many applications are in the pipeline that will further boost home security systems.

This technology hopes to deliver higher standards of comfort and security within our homes.

AI, Machine Learning, and Deep Learning

Artificial intelligence is the umbrella term for several data analytics processes. Machine learning is a subdivision of AI; it refers to a process that uses statistical techniques that give computers the ability to "learn" using data, without distinctly programming the computer system to do so.

Deep learning is a further subset of machine learning, involving processes based on deciphering the significance and meaning to be derived from input data.

The Beginnings of AI and Home Security Systems

There are two current applications that employ artificial intelligence in our home security systems.

The first is present in home security systems linked with consumer video cameras. In these systems, the video cameras use facial recognition software to identify whether a moving object is a family member or an intruder.

In these specific environments, facial recognition represents a form of machine learning, where the security systems analyze any objects detected in the video footage against a pre-determined set of approved images that have been previously uploaded. Based on this analytical process, the system will sound an alarm if the objects scanned fail to match any of the images stored.

The second application that utilizes AI tech is voice assisted intruder alarm systems. In these systems, the voice assistant is developed using AI methodologies to ensure smooth user and device interactions.

The Potential Scope of AI and Home Security in the Future

There are many possibilities that AI offer for home security systems in the future.

For example, the use of artificial intelligence could lead to the creation of smart homes capable of learning the habits, ways, and preferences of all the occupants of a building. This technology could identify changes in movement, differences in height, and variable in the tonation of peoples voices, immediately identifying strangers within a building.

These technologies could automatically adjust their settings across various systems to accommodate both standard patterns and changes in behavior. As more intruder alarm systems become integrated with home automation devices, the security of our homes could become significantly improved.

Current home automation systems rely heavily on pre-determined scenarios which must be set up by the user, following specific criteria. All changes to the settings for these systems must be entered manually by the designated system operator.

Eventually, AI software could monitor activity within our houses and activate processes when home occupants go outside of the property, leaving it unlocked.

In these circumstances, if a family member should enter the house while the system is armed, the cameras could identify them immediately and choose not to sound the alarm.

AI processes could also be used to predict false alarms across the world. This would be monitored by analyzing the circumstances that are prevalent in false alarm cases. Eventually, the AI could learn to predict the likelihood of a false alarm with near-accurate certainty, leading to reduced costs and fewer wasted resources for home security and police services.

Intrusion systems integrated with cameras could also help protect our children against kidnappings.

Cameras that monitor areas occupied by a child could sound an alarm upon the approach of a kidnapper, while also recording the image of the kidnapper and forwarding it directly to a monitoring center or the relevant police authorities.

Words & Expressions

burglary/'bɜːgləri/*n.* 入室盗窃，入室盗窃罪

witness/'wɪtnəs/*n.*（尤指犯罪或事故的）目击者；（法庭等的）证人；*v.* 目击，目睹；见证，经历

intruder/ɪn'truːdə(r)/*n.* 闯入者，侵入者；不速之客

mechanism/'mekənɪzəm/*n.* 机械装置，机件；途径，方法；（生物体内的）机制，构

造；机械论；（产生自然现象等的）物理过程
enhance/ɪn'hɑːns/v. 增强，提高，改善
pipeline/'paɪplaɪn/n.（常指地下的）输送管道；（供应货物、信息等的）渠道，途径；研发生产系统（the pipeline）
umbrella term 泛指：一个用于涵盖一组相关概念或事物的通用术语
subdivide/'sʌbdɪvaɪd/vi. 细分，再分；vt. 把…再分，把…细分
distinctly/dɪ'stɪŋktli/adv. 清楚地，明白地；明显地；非常，很
subset/'sʌbset/n. [数] 子集；子设备；小团体
decipher/dɪ'saɪfə(r)/v. 破译，辨认（难认、难解的东西）；理解（神秘或难懂的事物）
footage/'fʊtɪdʒ/n. 一组（电影，电视）镜头；（以英尺表示的）尺码，长度
methodology/ˌmeθə'dɒlədʒi/n. 方法论，一套方法
occupant/'ɒkjəpənt/n. 居住者，住户；（某一时刻房间、交通工具、床等的）占用者
variable/'veəriəb(ə)l/adj. 易变的，多变的；时好时坏的；n. 可变性，可变因素
automatically/ˌɔːtə'mætɪkli/adv. 自然地，必然地；不假思索地，无意识地；自动地
accommodate/ə'kɒmədeɪt/v. 为…提供住宿；容纳，提供空间；考虑到，顾及
pre-determined/ˌpriːdɪ'tɜːmɪnd/v. 预先决定；命中注定；adj. 预先确定的
scenario/sə'nɑːriəʊ/n. 设想，可能发生的情况；（电影、戏剧等的）剧情梗概；（艺术或文学作品中的）场景
activate/'æktɪveɪt/v. 激活，使活化；使参战；（尤指透过加热）加速…的反应
monitor/'mɒnɪtə(r)/n. 显示器，监控器；班长，级长；v. 监视；监听（外国广播或电话）；监控（无线电或电视传输信号）
likelihood/'laɪklihʊd/n. 可能，可能性；可能的事
kidnap/'kɪdnæp/v. 绑架，劫持；n. 绑架，诱拐

 Notes

IoT：物联网技术（Internet of Things，IoT）起源于传媒领域，是信息科技产业的第三次革命。物联网是指通过信息传感设备，按约定的协议，将任何物体与网络相连接，物体通过信息传播媒介进行信息交换和通信，以实现智能化识别、定位、跟踪、监管等功能。

 Exercises

I. Getting the Message

There are 5 questions in this section. Read the questions and complete the answers according to the text.

1. What is Deep learning?

2. What are the two current applications that employ artificial intelligence in our home security systems?
___

3. How does the video camera work in home security systems?
___

4. What are the disadvantages of current home automation systems?
___

5. How could the intrusion systems integrated with cameras help protect our children against kidnappings?
___

II. Languages Focus

A. *Match the following words in left with their explanations in right.*

1. witness
2. intruder
3. enhance
4. subdivide
5. decipher
6. occupant
7. methodology
8. accommodate
9. activate
10. kidnap

a. to provide sb. with a room or place to sleep, live or sit
b. to divide sth. into smaller parts
c. to increase or further improve the good quality, value or status of sb./sth.
d. to make sth. such as a device or chemical process start working
e. a person who sees sth. happen and is able to describe it to other people
f. a person who enters a building or an area illegally
g. a person who lives or works in a particular house, room, building, etc.
h. to take sb. away illegally and keep them as a prisoner, especially in order to get money or sth. else for returning them
i. a set of methods and principles used to perform a particular activity
j. to succeed in finding the meaning of sth. that is difficult to read or understand

B. *Fill in the blanks with the words or expressions given below. Change the form where necessary.*

| witness | intrude | enhance | subdivide | occupy |
| automatic | scenario | variable | methodology | monitor |

1. Rainfall is not completely absent in desert areas, but it is highly _____.
2. As a general rule, all muscular effort is _____ by breathing in as the effort is

made.

3. There was no mail except the usual junk addressed to the _____.

4. The judge reminded the _____ that he was still under oath.

5. A robot has to identify the players, conditions, and possible outcomes for various _____.

6. Together we decide on the _____ and the objectives of the research.

7. An _____ broke into the campaign headquarters and managed to erase 17,000 names from computer files.

8. Each Android application can be further _____ into distinct functional units.

9. If you should be fired, your health and pension benefits will not be _____ cut off.

10. A shortage of funds is preventing the UN from _____ relief.

III. Translation

Translate the following sentences into Chinese.

1. As home security systems and IoT technologies combine, we're seeing a new class of smarter intruder alarms emerging.

2. Artificial intelligence is the umbrella term for several data analytics processes.

3. In these systems, the video cameras use facial recognition software to identify whether a moving object is a family member or an intruder.

4. Based on this analytical process, the system will sound an alarm if the objects scanned fail to match any of the images stored.

5. These technologies could automatically adjust their settings across various systems to accommodate both standard patterns and changes in behavior.

IV. Discussion

Today, we can connect our home security system to a mobile phone, we can confidently leave home, knowing that we can view your home through live-streaming cameras, which allow us to monitor belongings and loved ones from wherever we are. This can relieve our stress when we forgot to turn on the security system before we left home or provide reassurance if we're travelling away from home for an extended period. The advanced Apps can help us remotely arm and disarm our security system, and turn appliances on or off to save energy.

Work in pairs and discuss about your opinions on the role of modern technology in keeping home security, and then write down your opinions.

Don't Put Home Security Cameras in These 3 Places

Live streaming cameras are ideal for monitoring multiple areas around the home and can be a strong deterrent to potential thieves. With ADT Security wi-fi cameras, view people coming and going from your home, such as tradespeople or cleaners, and keep an eye on online shopping deliveries that arrive. Indoor video monitoring capabilities can also be used as a pet or baby monitor, allowing users to watch a live feed from a phone, tablet or computer. There is even the option to remotely set predefined parameters to track entry and exit into your home, as well as communicate with people via a 2-way communication system.

Here's where you really shouldn't put your home security cameras around your property.

The appeal of home security cameras is simple: You can essentially set them up and forget them. With a few well-placed cameras, you can deter would-be burglars, protect your home and privacy, and keep a remote eye on your property and family or pets. With more affordable options on the market and improvements in wireless technology, it's now possible for just about anyone to set up a wired or wireless security camera system that fits your home's specific needs and budget.

But it's also possible to set up a home camera security system the wrong way. The last thing that you want to do is place a camera in a spot where it's rendered ineffective and find out too late that its footage is useless. This guide will steer you away from bad camera placements and help you establish a more effective home security camera system.

For more on home security, check out how to keep your security cameras from being hacked and read up on using an old smartphone as a security camera. Plus, read about the most ideal locations for your home security cameras.

Spot 1: Difficult-to-see locations

You might be tempted to point cameras at the spots around your home that are difficult to see. There is an intuitive reason for this: if you can't see a location from your windows or doors, it feels possible that someone might be lurking there. You might think these hidden areas are a burglar's preferred place to break and enter.

But the fact is, most burglars enter a home through the most obvious paths. According to data collected by security company ADT, 34% of burglars enter through the front door and 22% use a first-floor window. You might imagine that these are spaces where your eyes or your neighbors can spot any malicious activity, but they are also the most used-routes for break-ins. Pointing a camera at these spaces can deter a potential break-in and can help identify anyone who attempts to get in.

Placing a security camera in a side alley or the back of your home might seem like it will catch someone sneaking around, but it's more likely to miss the action that you intend to catch on camera.

Spot 2: Behind obstructions

This might sound like a no-brainer, but camera obstructions aren't always so obvious. Outdoors, this might mean allowing space for tree branches to swing in the wind. Be careful of quick-growing plants that will require you to move your camera every year or two.

Consider your camera's range of view inside, too. Will your camera see everything you want it to when interior doors are opened and closed? You'll also want to avoid placing the camera in a spot where a pet might interact with it. If you place it on a shelf, will your cat knock it off? Will an energetic dog barreling through the house send it tumbling or adjust its angle? Find a spot that has good views of the space you want to watch and is also unlikely to be bumped by you, a guest or your four-legged friend.

Spot 3: Privacy-violating places

While you want your security camera to protect your home, the last thing that you want it to do in infringe upon the safety of others. For that reason, it's important to consider privacy concerns surrounding your camera's placement. Do not place a security camera in a bathroom or bedroom. No matter what your intentions are with this camera, it runs the risk of putting anyone caught on camera in an uncomfortable position and could put you in legal trouble for doing so.

Likewise, you'll want to consider where your camera is pointed outside. For the most part security cameras are allowed to capture public spaces like the sidewalk or street that runs past your home. However, you cannot point a security camera toward a private place that is not part of your property. You may also want to clear the placement of your camera with your neighbors if you think it may capture their home or activity.

As a general rule, make sure that your security cameras are pointed at the areas of your home that matter most to you. You want to keep an eye on who is approaching your home and be aware if anyone tries to enter it. The camera is there to provide a sense of security and serve as a tool to keep you and your home safe. Make sure that your cameras aren't located in places that will render them ineffective, or worse, actually undermine your security.

For more, read up on other home security mistakes you can make. Learn how to stop porch pirates, reduce the risk of car break ins and what you should keep in a safe.

Words & Expressions

deterrent/dɪ'terənt/*n.* 威慑，遏制；威慑武器；*adj.* 威慑的，遏制的
tradespeople/'treɪdzpiːpl/*n.* 商人；商界；开商店者及其家属
parameter/pə'ræmɪtə(r)/*n.* 界限，范围；参数，变量；（统计）人口参数

Unit 15 Technology and Home Security 229

security/sɪ'kjʊərəti/*n.* 保护措施，安全工作；安全，安全感；抵押品，保证金；证券，债券
deter/dɪ'tɜː(r)/*v.* 使打消念头，防止
render/'rendə(r)/*v.* 使成为，使处于某种状态；给予，提供；（以某种方式）表达，表现
steer/stɪə(r)/*v.* 驾驶（交通工具），掌方向盘；引导，指导（某人的行为）
hack/hæk/*v.* 砍，劈；非法侵入（他人计算机系统）；大幅删改（文章）
intuitive/ɪn'tjuːɪtɪv/*adj.* 直觉的；有直觉力的；易懂的，使用简便的
lurk/lɜːk/*vi.* 潜伏；潜藏；埋伏；*n.* 潜伏；埋伏
malicious/mə'lɪʃəs/*adj.* 恶意的，恶毒的，怀恨的
sneak/sniːk/*v.* 偷偷地走，潜行；偷带，私运
obstruction/əb'strʌkʃn/*n.* 阻挠，妨碍；堵塞；障碍物；阻塞，梗阻
no-brainer/ˌnəʊ'breɪnə(r)/*n.* 无须用脑的事；容易作的决定；愚蠢的人（或行为）
knock off 停止，结束（指停止做某事或结束某事）
barrel/'bærəl/*n.* 桶；一桶（的量）；（马等四足动物的）躯干；*v.* 飞奔，高速行驶；把…装入桶内
tumble/'tʌmb(ə)l/*v.* 翻滚，滚落；摔倒，跌倒；倒塌，坍塌；（价格、数量等）暴跌，骤降
bump/bʌmp/*v.* （使身体部位等）碰上，撞上；（无意地）碰，撞；颠簸行进；拖拽
infringe/ɪn'frɪndʒ/*v.* 违反，违背（法律、规则等）；侵犯，侵害（权益）
capture/'kæptʃə(r)/*v.* 俘获，捕获；夺取，占领；吸引，引起
undermine/ˌʌndə'maɪn/*v.* 逐渐削弱（损害）；故意破坏（某人）的形象（或威信）

Notes

ADT：ADT Inc.于 2015 年 5 月 15 日根据美国特拉华州法律注册成立。该公司是美国和加拿大监控安全，交互式家庭和商业自动化及相关监控服务的领先供应商。他们的使命是帮助他们的客户保护和连接最重要的事情——他们的家庭，家庭和企业。ADT 品牌是安全的代名词，作为业内最受认可和值得信赖的品牌，安全是他们成功的关键驱动力。2017 年的一项调查发现，ADT 品牌的品牌知名度约为 95%，受访的 ADT 客户近一半在购买过程中没有考虑任何其他安全警报提供商。排除监控但未拥有的合同，目前他们服务的住宅约为 720 万商业客户，使他们成为美国和加拿大同类中最大的公司。

Exercises

I. Comprehension of the Text

Read the text and answer the following questions. Write the answers on the lines.
1. What is the appeal of home security cameras?

2. What is the intuitive reason for you to point cameras at the spots around your home that are difficult to see?

_____

3. What is the disadvantage of placing a security camera in a side alley or the back of your home?

_____

4. Are camera obstructions always so obvious? Why?

_____

5. If you place a security camera in a bathroom or bedroom, what trouble will it bring you?

_____

II. Main Details Comprehension

Directions: *In this section, you are going to read a passage with ten statements attached to it. Each statement contains information given in one of the paragraphs. Identify the paragraph from which the information is derived. You may choose a paragraph more than once. Each paragraph is marked with a letter.*

Reaping the Rewards of Risk-Taking

A) Since Steve Jobs resigned as chief executive of Apple, much has been said about him as a peerless business leader who has created immense wealth for shareholders, and guided the design of hit products that are transforming entire industries, like music and mobile communications.

B) All true, but let's think different, to borrow the Apple marketing slogan of years back. Let's look at Mr. Jobs as a role model.

C) Above all, he is an innovator. His creative force is seen in products such as the iPod, iPhone, and iPad, and in new business models for pricing and distributing music and mobile software online. Studies of innovation come to the same conclusion: you can't engineer innovation, but you can increase the odds of it occurring. And Mr. Jobs's career can be viewed as a consistent pursuit of improving those odds, both for himself and the companies he has led. Mr. Jobs, of course, has enjoyed singular success. But innovation, broadly defined, is the crucial ingredient in all economic progress-higher growth for nations, more competitive products for companies, and more prosperous careers for individuals. And Mr. Jobs, many experts say, exemplifies what works in the innovation game.

D) "We can look at and learn from Steve Jobs what the essence of American innovation is," says John Kao, an innovation consultant to corporations and governments. Many other nations, Mr. John Kao notes, are now ahead of the United States in producing what are considered the raw materials of innovation. These include government financing for scientific research, national policies to support emerging industries, educational achievement, engineers and scientists graduated, even the speeds of Internet broadband service.

E) Yet what other nations typically lack, Mr. Kao adds, is a social environment that encourages diversity, experimentation, risk-taking, and combining skills from many fields into products that he calls "recombinant mash-ups (打碎重组)": like the iPhone, which redefined the smartphone category. "The culture of other countries doesn't support the kind of innovation that Steve Jobs exemplifies, as America does," Mr. John Kao says.

F) Workers of every rank are told these days that wide-ranging curiosity and continuous learning are vital to thriving in the modem economy. Formal education matters, career counselors say, but real life experience is often even more valuable.

G) An adopted child, growing up in Silicon Valley, Mr. Jobs displayed those traits early on. He was fascinated by electronics as a child, building Heath kit do-it-yourself projects, like radios. Mr. Jobs dropped out of Reed College after only a semester and traveled around India in search of spiritual enlightenment, before returning to Silicon Valley to found Apple with his friend, Stephen Wozniak, an engineering wizard (奇才). Mr. Jobs was forced out of Apple in 1985, went off and founded two other companies, Next and Pixar, before returning to Apple in 1996 and becoming chief executive in 1997.

H) His path was unique, but innovation experts say the pattern of exploration is not unusual. "It's often people like Steve Jobs who can draw from a deep reservoir of diverse experiences that often generate breakthrough ideas and insights", says Hal Gregersen, a professor at the European Institute of Business Administration.

I) Mr. Gregersen is a co-author of a new book, *The Innovator's DNA*, which is based on an eight-year study of 5,000 entrepreneurs (创业者) and executives worldwide. His two collaborators and co-authors are Jeff Dyer, a professor at Brigham Young University, and Clayton Christensen, a professor at the Harvard Business School, whose 1997 book *The Innovator's Dilemma* popularized the concept of disruptive（颠覆性的）innovation".

J) The academics identify five traits that are common to the disruptive innovators: questioning, experimenting, observing, associating and networking. Their bundle of characteristics echoes the ceaseless curiosity and willingness to take risks noted by other experts. Networking, Mr. Hal Gregersen explains, is less about career-building relationships than a consistent search for new ideas. Associating, he adds, is the ability to make idea-producing connections by linking concepts from different disciplines.

K) "Innovators engage in these mental activities regularly," Mr. Gregersen says. "It's a habit for them. Innovative companies, according to the authors, typically enjoy higher valuations in the stock market, which they call an innovation premium. It is calculated by estimating the share of a company's value that cannot be accounted for by its current products and cash flow. The innovation premium tries to quantify（量化）investors' bets that a company will do even better in the future because of innovation.

L) Apple, by their calculations, had a 37 percent innovation premium during Mr.

Jobs's first term with the company. His years in exile resulted in a 31 percent innovation discount. After his return, Apple's fortunes improved gradually at first, and improved markedly starting in 2005, yielding a 52 percent innovation premium since then.

M) There is no conclusive proofs but Mr. Hal Gregersen says it is unlikely that Mr. Jobs could have reshaped industries beyond computing, as he has done in his second term at Apple, without the experience outside the company, especially at Pixar — the computer-animation studio that created a string of critically and commercially successful movies, such as "*Toy Story*" and "*Up*".

N) Mr. Jobs suggested much the same thing during a commencement address to the graduating class at Stanford University in 2005. "It turned out that getting fired from Apple was the best thing that could have ever happened to me," he told the students. Mr. Jobs also spoke of perseverance and will power. "Sometimes life hits you in the head with a brick", he said, "don't lose faith".

O) Mr. Jobs ended his commencement talk with a call to innovation, both in one's choice of work and in one's life. Be curious, experiment, take risks, he said to the students. His advice was emphasized by the words on the back of the final edition of *The Whole Earth Catalog*, which he quoted: "Stay hungry, Stay foolish." "And," Mr. Jobs said, "I have always wished that for myself And now, as you graduate to begin anew, I wish that for you".

_____1. Steve Jobs called on Stanford graduates to innovate in his commencement address.

_____2. Steve Jobs considered himself lucky to have been fired once by Apple.

_____3. Steve Jobs once used computers to make movies that were commercial hits.

_____4. Many governments have done more than the US government in providing the raw materials for innovation.

_____5. Great innovators are good at connecting concepts from various academic fields.

_____6. Innovation is vital to driving economic progress.

_____7. America has a social environment that is particularly favorable to innovation.

_____8. Innovative ideas often come from diverse experiences.

_____9. Real-life experience is often more important than formal education for career success.

_____10. Apple's fortunes suffered from an innovation discount during.

Ⅲ. Translation

Translate the five following sentences into English, using the words or expressions given in brackets.

Unit 15　Technology and Home Security

1. 我们已请邻居在我们离开时帮我们照看一下房子。(keep an eye on)

2. 他设法把话题从他离婚一事上引开。(steer away from)

3. 幸运的是，你无须立马走到门外，虽然你可能尝试这么做。(be tempted to)

4. 如果你现在买不起房的话，那就租一个好了，这还用想吗？（no-brainer）

5. 如果我完成这个报告就会早点儿下班。(knock off)

Product Manual
产品说明书的翻译策略 5——平行结构

平行结构在说明书中常用于列举、强调和并列相关信息。在翻译平行结构时，保持结构的一致性和平衡是关键，以确保翻译文本流畅、易读。以下是针对翻译平行结构的一些建议：

（1）词汇的一致性。在平行结构中，使用相似的词汇或短语，以保持句子的平衡感。例如：

To assemble the product, you will need a screwdriver, pliers, and a wrench.

组装产品时，您需要一个螺丝刀、一把钳子和一个扳手。

（2）保持结构平衡。确保平行结构中的各个元素在语法结构上保持平衡，以使翻译更加自然。例如：

The system allows you to view, edit, and save your documents.

该系统允许您查看、编辑和保存文档。

（3）注意语气和风格。在平行结构中，注意保持语气和风格的一致性，以确保翻译文本整体的连贯性。例如：

The software is user-friendly, efficient, and reliable.

这个软件用户友好、高效可靠。

（4）维持语序一致。在平行结构中，尽量保持中文语序的一致性，以确保读者更容易理解。例如：

To troubleshoot the issue, you can check the connections, restart the device, or contact customer support.

要解决问题，您可以检查连接、重新启动设备或联系客户支持。

（5）避免过度翻译。在翻译平行结构时，不要过度翻译，保持简练和清晰。例如：

The product is durable, reliable, and resistant to water.

产品坚固、可靠，耐水性强。

（6）考虑语境。确保平行结构的翻译在整个句子和段落的语境中是合适的，不会引起歧义。

通过使用这些策略，翻译者可以有效地处理说明书中的平行结构，确保翻译文本保持一致、清晰，读者易于理解。

1. *Read the following paragraphs and then answer the questions.*

DWARFLAB DWARF II Smart Telescope User Guide

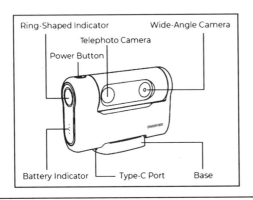 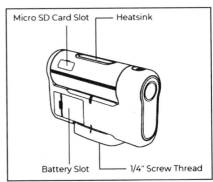

Let's Play

1. **Power on/off**

   Short press the power button to power it on. Long press the power button for above 2s to power off.

2. **Download DWARFLAB App**

   Please download DWARFLAB App at dwarflab.com You can also get it at App Store or Google Play. Please search DWARFLAB.

3. **Wireless Connection**

   After DWARF II powers on, please open the DWARFLAB App and make sure that the Bluetooth and WiFi of your smartphone/tablet are open. Click the camera button in DWARFLAB App to retrieve the DWARF II, and click the device name in the device list window to start the connection. Then the connection will be established automatically. When the connection is successful, DWARFLAB App will prompt to the photography page.

4. **Enjoy it!**

   Enjoy it! Please stably place DWARF II on a flat surface, or fix it on a tripod through the 1/4″ screw thread at the bottom of the base. To unlock more interesting features, please visit dwarflab.com.

Attention

1. Please do not disassemble or remodify the product.
2. Please do not use the product in heavy rain or high temperature (sun exposure) environments, or put it in water.
3. Please do not touch the lens with hard, sharp objects or corrosive solutions to avoid damage.
4. If the lens is dirty, please use a clean lens cloth to wipe it.
5. Never charge the DWARF II if the temperature is under 0 °C / 32 °F. It could cause irreversible damage to the DWARF II's battery. Always charge it between 5 °C / 41 °F and 45 °C / 113 °F.

Unit 15　Technology and Home Security 　235

(1) What is the procedure for turning off DWARF Ⅱ?

(2) Name two alternative sources for downloading the DWARFLAB App.

(3) What are the recommended placement options for DWARF Ⅱ during use?

(4) Where can you unlock more interesting features for DWARF Ⅱ?

(5) Why is it advised not to charge DWARF Ⅱ if the temperature is below 0℃/32℉?

2. *Map reading and translation.*

| This equipment complies with FCC radiation exposure limits set forth for an uncontrolled environment. This equipment should be installed and operated with a minimum distance of 20cm between the radiator & your body. |

 ①_____

| Please do not use the product in heavy rain or high temperature (sun exposure) environments, or put it in water. |

 ②_____

| Please do not touch the lens with hard, sharp objects or corrosive solutions to avoid damage. |

 ③_____

| **This device complies with Part 15 of the FCC Rules. Operation is subject to the following two conditions:** |
| 1. This device may not cause harmful interference. and |
| 2. This device must accept any interference received. including interference that may cause undesired operation. |

 ④_____

| **Enjoy it!** |
| Enjoy it! Please stably place DWARF Ⅱ on a flat surface, or fix it on a tripod through the 1/4″ screw thread at the bottom of the base. To unlock more interesting features, please visit dwarflab.com. |

 ⑤_____

Workshop

Background

While a safe and crime-free society would be ideal, the reality is that thousands of homes are broken into every year. Property related crimes, including break-ins and theft, are mostly opportunistic in nature. Fortunately, advancements in home security technology and real-time monitoring capabilities have made it easier for property owners to better protect their assets. Take appropriate actions to address urgent maintenance and upgrade your security system to help close the gaps.

Task

1. Interview some classmates and your friends on this topic.
2. Search more information online.

Process

Step 1. Complete the task in groups. Form small groups with 5－6 students respectively.

Step 2. Interview your friends and search information online.

Step 3. Have a discussion with your classmates on the relationship between Technology and Home Security, and summarize some practical tips to keep our homes safe and secure.

Step 4. Make an oral presentation and introduce those tips in class.